the pasta book

WILLIAMS·SONOMA

the pasta book

AUTHOR **JULIA DELLA CROCE**
PHOTOGRAPHER **RAY KACHATORIAN**

weldon**owen**

THE WORLD OF PASTA

Few foods are more universal than pasta. In Italy, which boasts a wealth of recipes for both making noodles and for dressing them with an unbelievable array of sauces, it is a gastronomical passion. In nearly every culture where pasta is enjoyed, its myriad forms engage the cook's imagination. Whether fresh or dried, stuffed or baked, sauced, in soup, steamed, or stir-fried, pasta is one of the most welcome sights on the dinner table.

Pasta has long been a part of the Italian national diet. Dried pasta, called *maccheroni* or *pasta secca,* is typically made of nothing more than hard-wheat flour (semolina) and water and comes in countless forms: long or short, flat or cylindrical, wide or narrow, with holes, twists, or divots. In contrast, most fresh pasta, or *pasta fresca,* is made from soft-wheat flour and includes eggs and sometimes also vegetable purées for color and a hint of flavor. Like its dried counterpart, fresh pasta comes in a wide assortment of shapes and sizes, and includes strand pastas, stuffed pastas, such as ravioli and cannelloni, as well as layered pastas, like lasagne. Italians make dumplings known as gnocchi, too, creating a dough from flour, potatoes, pumpkin, stale bread, or even ricotta cheese before rolling the dough into ropes and cutting into small pieces.

The term *pasta* is also a broad umbrella for numerous other noodles and dumplings found around the world, from the spaetzle of eastern Europe to the *fideo* of Mexico to the *tallarines verdes* of Peru. But Asia offers the largest variety of noodles and dumplings outside of Italy. Cooks in kitchens from Saigon to Bangkok, Beijing to Seoul turn out pastas that honor both culinary tradition and local ingredients. They fashion them primarily from wheat flour, rice flour, buckwheat, or mung bean starch and serve them in soups or tossed with sauces. Asian cooks are also famed dumpling makers, as both Japanese *gyoza* and Chinese *shumai* attest.

A VERSATILE FOOD

Pasta is a food fit for all occasions. It can be dressed down for weeknight meals or dressed up for dinner parties. Anointed with only fruity olive oil, garlic, and parsley, it is a quick, satisfying supper. Layered with béchamel and *ragù* to make *lasagne al forno,* it is an elegant main course. It can be added to soups or salads, wrapped around a filling, or layered with meats, vegetables, cheeses, and sauce. In Italy, pasta is traditionally served as a first course, but elsewhere it is often eaten as a main course. In Asia, noodles and dumplings are eaten at breakfast, lunch, and dinner.

PASTA-MAKING TOOLS & EQUIPMENT

Food mill For creating fine-textured sauces.

Food processor For making pasta doughs, bread crumbs, and fillings for stuffed pastas.

Frying pan or sauté pan Large, for cooking sauce and then accommodating both the sauce and the cooked pasta.

Graters and grinders A box grater for slicing and shredding vegetables and cheese; rasp graters in different sizes for grating spices and cheeses; and a pepper mill for freshly ground pepper.

Knives A heavy chef's knife and a paring knife for general cutting tasks.

Measuring cups and spoons Standard set of dry measuring cups, one small and one large liquid measuring cup, and measuring spoons for measuring ingredients.

Mixing bowls Small bowls for prepped ingredients; medium and large bowls for ice-water baths, for mixing fillings, and for covering dough while it rests.

Pasta machine Manual or electric machine for rolling and sometimes cutting fresh pasta.

Pasta pot and colander A heavy 8-quart (8-l) pot for cooking pasta and a colander for draining pasta.

Pastry wheel and pizza cutter A fluted pastry wheel for creating fluted edges on stuffed pasta, and a pizza cutter for cutting pasta sheets and straight edges on stuffed pastas.

Slotted spoon or skimmer For lifting stuffed pastas, dumplings, and vegetables out of cooking water.

Steamer One or more bamboo steamers or a steamer insert for steaming dumplings.

Wok or nonstick frying pan For stir-frying or sautéing Asian pasta dishes.

Wooden spoon Long-handled spoon for stirring pasta in boiling water and for stirring sauces.

OUTFITTING YOUR KITCHEN

Most of the equipment you will need for making pasta you probably already have on your shelves, such as graters, good knives, pots and pans, a colander, and the like. More specialized equipment, such as a large pasta pot and a pasta machine, are easily found in cookware shops. The list to the left briefly describes the basics.

STOCKING YOUR PANTRY

Pastas are often simple dishes, fashioned from just noodles and no more than a handful of ingredients for the sauce. That simplicity means that every element must be of the highest quality your budget allows: the finest cheeses and the freshest eggs, seafood, meats, and vegetables. But to make planning your meals and shopping for them easier, keep your pantry filled with a variety of staples, so that only a few fresh ingredients are needed to complete a dish. For example, stock a selection of dried Italian and Asian noodles, canned plum tomatoes for sauces, a variety of oils for sautéing and stir-frying, and extra-virgin olive oil for finishing sauces and soups. Have on hand kosher salt for cooking pasta and vegetables and sea salt for finishing sauces.

Homemade meat and vegetable broths are ideal, but high-quality commercial low-sodium broths are great time-savers. Other good candidates for your pantry shelves include capers, olives, oil-packed tuna, anchovies, dried mushrooms, mirin, Thai curry paste, Asian chile oil, fish sauce, and soy sauce—ingredients and seasonings that will complete countless pasta dishes.

COOKING ITALIAN PASTA

To ensure your pasta moves freely as it cooks, use at least 5 quarts (5 l) of water to cook 1 pound (500 g) of fresh or dried pasta. Add 2 tablespoons kosher salt at the same time you add the pasta to the water. This may seem like a lot of salt, but the amount is necessary to flavor the pasta properly. Do not, as some books suggest, add oil to the water. It will coat the pasta, which will cause it to repel the sauce. Stir the pasta often as it cooks to keep it from sticking together, and maintain the pot's high heat to keep the water moving. Cook stuffed pastas, such as tortellini and ravioli, at a slightly lower temperature to prevent them from knocking against one another and breaking open.

Because most dried pasta cooks within 10 to 12 minutes and most fresh pasta cooks within a fraction of that time, keep an eye on the pot to prevent overcooking. The recipes that follow provide cooking times for fresh pasta and direct you to the package directions for dried. But with practice, you will learn to judge doneness by physical cues and tasting, rather than by the clock.

As soon as the pasta is ready, add a glass of cold water to the pot to immediately stop the cooking. Scoop out a little of the cooking water, in case you need to add moisture to encourage smooth and easy distribution of the sauce, and then drain the pasta. Don't overdrain it, however, or it may stick together and/or absorb too much sauce. (See each chapter's introduction for more details on cooking fresh, dried, and stuffed pastas and dumplings.)

COOKING ASIAN PASTA

Fresh and dried Asian noodles—wheat, rice, buckwheat—are typically cooked in boiling water before they are added to soups, to remove the starchy coating that would otherwise cloud the broth. These same noodles are also boiled before they are combined with other ingredients in a stir-fry. Some dried Asian noodles, such as cellophane (bean thread) noodles, need only be soaked in hot water to cover until pliable before they can be used in stir-fries or other dishes. Asian dumplings are steamed, boiled, or fried, depending on the type. (See each chapter's introduction for more details on cooking Asian noodles and dumplings.)

SEASONING AND SERVING PASTA

Although every recipe indicates amounts for seasonings, it is always important to taste and adjust the seasoning of a dish as it cooks. When making a slow-cooked sauce, it is best to add a minimal measure of salt in the beginning, and then adjust the seasoning after the sauce has reduced fully.

Dress Italian pastas immediately after draining them, while they are still piping hot, by either adding them to the sauce in the pan or combining them with the sauce in an ample serving bowl. If you have tossed them together in a pan, serve the sauced pasta directly in individual shallow bowls or plates.

With the exception of lasagne and other baked pasta dishes, Italians traditionally eat pasta as a first course, preceding a meat or seafood course. Outside of Italy, pasta is often served as a main course, typically accompanied by a salad or vegetable. The recipes in this book reflect this latter custom, with most of them serving four to six diners as a main course. The Asian noodle recipes in this book are also portioned as main courses.

Many cooks have the mistaken notion that whenever they serve Italian pasta, they should pass freshly grated cheese at the table. The recipes in this book follow Italian tradition and do not add cheese to pasta dishes dressed with fish, shellfish, game, or mushroom sauces.

STORING SAUCES AND SOUPS

Most pasta sauces can be stored in the refrigerator for up to 2 days, and most soups containing pasta can be refrigerated for up to 4 days. In general, tomato-based sauces and other liquid-heavy sauces are good candidates for freezing. Let cool to room temperature and transfer to airtight containers in 2-cup (16–fl oz/500-ml) portions for 1 lb (500 g) pasta. Leave 1 inch (2.5 cm) headroom to allow for expansion during freezing.

FRESH PASTA

ABOUT FRESH PASTA

Pasta fresca (fresh pasta), *pasta fatta in casa* (pasta made at home), *pasta fatta a mano* (pasta made by hand), *sfoglia* ("thin sheets" of pasta), and *pasta all'uovo* (egg pasta) are all terms Italians use when referring to homemade pasta. Although the dough calls for just a handful of ingredients and the method is simple, making fresh pasta takes time. There is, however, nothing more satisfying than enjoying the delicate results of your labor at the dinner table.

HOMEMADE PASTA BASICS

Fresh pasta can be made by mixing together only eggs and flour until they form a soft, smooth, uniform dough, which is then rolled out and cut into myriad shapes. But in this book, the basic dough recipe also includes a little salt and olive oil for a more flavorful and silky-textured dough. In Italy, fresh pasta is usually either made at home or purchased from a specialty shop that makes a selection of fresh pastas daily. In both cases, it is served the same day it is made. Nowadays, however, so-called fresh pasta is made in factories and packaged for supermarket shelves, where it can sit for weeks until it is purchased or its expiration date is reached. Not surprisingly, these products bear no resemblance to true fresh pasta. If you don't have the time or the inclination to make fresh pasta or to seek it out from a specialty shop that makes it daily, use dried pasta.

CHOOSING INGREDIENTS

Because homemade pasta dough calls for only a few ingredients, every one of them must be of the highest quality. Fresh organic eggs, preferably from chickens that can wander beyond the coop, will give you the best-tasting pasta. Italians use "00" flour *(doppio zero)* in their fresh pastas; it is a soft-wheat flour that is almost powdery and yields a particularly light and porous dough. If you cannot find it, unbleached all-purpose flour is the best substitute. Milled from a blend of hard and soft wheats, it is more wholesome than its chemically

bleached all-purpose counterpart, which means it tastes better, too. Whole-wheat and buckwheat flours are commonly used for a heartier, nutty-tasting pasta dough. When a recipe calls for coloring and flavoring dough with spinach, saffron, or tomato paste, follow the same rule: start with the best-quality ingredients.

TYPES OF FRESH PASTA

The most commonly made fresh pastas are called ribbon or strand pasta. Among the most well-known types are fettuccine, tagliatelle, pappardelle, and taglierini. They are formed by rolling up a sheet of pasta dough into a loose, flat cylinder and then cutting the cylinder crosswise to make noodles 10 to 14 inches (25 to 35 cm) long. The width varies with the type of noodle; see the fresh pasta gallery on pages 14 and 15 for widths of the most popular types. Other pastas, such as maltagliati, are roughly cut from a pasta sheet that is folded in half or rolled into a cylinder (see page 23).

The thickness and width of strand pastas define the sauces that accompany them. For most ribbon noodles, including tagliatelle and pappardelle, the dough is rolled out as thinly as possible to ensure a light, delicate result when dressed with a sauce. Others, such as fettuccine and trenette, are rolled slightly thicker because they are intended for heavier, more unctuous sauces, such as a pesto or a *ragù*. Very narrow noodles, like taglierini, are dressed with sauces with finely cut ingredients, because large pieces would get trapped underneath the strands. Wide noodles, such as pappardelle, can handle thicker, heavier sauces and bigger ingredients, which will catch in the broad loops of the ribbons. (For information on stuffed fresh pastas, see pages 132–133.)

MIXING THE DOUGH

The traditional way to make pasta dough is to mix it by hand on a work surface: the dry ingredients are shaped into a mound with a well in the center, the liquid ingredients are added to the well, and the dry and liquid ingredients are worked together. The benefit of making the dough by hand is that you can easily feel if it is too dry and needs more liquid or if it is too sticky and needs more flour. However, a food processor will save you time without sacrificing quality. After the pasta dough rests for 15 minutes, it is ready to be rolled out by hand or by machine.

ROLLING AND CUTTING DOUGH

Italian home cooks have long used hand-cranked pasta machines to roll out and cut pasta dough; these same machines still produce the most consistent results. If you are shopping for a new pasta machine, don't skimp. Investing in a well-made model over a lesser one is worth the expense: it will have more sophisticated mechanisms for controlling the thickness of the finished sheets. Manual pasta machines typically come with a single cutting attachment with two blades, one for cutting noodles 1/16 inch (2 mm) wide (for taglierini) and one for cutting noodles 1/4 inch (6 mm) wide (for fettuccine and tagliatelle). You can usually purchase additional cutting attachments for other widths.

A second option is to purchase rolling and cutting attachments for your stand mixer. Powered by the motor of the mixer, the rolling attachment kneads and rolls out the dough to the desired thickness, and then the cutting attachment—a separate one is needed for each width—cuts the dough into strands. You can also purchase extrusion attachments for

your stand mixer. These allow you to feed a piece of dough into the machine, which then pushes it through a perforated disk that yields a specific shape and size. These attachments are easy to use, but skip the important step of rolling, which kneads as well as stretches the dough, ensuring pasta with a good consistency.

Fresh pasta dough can also be rolled out and cut by hand, and some irregular shapes, such as maltagliati, must be cut by hand (see pages 22 and 23).

DRYING AND STORING

If you plan to cook fresh pasta strands within a few hours of cutting them, spread them out on clean, barely damp kitchen towels or hang them on a drying rack or the back of a chair and leave them to dry for at least 30 minutes, or until they develop a thin skin, up to 3 hours. Just before cooking, shake the strands to separate them. If you plan to refrigerate or freeze the fresh pasta strands, let them dry for 30 minutes, then half-cook them in salted boiling water (this prevents the strands from sticking together), drain immediately, rinse under cold running water to halt the cooking, and store in resealable plastic bags in the freezer. To cook, drop the frozen pasta into salted boiling water and cook as for fresh pasta (it may take a few more seconds to cook).

COOKING AND SERVING

In general, plan on about 1/4 pound (4 oz/125 g) fresh pasta per serving, though the amount will vary with the nature of the sauce. If the pasta is combined with a rich, cream-based sauce, 1 pound (500 g) for four persons should be sufficient. If it is dressed with a lighter, meatless sauce, you may need slightly more pasta per diner. Because fresh pasta is soft even before it is cooked, it can never be cooked al dente, a term appropriate only for dried pasta. Fresh pasta is also porous, which makes it an ideal canvas for rich, slow-cooked meat sauces and cream- or cheese-based sauces.

FRESH PASTA SHAPES

1 **TAGLIATELLE** Resembles fettuccine but is rolled out 1/32 inch (1 mm) thick and cut into strands 1/4 inch (6 mm) to 3/8 inch (1 cm) wide.

2 **MALTAGLIATI** Thin, irregular, scraplike pieces that are either triangular or diamond-shaped and 2 to 3 inches (5 to 7.5 cm) long.

3 **TRENETTE** Rolled out 1/16 inch (2 mm) thick and cut into strands 1/4 inch (6 mm) wide or less.

4 **TAGLIERINI** Rolled out 1/32 inch (1 mm) thick and cut into narrow strands about 1/16 inch (2 mm) wide.

5 **PAPPARDELLE** Rolled out 1/32 inch (1 mm) thick and cut into strands 3/4 to 1 inch (2 to 2.5 cm) wide with either straight or fluted edges.

6 **FETTUCCINE** Rolled out 1/16 inch (2 mm) thick and cut into strands 1/4 to 3/8 inch (6 mm to 1 cm) wide.

MAKING PASTA DOUGH BY HAND

EGG PASTA I
For strand pasta

2½ cups (12½ oz/390 g)
unbleached all-purpose
or "00" flour (see page 12),
plus more flour as needed

¼ teaspoon fine sea salt

4 large eggs, at room temperature

2 teaspoons olive oil

MAKES 1 LB (500 G)

EGG PASTA II
For stuffed and baked pasta

3 cups (15 oz/470 g) unbleached
all-purpose or "00" flour (see
page 12), plus more flour as needed

Scant ½ teaspoon fine sea salt

5 large eggs, at room temperature

1 tablespoon olive oil

MAKES 1¼ LB (625 G)

1 MAKE A WELL

Measure the flour onto a work surface,
mix in the salt, and shape the flour into
a mound. Using your fingertips, make a
well in the center.

2 ADD THE EGGS AND OIL

Break the eggs into the center of the
well and add the oil. Using a fork, beat
until the eggs and oil are blended,
making sure the liquid doesn't breach
the walls of the well.

3 DRAW IN THE FLOUR

Using the fork, gradually draw the flour
from the sides of the well into the egg
mixture and beat gently, always in the
same direction, to combine the flour
with the liquid. Secure the wall of the
well with your other hand until the liquid
has absorbed enough flour that it won't
flow over the wall.

4 USE YOUR HANDS

When the mixture is too stiff to use the fork, begin using both hands, gradually drawing in the flour from the bottom of the wall, until you have a soft, moist, but not sticky ball of dough. If the dough will not absorb more flour without becoming stiff, don't use it all. If it is too soft, add more flour, a spoonful at a time.

5 KNEAD THE DOUGH

Clean the work surface, dust it lightly with flour, and flatten the ball of dough into a disk. Using the heel of your hand, push the dough down and away from you, fold it in half back toward you, rotate a quarter turn, and repeat the kneading motion. After about 10 minutes, the dough should be smooth and elastic.

6 LET THE DOUGH REST

Shape the dough into a ball, cover with an overturned bowl, and let rest for 15 minutes before you roll it out. The gluten in the flour will relax, making the dough easier to roll. Do not let it rest longer or it will be too dry.

MAKING PASTA DOUGH IN A MACHINE

EGG PASTA I
For strand pasta

2½ cups (12½ oz/390 g) unbleached all-purpose or "00" flour (see page 12), plus more flour as needed

¼ teaspoon fine sea salt

4 large eggs, at room temperature

2 teaspoons olive oil

MAKES 1 LB (500 G)

EGG PASTA II
For stuffed and baked pasta

3 cups (15 oz/470 g) unbleached all-purpose or "00" flour (see page 12), plus more flour as needed

Scant ½ teaspoon fine sea salt

5 large eggs, at room temperature

1 tablespoon olive oil

MAKES 1¼ LB (625 G)

1 MIX THE FLOUR	2 ADD THE EGGS AND OIL	3 MIX THE DOUGH

Fit a food processor with the metal blade. Add all but ½ cup (2½ oz/75 g) of the flour and the salt to the food processor work bowl and pulse to mix. Set the reserved ½ cup flour aside; you will use it later to adjust the consistency of the dough.

Crack the eggs into a liquid measuring cup and check for and remove any stray shells. Add the oil; there is no need to stir. Pour the eggs and oil into the food processor work bowl.

Process until the flour is evenly moistened and crumbly, about 10 seconds. Test the dough by pinching it; if it is very sticky, add more flour, 1 tablespoon at a time, processing until it is incorporated. After about 30 seconds total, the dough should come together in a loose ball and feel moist but not sticky.

4 FLOUR A WORK SURFACE	5 KNEAD THE DOUGH	6 LET THE DOUGH REST
Dust a clean work surface with flour. Remove the ball of dough from the food processor and place it in the center of the floured surface. Using your hands, flatten the dough into a disk.	Using the heel of your hand, push the dough down and away from you, fold it in half back toward you, rotate a quarter turn, and repeat the kneading motion. After about 10 minutes, the dough should be smooth and elastic.	Shape the dough into a ball, cover with an overturned bowl, and let rest for 15 minutes before you roll it out. The gluten in the flour will relax, making the dough easier to roll. Do not let it rest longer or it will be too dry.

ROLLING AND CUTTING PASTA DOUGH BY MACHINE

1 SET UP THE MACHINE	2 KNEAD THE DOUGH	3 ROLL OUT THE DOUGH
Set up the pasta machine according to the manufacturer's directions. Set the rollers at the widest setting and dust with flour to prevent sticking. Cut the dough into 4 equal pieces and slip 3 pieces back under the bowl.	Flatten the remaining piece into a disk and dust with flour. Turning the crank, feed the dough through the rollers. Fold the dough into thirds like a letter. Lightly flour botah sides and feed it through again; this process further kneads the dough. Repeat the folding and rolling twice, dusting with flour as needed.	Narrow the rollers to the next notch, dust the dough with flour, and pass it through the rollers again. Catch the sheet with your hand and carefully guide it onto the work surface. Narrow the rollers to the next notch and feed the dough through again. If the dough tears, start again at the widest setting.

4 ROLL OUT THINNER

Continue in this fashion, dusting with flour and repairing holes as needed. For tagliatelle, taglierini, pappardelle, maltagliati, all stuffed pastas, cannelloni, and lasagne, end with the narrowest setting (1/32 inch/1 mm). For fettuccine and trenette, stop at the second-to-last notch (1/16 inch/2 mm).

5 CUT INTO SECTIONS

At the end of rolling, you will have a long, smooth sheet 4–5 inches (10–13 cm) wide from each of the 4 pieces of dough. To cut pasta sheets into strands, place the rolled-out sheet flat on a clean work surface and cut it crosswise into 14-inch (35-cm) lengths.

6 CUT INTO STRANDS

Fasten the machine's cutting attachment and insert the crank. Most standard cutters have two widths, 1/4 inch (6 mm) for fettuccine/tagliatelle and 1/16 inch (2 mm) for taglierini. Feed the pasta sheets through the desired blade and catch gently. See page 23 for cutting other noodles by hand.

ROLLING PASTA DOUGH BY HAND

1 ROLL OUT THE DOUGH

2 TEST FOR THINNESS

3 CUT INTO SECTIONS

Cut the dough into 4 equal pieces and slip 3 pieces back under the bowl. Flatten the remaining piece into a disk and dust with flour. Using a floured rolling pin, roll the dough away from you. Lift the dough, flour the work surface again, if necessary, and turn the dough 90 degrees. Roll out again.

Continue rolling the dough until you can see your hand through it. For tagliatelle, taglierini, pappardelle, maltagliati, all stuffed pastas, cannelloni, and lasagne, roll out to ⅟₃₂ inch (1 mm) thick. For fettuccine and trenette, roll out to ⅟₁₆ inch (2 mm) thick. Transfer to a floured baking sheet and let rest for 10–20 minutes.

Place the rolled-out pasta sheet on a clean work surface. Using a pizza cutter or paring knife, cut the pasta sheet into sections 4–5 inches (10–13 cm) wide and 14 inches (35 cm) long. You may find it helpful to use a ruler for guidance.

CUTTING FRESH PASTA SHAPES

CUTTING STRANDS

On a lightly floured work surface, starting on a short side, roll up a pasta sheet into a loose, flat cylinder. Using a chef's knife, cut the cylinder crosswise to create strands. To make fettuccine and tagliatelle, cut at about ¼-inch (6-mm) intervals. For pappardelle, cut at ¾–1 inch (2–2.5-cm) intervals. For trenette, cut just shy of ¼-inch (6-mm) intervals. For taglierini, cut at ¹⁄₁₆-inch (2-mm) intervals. Gently shake out the noodles to separate them.

CUTTING MALTAGLIATI

Fold a section of dough in half or roll it up so that it is 2–3 inches (5–7.5 cm) wide. Using a knife, cut off both corners of one end of the folded dough on a diagonal, then cut straight across so that a triangle has been cut off. Repeat, cutting off the corners and the triangles, until all of the dough has been cut up. Shake out the cut noodles to separate them. The noodles will be somewhat unevenly shaped.

FETTUCCINE *alla* BOLOGNESE

Here is one of the many versions of the complex, robust meat sauce that is typically paired with fresh fettuccine in Emilia-Romagna, a region famed for its homemade egg pasta. Unlike other *ragù*, tomato is not the focus of this velvety sauce, which relies on milk to impart sweetness to the meat.

FOR THE BOLOGNESE SAUCE

1 can *(28 oz/875 g)* plum tomatoes

2 tablespoons unsalted butter

1 tablespoon extra-virgin olive oil

1 small white or yellow onion, finely chopped

1 small rib celery, including leaves, finely chopped

½ small carrot, peeled and finely chopped

1 tablespoon chopped fresh flat-leaf parsley

¾ lb *(375 g)* ground beef, preferably chuck, or equal parts beef, veal, and pork

2 oz *(60 g)* thinly sliced prosciutto or mortadella, chopped, including fat

½ cup *(4 fl oz/125 ml)* dry white wine

Fine sea salt and freshly ground pepper

⅔ cup *(5 fl oz/160 ml)* milk

⅛ teaspoon freshly grated nutmeg

Egg Pasta I *(page 16 or 18)*

Kosher salt for cooking pasta

Freshly grated Parmigiano-Reggiano cheese for serving

To make the Bolognese Sauce, drain the tomatoes, reserving their juice. Strain the captured juice to hold back the seeds. Using your fingers, push out the excess seeds from the tomatoes, then chop the tomatoes and set aside with the juice.

In a Dutch oven or large, deep frying pan over low heat, melt the butter with the olive oil. Add the onion, celery, carrot, and parsley and cook, stirring occasionally, until the vegetables are softened but the onions are not colored, about 12 minutes. Keeping the heat low, add the beef and prosciutto and cook gently, stirring to break up any clumps, until the meat is just lightly colored on the outside and uniformly pink inside, about 8 minutes. Stir in the wine and ½ teaspoon sea salt and simmer very gently until most of the alcohol has evaporated and the liquid begins to be absorbed by the meat and vegetables, 3–5 minutes.

Add the milk and nutmeg, return to a gentle simmer, and cook over low heat for 10 minutes. Add the tomatoes and their juice, and as soon as the sauce begins to simmer again, turn the heat down as low as possible so that the sauce barely simmers and only a few bubbles at a time break on the surface. Cover partially and continue to simmer, always over the lowest heat possible and stirring occasionally, for about 4 hours. The sauce should be deeply colored, aromatic, and nicely thickened. Taste and adjust the seasoning with sea salt and pepper.

While the sauce is cooking, make the pasta dough as directed, then roll out and cut into fettuccine as directed on pages 20–21 or 22–23. Let dry for 30 minutes or up to 3 hours (see page 13).

When the sauce is ready, in a large pot, bring 5 qt (5 l) water to a rapid boil. Add 2 tablespoons kosher salt and the pasta and cover the pot. When the water returns to a boil, uncover, cook for about 5 seconds, and then drain. Transfer the pasta to a warmed large, shallow serving bowl or individual shallow bowls. Top with the sauce and serve right away. Pass the cheese at the table.

TAGLIATELLE *with* ARTICHOKES AND THYME

While cleaning fresh artichokes adds an extra step to the cooking process, frozen or canned artichokes can't compare in flavor. Look for artichokes that are bright green, have firm, rigid stems, and are heavy for their size. Small or medium artichokes will be the most tender.

Egg Pasta I *(page 16 or 18)*

1 tablespoon fresh
lemon juice

10 artichokes, about
7 oz *(220 g)* each

Kosher salt for cooking
artichokes and pasta

6 tablespoons *(3 oz/90 g)*
unsalted butter

2 tablespoons extra-virgin
olive oil

2 large shallots, thinly sliced

3 large cloves garlic, bruised
(see page 233)

1 teaspoon minced fresh
thyme, or ½ teaspoon
crumbled dried thyme,
plus more for serving

½ cup *(4 fl oz/125 ml)*
dry white wine

1 cup *(8 fl oz/250 ml)*
low-sodium chicken broth

Fine sea salt and freshly
ground pepper

¼ cup *(2 fl oz/60 ml)*
crème fraîche

½ cup *(2 oz/60 g)* freshly
grated Parmigiano-Reggiano
cheese, plus more for serving

Make the pasta dough as directed, then roll out and cut into tagliatelle as directed on pages 20–21 or 22–23. Let dry for 30 minutes or up to 3 hours (see page 13).

Fill a large bowl with water and add the lemon juice. Working with 1 artichoke at a time, pare away the dark skin from the stem. Cut off the top 2 inches (5 cm) of the leaves, then pull off and discard the tough outer leaves until you reach the tender, pale leaves. Cut the artichoke in half lengthwise and then cut out the hairy choke and the inner purple leaves. Drop the halves into the lemon water. When all of the artichokes have been trimmed, drain them. Place each half on a cutting board, cut side down, and cut lengthwise into slices ¼ inch (6 mm) thick.

Bring a large saucepan three-fourths full of water to a boil and add ¼ teaspoon kosher salt. Add the artichokes and boil until half-cooked and barely tender, 2–4 minutes, depending on their freshness. Drain the artichokes and set aside.

In a frying pan large enough to accommodate the pasta later, melt the butter with the olive oil over medium heat. Add the shallots, garlic, and thyme and sauté until the shallots are softened, about 3 minutes. Add the artichokes and sauté for 5 minutes. Add the wine and cook until most of the alcohol has evaporated, 2–3 minutes. Add the broth and ½ teaspoon sea salt, cover, and cook over low heat until the artichokes are tender and a cohesive sauce is formed, about 10 minutes. Uncover and remove and discard the garlic. Stir in the crème fraîche, bring to a simmer, and remove from the heat. Season to taste with pepper and stir in the ½ cup (2 oz/60 g) grated cheese. Remove from the heat and cover to keep warm.

In a large pot, bring 5 qt (5 l) water to a rapid boil. Add 2 tablespoons kosher salt and the pasta and cover the pot. When the water returns to a boil, uncover, cook for about 5 seconds, and drain. Add the pasta to the sauce in the pan and toss until the strands are well coated with the sauce. Transfer to a warmed large, shallow serving bowl or individual shallow bowls, and sprinkle with the additional thyme and cheese. Serve right away.

Maltagliati *with* Zucchini Blossoms and Basil

If you have a zucchini plant in your yard, this delicate sauce is a rewarding way to use the colorful, bittersweet blossoms. Select male flowers about 2 inches (5 cm) long. Avoid picking the female flowers (the ones with a baby squash attached) if you want your plant to produce a good harvest.

Egg Pasta I *(page 16 or 18)*

10–15 zucchini blossoms *(see Note)*

4 tablespoons *(2 oz/60 g)* **unsalted butter**

2 tablespoons extra-virgin olive oil

1 shallot, minced

10 fresh basil leaves, cut crosswise into thin ribbons

Fine sea salt and freshly ground black or white pepper

Kosher salt for cooking pasta

3 tablespoons freshly grated Parmigiano-Reggiano cheese

Make the pasta dough as directed, then roll out (pages 20–21 or 22) and cut into maltagliati as directed on page 23. Let dry for 30 minutes or up to 3 hours (see page 13).

Rinse the blossoms briefly under cold running water, checking inside for insects. Remove the stamens and gently pat the blossoms dry on paper towels. Cut the blossoms lengthwise into narrow ribbons.

In a large pot, bring 5 qt (5 l) water to a rapid boil.

While the water is heating, make the sauce. In a frying pan large enough to accommodate the pasta later, melt the butter with the olive oil over medium-low heat. Add the shallot and sauté until translucent, about 3 minutes. Add the blossoms and sauté until tender, about 3 minutes longer. Add the basil and toss to combine. Season to taste with sea salt and pepper. Remove from the heat and cover to keep warm.

Add 2 tablespoons kosher salt and the pasta to the boiling water and cover the pot. When the water returns to a boil, uncover, cook for about 5 seconds, and then drain. Add the pasta and the cheese to the sauce in the pan and stir and toss until the cheese is evenly distributed and the pasta is well coated with the sauce. Transfer to a warmed large, shallow serving bowl or individual shallow bowls and serve right away.

TRENETTE *with* POTATOES, GREEN BEANS, AND PESTO

In this recipe, pesto brings together three foods for which it has a natural affinity: pasta, potatoes, and green beans. Pesto was invented for dressing egg pasta in the Italian region of Liguria, but cooks there also use it with potato dishes of various kinds, including potato gnocchi.

Egg Pasta I *(page 16 or 18)*

Kosher salt for cooking vegetables and pasta

¼ lb *(125 g)* green beans, trimmed and cut crosswise into thirds

1 Yukon gold potato, about ¼ lb *(125 g)*

FOR THE BASIL PESTO

2 cups *(2 oz/60 g)* firmly packed fresh basil leaves

2 cloves garlic, coarsely chopped

⅓ cup *(1½ oz/45 g)* pine nuts, lightly toasted

½ cup *(4 fl oz/125 ml)* extra-virgin olive oil

Fine sea salt and freshly ground pepper

2 tablespoons unsalted butter, at room temperature

¾ cup *(3 oz/90 g)* freshly grated Parmigiano-Reggiano cheese

Freshly grated Parmigiano-Reggiano cheese for serving

Make the pasta dough as directed, then roll out (pages 20–21 or 22) and cut into trenette as directed on page 23. Let dry for 30 minutes or up to 3 hours (see page 13).

Have ready a bowl of ice water. In a saucepan, bring 2 qt (2 l) water to a boil over high heat. Add 2 teaspoons kosher salt and the green beans and cook until tender, about 6 minutes. Using a wire skimmer or a sieve, remove the beans and immediately immerse them in the ice water to halt the cooking. Drain and set aside. Add the potato to the same boiling water, reduce the heat to medium, and cook until tender when pierced with a knife, about 20 minutes. Drain, and when cool enough to handle, peel the potato and cut into small dice; set aside.

To make the pesto, in a food processor, combine the basil, garlic, pine nuts, olive oil, ½ teaspoon sea salt, and a few grinds of pepper. Process to a paste, stopping occasionally to scrape down the sides of the work bowl. Be careful not to overprocess; the consistency of the pesto should be thick and fluid and have a slightly grainy texture. Transfer to a bowl and stir in the butter and the cheese. Transfer the pesto to a serving bowl large enough to accommodate the pasta later. Set aside.

In a large pot, bring 5 qt (5 l) water to a rapid boil. Add 2 tablespoons kosher salt and the pasta and cover the pot. When the water returns to a boil, uncover, cook for about 5 seconds, and then drain, reserving about ½ cup (4 fl oz/125 ml) of the cooking water. Stir a few tablespoons of the cooking water into the pesto to make a creamy consistency, then add the pasta, green beans, and potato to the bowl and stir and toss with the pesto until evenly distributed and the strands are well coated with the sauce, adding a little more of the cooking water if needed to loosen the sauce. Serve right away. Pass the additional cheese at the table.

TAGLIATELLE AND CHICKPEA SOUP *with* PANCETTA

This soup, called *pasta e ceci* in Italian, is a favorite dish of Romans. In Italy, it is served as a first course, but it is hearty enough to be enjoyed as a main dish. Because chickpeas are dense, they take a long time to soak and soften; here, baking soda is added to the soaking water to speed up the process.

1½ cups *(10½ oz/330 g)* dried chickpeas

½ teaspoon baking soda

1 large clove garlic, unpeeled, plus 2 cloves garlic, minced

1 rib celery with leaves

1 small fresh rosemary sprig

Egg Pasta I *(page 16 or 18)*

Fine sea salt and freshly ground pepper

3 tablespoons extra-virgin olive oil

2 oz *(60 g)* pancetta, finely diced

2 tablespoons tomato paste

Pick over the chickpeas, discarding any grit or misshapen chickpeas. Rinse well, place in a bowl with cold water to cover by 3 inches (7.5 cm), and stir in the baking soda. Let stand for 24 hours. Drain and rinse well.

In a large saucepan, combine the rehydrated chickpeas, the unpeeled garlic clove, the celery rib, rosemary, and 7 cups (56 fl oz/1.75 l) water. Bring to a gentle boil over medium-high heat. Adjust the heat to maintain a steady simmer, cover partially, and cook until the chickpeas are tender, about 1½ hours.

Meanwhile, make the pasta dough recipe as directed to yield 1 lb (500 g), then roll out one-fourth of the dough and cut into tagliatelle as directed on pages 20–21 or 22–23. (Reserve the remaining dough for another use.) Cut the tagliatelle into 2-inch (5-cm) lengths. Let dry for 30 minutes or up to 3 hours (see page 13).

When the chickpeas are ready, remove the pan from the heat. Stir in 2 teaspoons sea salt and let the chickpeas stand for 5 minutes to absorb the salt. Remove and discard the garlic clove, celery, and rosemary. Remove 1 cup (7 oz/220 g) of the chickpeas and mash them with a fork or potato masher. Return them to the pot and stir to combine.

In a frying pan over medium-low heat, warm the olive oil. Add the diced pancetta and sauté until golden brown, about 3 minutes. Stir in the minced garlic, reduce the heat to low, and sauté until the garlic is softened, about 1 minute. Add the tomato paste and ½ cup (4 fl oz/125 ml) of the broth from the chickpeas and stir well.

Add the pancetta mixture to the chickpeas, place the pot over medium heat, and bring to a gentle boil. Cook for 10 minutes to allow the flavors to blend. Add the pasta and continue to cook until the pasta is just shy of tender, about 2 minutes. (It will continue to cook in the heat of the soup.) Season with sea salt and pepper, ladle into warmed shallow bowls, and serve right away.

FETTUCCINE *with* CRAB AND FENNEL

The anise notes of fennel are a good match for the rich, sweet flavor of crab in this dish. Seek out the freshest premium lump crabmeat you can find; it should be moist, not dry. Since lump crabmeat comes precooked, it should be just heated through when added to the sauce.

Egg Pasta I *(page 16 or 18)*

1 fennel bulb

3 tablespoons unsalted butter

1 carrot, peeled and minced

1 large shallot, minced

1 clove garlic, bruised
(see page 233)

1 tablespoon minced
fresh flat-leaf parsley

½ cup *(4 fl oz/125 ml)*
dry sherry

1 cup *(8 fl oz/250 ml)*
heavy cream

¾ lb *(375 g)* lump crabmeat
(see Note), picked over for
shell fragments and cartilage
and flaked

Fine sea salt and freshly
ground white pepper

Kosher salt for cooking pasta

Make the pasta dough as directed, then roll out and cut into fettuccine as directed on pages 20–21 or 22–23. Let dry for 30 minutes or up to 3 hours (see page 13).

Cut off the stems and feathery tops and remove any bruised outer stalks from the fennel bulb. Pinch off a handful of tiny sprigs from the feathery tops and reserve for garnish. Slice off the tough bottom of the bulb, then quarter the bulb lengthwise. Cut out and discard the tough core. Remove the outer stalks and reserve for another use. Mince the light green heart of the bulb (you should have about 3 tablespoons) and set aside.

In a large pot, bring 5 qt (5 l) water to a rapid boil.

While the water is heating, make the sauce. In a frying pan large enough to accommodate the pasta later, melt the butter over medium heat. Add the carrot, shallot, garlic, parsley, and minced fennel and cook gently, stirring occasionally to prevent browning, until the vegetables are thoroughly softened and aromatic, about 7 minutes. Stir in the sherry and cook gently, stirring occasionally, until most of the alcohol has evaporated, about 3 minutes. Reduce the heat to low, add the cream, and warm just until heated through, 2–3 minutes. Add the crab and stir just until heated through, about 1 minute. Remove from the heat, season to taste with sea salt and white pepper, and cover to keep warm.

Just before the sauce is ready, add 2 tablespoons kosher salt and the pasta to the boiling water and cover the pot. When the water returns to a boil, uncover, cook for about 5 seconds, and then drain. Add the pasta to the sauce in the pan and and toss until the strands are well coated with the sauce. Transfer to a warmed large, shallow serving bowl or individual shallow bowls and garnish with the fennel sprigs. Serve right away.

Pappardelle *with* Braised Duck Ragù

This sauce, adapted from a traditional Hungarian duck stew, produces a succulent and winy, paprika-rich topping. Pappardelle, the traditional type of fresh pasta paired with duck in Italy, is wide and hefty enough to support this luxurious braise.

Egg Pasta I *(page 16 or 18)*

1 skin-on, boneless whole duck breast, about 1 lb *(500 g)*

Fine sea salt and freshly ground pepper

1 tablespoon rendered duck fat or unsalted butter

1 tablespoon extra-virgin olive oil

1 yellow onion, minced

2 large cloves garlic, bruised *(see page 233)*

1 small carrot, peeled and minced

1 small celery heart, minced

½ cup *(4 fl oz/125 ml)* dry red wine

4 teaspoons sweet paprika

2 teaspoons chopped fresh marjoram, or 1 teaspoon crumbled dried marjoram

½ teaspoon caraway seeds

1 cup *(8 oz/250 g)* canned plum tomatoes with juice, seeded and chopped

3½ cups *(28 fl oz/875 ml)* low-sodium chicken broth, or as needed

Kosher salt for cooking pasta

Make the pasta dough as directed, then roll out (pages 20–21 or 22) and cut into pappardelle as directed on page 23. Let dry for 30 minutes or up to 3 hours (see page 13).

Pat the duck breast dry with paper towels, then sprinkle on both sides with sea salt and pepper. In a Dutch oven or large, deep frying pan over medium heat, warm the duck fat with the olive oil over medium heat. Place the duck breast skin side down in the pan and cook, turning once, until deep gold on both sides, about 10 minutes total. Transfer to a plate.

Add the onion, garlic, carrot, and celery to the fat remaining in the pan and cook over medium heat, stirring occasionally, until tender, about 4 minutes. Return the duck breast, skin side up, to the pan, along with any accumulated juices. Add the wine and simmer until most of the alcohol has evaporated, about 1 minute. Stir in the paprika, marjoram, and caraway, and then add the tomatoes and their juice and the broth. Raise the heat and bring to a boil, then reduce the heat to low. Cover partially and simmer until the duck is tender and a thick sauce has formed, about 1 hour. If needed, add more broth in small quantities to prevent the sauce from drying out.

Remove the sauce from the heat, transfer the duck breast to a plate, and cover the pan to keep the sauce warm. When cool enough to handle, remove and discard the skin and excess fat from the breast. Shred the meat into small pieces. Using a large spoon, skim off the excess fat from the sauce. Stir the duck into the sauce, then taste and adjust the seasoning. Cover to keep the sauce warm.

In a large pot, bring 5 qt (5 l) water to a rapid boil. When the water is boiling, warm the sauce over medium heat until heated through. Add 2 tablespoons kosher salt and the pasta to the boiling water and cover the pot. When the water returns to a boil, uncover, cook for about 5 seconds, and then drain. Transfer the pasta to a warmed large, shallow serving bowl. Add the sauce and toss with the pasta until well combined. Serve right away.

Spinach Fettuccine *with* Creamy Sausage Sauce

This recipe comes from the northern Italian region of Emilia-Romagna, where the making of both fresh pasta and refined meat sauces is an art. In the local cuisine, a handmade, spiral-shaped spinach noodle called *gramigna* is typically paired with this sauce, but for ease fettuccine is used here.

FOR THE SPINACH PASTA

4 oz *(125 g)* fresh spinach, tough stems removed

Kosher salt for cooking spinach

1 teaspoon olive oil

2½ cups *(12½ oz/390 g)* unbleached all-purpose flour, plus more as needed

¼ teaspoon fine sea salt

3 large eggs, at room temperature

2 tablespoons unsalted butter

1 tablespoon extra-virgin olive oil

1 carrot, peeled and minced

1 small celery heart, minced

2 shallots, minced

½ lb *(250 g)* sweet Italian sausages, casings removed

½ teaspoon grated nutmeg

Fine sea salt and freshly ground pepper

½ cup *(4 fl oz/125 ml)* milk

2 tablespoons tomato paste

1 cup *(8 oz/250 g)* drained canned plum tomatoes, seeded and chopped

1 cup *(8 fl oz/250 ml)* low-sodium beef broth

Kosher salt for cooking pasta

Freshly grated Parmigiano-Reggiano cheese for serving

To make the spinach pasta, bring a saucepan three-fourths full of water to a boil and add the spinach and 1 teaspoon kosher salt. Cook, stirring several times, just until tender, about 30 seconds. Drain into a colander or sieve and let stand until cool. Squeeze the spinach to remove excess moisture, then wring it as dry as possible in a clean, dry kitchen towel. Chop very finely, by hand or preferably in a food processor or blender.

Proceed by following the method for Egg Pasta (page 16 or 18), stirring the spinach in with the eggs and oil before combining it with the flour and sea salt. Roll out and cut into fettuccine as directed on pages 20–21 or 22–23. Let dry for 30 minutes or up to 3 hours (see page 13).

In a frying pan large enough to accommodate the pasta later, melt the butter with the olive oil over medium heat. Add the carrot, celery, and shallots and sauté until tender, about 12 minutes. Add the sausage meat and stir to break up any clumps. Sprinkle with the nutmeg and season with sea salt and pepper, then reduce the heat to medium-low and sauté until the sausage is lightly colored on the outside but still pink inside, about 8 minutes. Add the milk, stir well, and cook gently until the milk begins to simmer, about 8 minutes. Stir the tomato paste and tomatoes into the sauce, mixing well. Reduce the heat to the lowest possible setting, cover partially, and cook, stirring in the broth a little at a time during the cooking to keep the sauce moist, for about 1½ hours. The sauce should be dense and aromatic. Uncover during the last 10 minutes to thicken, if necessary. Remove from the heat and cover to keep warm.

When the sauce is ready, in a large pot, bring 5 qt (5 l) water to a rapid boil. Add 2 tablespoons kosher salt and the pasta and cover the pot. When the water returns to a boil, uncover, cook for about 5 seconds, and then drain. Add the pasta to the sauce in the pan and toss until the strands are well coated with the sauce. Transfer the pasta to a warmed large, shallow bowl or individual shallow bowls and serve right away. Pass the grated cheese at the table.

WHOLE-WHEAT FETTUCCINE *with* ARUGULA PESTO

For those who find basil pesto too sweet, here is a nice alternative that uses the more assertive arugula. The vibrant sauce is cut with parsley to temper the bold, peppery flavor of the arugula, and Spanish Manchego, a sheep's milk cheese, lends a unique flavor in place of Parmigiano-Reggiano.

FOR THE WHOLE-WHEAT PASTA

1½ cups (7½ oz/235 g) whole-wheat flour

½ cup (2½ oz/75 g) unbleached all-purpose flour, plus more for dusting

¼ teaspoon fine sea salt

3 large eggs, at room temperature

1 tablespoon olive oil

FOR THE ARUGULA PESTO

2 cups (2 oz/60 g) firmly packed baby arugula leaves

1 cup (1 oz/30 g) firmly packed fresh flat-leaf parsley leaves

1 large clove garlic, coarsely chopped

¼ cup (1 oz/30 g) pine nuts, lightly toasted

½ cup (2 oz/60 g) freshly grated Manchego cheese

½ cup (4 fl oz/125 ml) extra-virgin olive oil

Fine sea salt and freshly ground pepper

Kosher salt for cooking pasta

To make the whole-wheat pasta, follow the method for Egg Pasta (page 16 or 18), but increase the kneading time to 12–14 minutes. Roll out and cut into fettuccine as directed on pages 20–21 or 22–23. Let dry for 30 minutes or up to 3 hours (see page 13).

To make the pesto, in a food processor, combine the arugula, parsley, garlic, pine nuts, cheese, olive oil, and a pinch each of sea salt and pepper. Process to a paste, stopping occasionally to scrape down the sides of the work bowl. Be careful not to overprocess; the consistency of the pesto should be thick and fluid and have a slightly grainy texture. Transfer to a serving bowl large enough to accommodate the pasta later.

In a large pot, bring 5 qt (5 l) water to a rapid boil. Add 2 tablespoons kosher salt and the pasta and cover the pot. When the water returns to a boil, uncover, cook for about 5 seconds, and then drain, reserving about ½ cup (4 fl oz/125 ml) of the cooking water. Blend a few tablespoons of the cooking water with the pesto to make a creamy consistency, then add the pasta to the bowl and stir and toss with the pesto until the strands are well coated with the sauce, adding a little more of the cooking water if needed to loosen the sauce. Serve right away.

TAGLIERINI *with* SHRIMP AND TARRAGON

South American white shrimp are the ideal choice for this recipe because they are usually firmer than other varieties and hold up well when sautéed. Pernod gives this dish a pleasant anise flavor, which marries well with the seafood and the warm, sweet hint of saffron.

Egg Pasta I *(page 16 or 18)*

1½ lb *(750 g)* large shrimp, preferably South American white, peeled and deveined

7 tablespoons *(3½ oz/105 g)* unsalted butter

2 shallots, minced

¼ cup *(2 fl oz/60 ml)* Pernod

2 cups *(16 fl oz/500 ml)* heavy cream

¼ teaspoon saffron threads, or ⅛ teaspoon powdered saffron

2 tablespoons chopped fresh tarragon

Fine sea salt

Kosher salt for cooking pasta

2 tablespoons snipped fresh chives

Make the pasta dough as directed, then roll out and cut into taglierini as directed on pages 20–21 or 22–23. Let dry for 30 minutes or up to 3 hours (see page 13).

Cut each shrimp in half lengthwise. Rinse and pat dry, then set aside.

In a frying pan large enough to accommodate the pasta later, melt 6 tablespoons (3 oz/90 g) of the butter over medium heat. Add the shallots and sauté until softened, about 4 minutes. Stir in the shrimp and sauté, stirring to heat evenly, just until they color, 1–2 minutes. Reduce the heat to medium-low, add the Pernod, and cook until most of the alcohol has evaporated, 2–3 minutes.

Meanwhile, in a saucepan over medium heat, warm the cream just until small bubbles begin to form around the edges of the pan. Do not let the cream boil. If using saffron threads, in a small, dry frying pan over low heat, warm the threads for 1 minute, then crush them between your fingers and drop into the hot cream. If using powdered saffron, add it to the hot cream and stir briefly to dissolve. Remove from the heat.

Add the saffron cream to the pan with the shrimp, reduce the heat to low, and cook to allow the flavors to blend, about 2 minutes. Using a slotted spoon, transfer the shrimp to a warmed plate, cover, and set aside. Return the heat to medium-low and simmer the sauce until it is thick enough to coat the back of a spoon, about 5 minutes. Add the remaining 1 tablespoon butter and the tarragon and stir until the butter has melted. Return the shrimp to the pan, stir well, and season to taste with sea salt. Remove from the heat and cover to keep warm.

In a large pot, bring 5 qt (5 l) water to a rapid boil. Add 2 tablespoons kosher salt and the pasta and cover the pot. When the water returns to a boil, uncover, cook for about 5 seconds, and then drain. Add the pasta to the sauce in the pan and toss until the strands are well coated with the sauce. Transfer to a warmed large, shallow serving bowl or individual shallow bowls and garnish with the chives. Serve right away.

TAGLIATELLE *with* LEEKS AND PEAS

This is a beautiful and bright-tasting dish that makes the most of the bounty of spring vegetables. The tagliatelle must be cut from pasta sheets that are rolled out as thinly as possible—you should be able to see your hand through a sheet when you hold it up to the light—to ensure a delicate dish.

Egg Pasta I *(page 16 or 18)*

FOR THE SAUCE

2 large leeks, thoroughly cleaned

Kosher salt for blanching leeks

½ cup *(2½ oz/75 g)* fresh or frozen shelled English peas

4 tablespoons *(2 oz/60 g)* unsalted butter

2 shallots, minced

1 small white onion, sliced lengthwise paper-thin

½ cup *(4 fl oz/125 ml)* dry sherry

1½ cups *(12 fl oz/375 ml)* heavy cream

Fine sea salt and freshly ground pepper

Kosher salt for cooking pasta

2 tablespoons chopped fresh flat-leaf parsley

Freshly grated Parmigiano-Reggiano cheese for serving

Make the pasta dough as directed, then roll out and cut into tagliatelle as directed on pages 20–21 or 22–23. Let dry for 30 minutes or up to 3 hours (see page 13).

To make the sauce, cut off and discard the dark green leaves from the leeks, and trim away the root end. Cut the white portion of each leek lengthwise into eighths, then cut the pieces crosswise on the diagonal into 1½-inch (4-cm) lengths.

Have ready a bowl of ice water. Bring 2 qt (2 l) water to a boil over high heat and add 1 tablespoon kosher salt. Add the leeks and blanch for 2 minutes. Using a wire skimmer or a sieve, remove the leeks and immediately immerse them in the ice water to halt the cooking. Drain and pat dry, then refill the bowl. If using fresh peas, add them to the same boiling water, blanch for 2 minutes, then drain and immediately immerse in the ice water. Drain again and pat dry. If using frozen peas, do not blanch.

In a frying pan large enough to accommodate the pasta later, melt the butter over medium heat. Add the shallots and onion and sauté until translucent and softened, 3–4 minutes. Add the leeks and peas, stir well, and then add the sherry. Reduce the heat to medium-low and cook, stirring occasionally, until most of the alcohol has evaporated, about 2 minutes. Add the cream, reduce the heat to low, and simmer until the sauce thickens, about 3 minutes. Season with sea salt and pepper. Remove from the heat and cover to keep warm.

In a large pot, bring 5 qt (5 l) water to a rapid boil. Add 2 tablespoons kosher salt and the pasta and cover the pot. When the water returns to a boil, uncover, cook for about 5 seconds, and then drain. Add the pasta to the sauce in the pan and toss until the strands are well coated with the sauce. Transfer to a warmed large, shallow serving bowl or individual shallow bowls, sprinkle with the parsley, and serve right away. Pass the cheese at the table.

TOMATO TAGLIATELLE *with* LOBSTER AND SAFFRON

This dish is time-consuming to make, but well worth the effort, yielding a luxurious and sophisticated show-stopping main course. The combination of onion, carrot, and celery in a classic *mirepoix* provides a naturally sweet foundation that complements the rich notes of the lobster meat.

1 live lobster, 1½ lb *(750 g)*

1 cup *(8 fl oz/250 ml)* heavy cream

6 tablespoons *(3 oz/90 g)* unsalted butter

¾ cup *(4 oz/125 g)* finely chopped white onion

⅔ cup *(3½ oz/105 g)* peeled and finely chopped carrot

2 large ribs celery, minced

1 clove garlic, bruised *(see page 233)*

½ cup *(4 fl oz/125 ml)* dry white wine

3 large fresh tomatoes, peeled, seeded, and chopped, or 6 canned plum tomatoes, seeded and chopped

Fine sea salt and freshly ground pepper

FOR THE TOMATO PASTA

Egg Pasta I *(page 16 or 18)*

1 tablespoon double-concentrated tomato paste

¼ teaspoon saffron threads, or ⅛ teaspoon powdered saffron

1 large shallot, finely chopped

Kosher salt for cooking pasta

3 tablespoons minced fresh flat-leaf parsley

In a pot, bring 4 cups (32 fl oz/1 l) water to a boil. Drop in the lobster, head first, and cover the pot. When the water returns to a boil, cook for about 5 minutes. The lobster is ready when it has turned red. Remove the lobster, and reserve the water in the pot.

When the lobster is cool enough to handle, working over a bowl to catch any juices, twist off the tail, claws, and legs. Crack the claws with a mallet and cut the tail in half lengthwise. Remove the meat from the claws and tail, cut into bite-size chunks, and set aside in a bowl. Add the cream to the bowl, cover, and refrigerate. Discard the claw shells. Break up the body (reserve the tomalley, if present), legs, and tail shell with a mallet and set aside.

In a large, deep frying pan over medium heat, melt 3 tablespoons of the butter. Add half of the onion and sauté until softened, about 3 minutes. Add half each of the carrot and celery and the garlic clove and cook, stirring occasionally, for 5 minutes. Add the body (with any tomalley), legs, tail shell, and any captured juices. Raise the heat to medium-high and cook, stirring, until the shells have deepened in color, 8–10 minutes. If the vegetables begin to dry out, reduce the heat. Add the wine, reduce the heat to low, and cook until most of the alcohol has evaporated, about 3 minutes. Add the tomatoes, ½ teaspoon sea salt, and several grinds of pepper and cook, stirring, for 3 minutes. Remove and discard the garlic. Add 3 cups (24 fl oz/750 ml) of the reserved lobster-cooking water and bring to a boil over medium-high heat. Immediately reduce the heat to low and simmer gently, uncovered, skimming off any foam that forms on the surface, until a flavorful stock is made, about 1 hour.

While the lobster stock is simmering, make the pasta dough. Prepare the Egg Pasta dough as directed, but reduce the olive oil to 1 teaspoon and stir the tomato paste in with the eggs and oil before combining with the flour. Cover the dough with an inverted bowl or slightly damp kitchen towel and let rest for 20 minutes, then roll out the dough and cut

Tomato tints fresh egg pasta
a beautiful pale red color that
is stunning when mixed with
pink-splotched lobster meat,
but plain egg pasta can be used
instead. Shrimp or crab can also
be substituted for the lobster.

into tagliatelle as directed on pages 20–21 or 22–23. The tomato dough
is more likely to stick to the work surface and pasta machine than plain
egg dough, so you may need more flour for dusting. Let dry for
30 minutes or up to 3 hours (see page 13).

Remove the stock from the heat. Line a large fine-mesh sieve with
a double layer of cheesecloth and place over a bowl. Pour the contents
of the pan into the sieve and press against the solids with the back of
a spoon to force through as much liquid as possible.

Transfer the strained stock to a frying pan and place over medium-low
heat. Without letting it boil, reduce the stock to about 1 cup (8 fl oz/
250 ml), about 10 minutes. Stir in the saffron, crushing it first between
your fingers if using saffron threads.

While the stock is reducing, rinse out the large frying pan, place over
medium-low heat, and melt the remaining 3 tablespoons butter. Add
the remaining onion and carrot and the shallot and cook gently, stirring
occasionally, until softened but not colored, 10–12 minutes. Stir in the
reduced stock, and then add the lobster meat and cream. Heat just until
warmed through, 4–5 minutes. Do not overcook the lobster, or it will
be tough. Remove from the heat, taste and adjust the seasoning with
sea salt and pepper, and cover to keep warm.

In a large pot, bring 5 qt (5 l) water to a rapid boil. Add 2 tablespoons
kosher salt and the pasta and cover the pot. When the water returns to
a boil, uncover, cook for about 5 seconds, and then drain. Add the pasta
to the sauce in the pan and toss until the strands are well coated with the
sauce. Transfer to a warmed large, shallow serving bowl or individual
shallow bowls, garnish with the parsley, and serve right away.

SERVES 4

Saffron Fettuccine *with* Prosciutto and Cream

The sunny tint of saffron in the fresh pasta dough and the garnish of crisp prosciutto strips and bright green flecks of chives make this an eye-catching dish. The light cream sauce, which comes together in just a few minutes, is also delicious tossed with thinner strand noodles such as tagliatelle.

FOR THE SAFFRON PASTA

Egg Pasta I *(page 16 or 18)*

½ teaspoon saffron threads, or ¼ teaspoon powdered saffron

FOR THE SAUCE

2 oz *(60 g)* prosciutto

1 tablespoon extra-virgin olive oil

7 tablespoons *(3½ oz/105 g)* unsalted butter

¾ cup *(6 fl oz/180 ml)* heavy cream

⅔ cup *(2½ oz/75 g)* freshly grated Parmigiano-Reggiano cheese

Freshly ground pepper

Kosher salt for cooking pasta

2 tablespoons snipped fresh chives

Freshly grated Parmigiano-Reggiano cheese for serving

To make the saffron pasta, make the Egg Pasta dough as directed, adding the saffron to the eggs and oil before combining with the flour. If using saffron threads, crush first between your fingers. Roll out the dough and cut into fettuccine as directed on pages 20–21 or 22–23. Let dry for 30 minutes or up to 3 hours (see page 13).

In a large pot, bring 5 qt (5 l) water to a rapid boil.

While the water is heating, make the sauce. Cut the prosciutto into strips about 1 inch (2.5 cm) long and ¼ inch (6 mm) wide. In a frying pan large enough to accommodate the pasta later, warm the olive oil over medium-low heat. Add the prosciutto and sauté gently until it is nicely colored and crisp, about 2 minutes. Using a slotted spoon, transfer to a plate. Add the butter to the pan over medium-low heat. As it melts, use a wooden spoon to scrape up any bits of prosciutto stuck to the bottom of the pan. When the butter has melted, stir in the cream, cheese, and several grinds of pepper and cook, stirring occasionally, until the cheese is incorporated and the sauce comes to a gentle simmer. Remove from the heat and cover to keep warm.

Add 2 tablespoons kosher salt and the pasta to the boiling water and cover the pot. When the water returns to a boil, uncover, cook for about 5 seconds, and then drain. Add the pasta to the sauce in the pan and toss until the strands are well coated with the sauce. Transfer to a warmed large, shallow serving bowl or individual shallow bowls and scatter the prosciutto and chives over the top. Pass the additional cheese at the table.

Fresh Herb Pappardelle *with* Veal and Lemon

Veal and lemon are harmonious companions in the kitchen, and this delicate dish is proof of that happy union. Adding fresh parsley to the egg dough is a pretty way of lacing the final dish with herbal brightness, and earthy mushrooms and a light sherry-cream sauce round out the flavors.

FOR THE HERB PASTA

Egg Pasta I *(page 16 or 18)*

3 tablespoons minced fresh flat-leaf parsley leaves

1 lb *(500 g)* veal shoulder, partially frozen and cut into thin strips 1 inch *(2.5 cm)* long and ¼ inch *(6 mm)* wide

4 tablespoons *(2 oz/60 g)* unsalted butter

2 tablespoons extra-virgin olive oil

2 large shallots, minced

½ lb *(250 g)* fresh white mushrooms, brushed clean and very thinly sliced

½ cup *(4 fl oz/125 ml)* dry sherry

1½ cups *(12 fl oz/375 ml)* low-sodium chicken broth

1 teaspoon chopped fresh thyme, or scant ½ teaspoon crushed dried thyme

1 lemon zest strip, 3 inches *(7.5 cm)* long and 1 inch *(2.5 cm)* wide

2 tablespoons chopped fresh flat-leaf parsley

Fine sea salt and freshly ground pepper

1 cup *(8 fl oz/250 ml)* heavy cream

Kosher salt for cooking pasta

To make the herb pasta dough, make the Egg Pasta dough as directed, mixing the parsley leaves into the flour and salt. Roll out the dough (pages 20–21 or 22) and cut into pappardelle as directed on page 23. Let dry for 30 minutes or up to 3 hours (see page 13).

Use paper towels to pat the veal dry thoroughly. Set aside.

In a large nonstick frying pan over medium heat, melt the butter with the olive oil. Add the shallots and sauté until tender, about 2 minutes. Raise the heat to medium-high and add the mushrooms. Sauté gently until softened, about 2 minutes. Using a slotted spoon, transfer the shallot and mushroom mixture to a plate and set aside.

Raise the heat to high and add the veal to the pan. Sauté until the meat colors on the surface, about 2 minutes. Add the sherry and reduce the heat to medium. Sauté until most of the alcohol evaporates, about 3 minutes. Add the broth, raise the heat to high, and bring to a boil. Add the thyme and immediately reduce the heat to low. Simmer, covered, for 15 minutes. Uncover, add the lemon zest and chopped parsley, and return the mushroom mixture to the pan. Season with sea salt and pepper and simmer, uncovered, until the veal is tender and the liquid is reduced to about 1¼ cups (10 fl oz/310 ml), about 15 minutes longer. Remove and discard the lemon zest. Add the cream and heat, stirring, just until small bubbles begin to form around the edges of the pan. Do not let the cream boil. Remove from the heat and cover to keep warm.

In a large pot, bring 5 qt (5 l) water to a rapid boil. Add 2 tablespoons kosher salt and the pasta and cover the pot. When the water returns to a boil, uncover, cook for about 5 seconds, and then drain. Add the pasta to the sauce in the pan and toss until the pasta is well coated with the sauce. Transfer to a warmed large, shallow serving bowl or individual shallow bowls and serve right away.

Pappardelle *with* Short Rib Ragù

The best beef to use for this *ragù* is short ribs, the prized cut that emerges falling-apart tender from slow cooking. If you prefer a fine-textured sauce, before you add the mushrooms, remove the ribs, bone them, shred the meat, and return the meat to the sauce to warm through.

4 lb *(2 kg)* beef ribs, each 2 inches *(5 cm)* long, or 2 lb *(1 kg)* beef top round

3 tablespoons extra-virgin olive oil

2 oz *(60 g)* pork fatback or prosciutto fat, cut into matchsticks, or 4 tablespoons *(2 oz/60 g)* unsalted butter

1 large yellow onion, chopped

1 carrot, peeled and chopped

1 large clove garlic, minced

2 bay leaves

1 cinnamon stick, 3 inches *(7.5 cm)* long

1 teaspoon ground cumin

½ teaspoon ground cloves

¼ teaspoon ground cardamom

Fine sea salt and freshly ground pepper

3 tablespoons tomato paste, diluted with 3–4 tablespoons water

½ cup *(4 fl oz/125 ml)* full-bodied dry red wine

3½ cups *(28 fl oz/875 ml)* low-sodium beef broth

Egg Pasta I *(page 16 or 18)*

2 tablespoons unsalted butter

3 oz *(90 g)* fresh wild or cultivated mushrooms, brushed clean, tough stems removed, and sliced

Kosher salt for cooking pasta

Trim the beef of excess fat. If using the beef round, cut into 1½-inch (4-cm) dice. Pat the meat dry thoroughly with paper towels.

In a Dutch oven or other large, heavy pot over medium heat, warm 1 tablespoon of the olive oil. If using the fatback or prosciutto fat, add to the pan with the olive oil and sauté until lightly browned, 2–3 minutes. Using a slotted spoon, transfer to a large platter and reserve. If using the butter, melt it with the olive oil. Working in batches to avoid crowding, add the beef to the pan and brown on all sides, about 12 minutes for each batch. Transfer the beef and its juices to the platter with the fatback.

Add the remaining 2 tablespoons olive oil to the pot over medium heat and stir in the onion, carrot, garlic, bay leaves, cinnamon, cumin, cloves, and cardamom. Sauté until the vegetables are softened, lightly colored, and aromatic, about 10 minutes. Return the beef and the fatback (if used) to the pan, add 1 teaspoon sea salt and several grinds of pepper, and stir well. Stir in the diluted tomato paste, the wine, and enough broth just to cover the meat. Cover partially, reduce the heat to low, and cook, stirring occasionally and adding additional broth or water as needed to prevent the pan from drying out, until the meat is tender, about 3 hours.

While the sauce is cooking, make the pasta dough as directed, then roll out (pages 20–21 or 22) and cut into pappardelle as directed on page 23. Let dry for 30 minutes or up to 3 hours (see page 13).

Just before the sauce is ready, in a frying pan over medium heat, melt the butter. Add the mushrooms and sauté until tender, about 4 minutes. Remove the sauce from the heat and remove and discard the bay leaves and cinnamon stick. Fold in the mushrooms, cover, and let rest while you cook the pasta. In a large pot, bring 5 qt (5 l) water to a rapid boil. Add 2 tablespoons kosher salt and the pasta and cover the pot. When the water returns to a boil, uncover, cook for about 5 seconds, and then drain. Transfer the pasta to a warmed large, shallow serving bowl or individual shallow bowls. Top with the sauce and serve right away.

FETTUCCINE *with* BEEF AND MUSHROOMS

This rich and elegant meat sauce is ideal not only with fresh fettuccine, but also with other fresh flat noodles, such as pappardelle; filled pasta, like cheese ravioli; or dried shapes like orecchiette. If you like, offer a tangy young pecorino cheese in place of the Parmigiano-Reggiano at the table.

¼ cup *(¼ oz/7 g)* dried porcini mushrooms, soaked in ¼ cup *(2 fl oz/60 ml)* hot water for 30 minutes

1 can *(28 oz/875 g)* plum tomatoes

2 tablespoons unsalted butter

2 tablespoons extra-virgin olive oil

1 carrot, peeled and finely chopped

1 rib celery, including leaves, finely chopped

1 small yellow onion, finely chopped

2 tablespoons chopped fresh flat-leaf parsley

1 teaspoon chopped fresh sage, or ½ teaspoon crumbled dried sage

½ lb *(250 g)* ground beef, preferably chuck, or equal parts beef and pork

2 tablespoons tomato paste

½ cup *(4 fl oz/125 ml)* dry red wine

Fine sea salt and freshly ground pepper

Egg Pasta I *(page 16 or 18)*

Kosher salt for cooking pasta

Freshly grated Parmigiano-Reggiano cheese for serving

Remove the mushrooms from the water and reserve the water. Rinse the mushrooms under cold running water to remove any sand or grit, squeeze dry, and chop coarsely. Line a fine-mesh sieve with cheesecloth or a paper towel, place over a cup, and strain the soaking water. Set the mushrooms and water aside separately.

Drain the tomatoes, reserving their juice. Strain the captured juice to hold back the seeds. Using your fingers, push out the excess seeds from the tomatoes, then chop the tomatoes and set aside with the juice.

In a saucepan over medium-low heat, melt the butter with the olive oil. Add the carrot, celery, onion, parsley, and sage and sauté until the vegetables are softened but the onions are not colored, 10–12 minutes. Add the beef and cook, stirring to break up any clumps, until the meat has taken on color but is still somewhat pink inside, about 8 minutes. Do not overcook. Stir in the tomato paste, wine, and the mushrooms and their soaking water, reduce the heat to low, and simmer until most of the alcohol has evaporated, about 5 minutes. Add the tomatoes and their juice, 1 teaspoon sea salt, and ¼ teaspoon pepper, cover partially, and simmer until a thick, fragrant sauce forms, about 40 minutes.

While the sauce is cooking, make the pasta dough as directed, then roll out and cut into fettuccine as directed on pages 20–21 or 22–23. Let dry for 30 minutes or up to 3 hours (see page 13).

In a large pot, bring 5 qt (5 l) water to a rapid boil. Add 2 tablespoons kosher salt and the pasta and cover the pot. When the water returns to a boil, cook for about 5 seconds and then drain. Transfer the pasta to a warmed large, shallow serving bowl or individual shallow bowls. Top with the sauce and serve right away. Pass the cheese at the table.

TAGLIATELLE *with* ASPARAGUS AND PINE NUTS

Pine nuts, famously ground with basil to make the classic *pesto alla Genovese,* are also delicious when toasted whole and tossed with vegetables, cheese, and butter, as in this recipe. The unique flavor of pine nuts pairs well with the asparagus and Parmesan, both of which have an inherent nuttiness.

Egg Pasta I *(page 16 or 18)*

1 lb *(500 g)* asparagus

Kosher salt for cooking asparagus and pasta

½ cup *(4 oz/125 g)* unsalted butter, clarified *(see page 233)*

1 cup *(5 oz/155 g)* pine nuts, lightly toasted

Fine sea salt

½ cup *(2 oz/60 g)* freshly grated Parmigiano-Reggiano cheese

Make the pasta dough as directed, then roll out and cut into tagliatelle as directed on pages 20–21 or 22–23. Let dry for 30 minutes or up to 3 hours (see page 13).

In a large pot, bring 5 qt (5 l) water to a rapid boil.

While the water is heating, snap off the tough ends of the asparagus. Using a vegetable peeler, peel away the thick skin to within about 2 inches (5 cm) of the tips. Cut the spears crosswise on the diagonal into 2-inch (5-cm) pieces, leaving the tips intact.

Add 2 tablespoons kosher salt and the asparagus to the boiling water and cook until tender, about 6 minutes. Using a wire skimmer or slotted spoon, transfer to a bowl and set aside. Reserve the water in the pot.

In a frying pan large enough to accommodate the pasta later, warm the clarified butter over low heat. Add the pine nuts and asparagus and toss to coat with the butter.

Return the water to a rapid boil. Add the pasta and cover the pot. When the water returns to a boil, uncover, cook for about 5 seconds, and then drain, reserving about ½ cup (4 fl oz/125 ml) of the cooking water. Add the pasta to the sauce in the pan and stir and toss until well combined, adding some of the reserved cooking water if needed to moisten the sauce so that it coats the pasta nicely. Season to taste with sea salt and transfer to a warmed large, shallow serving bowl or individual shallow bowls. Top with the cheese and serve right away.

MALTAGLIATI *with* CREAMY SWISS CHARD

Swiss chard is commonly used in fillings for ravioli and other stuffed pastas, but it also makes an easy, full-flavored topping for fresh or dried noodles. Here, roughly cut maltagliati are tossed with a sauce of tender chard leaves, cream, and nutmeg. Baby spinach or beet greens can be used instead.

Egg Pasta I *(page 16 or 18)*

1½ lb *(750 g)* Swiss chard

4 tablespoons *(2 oz/60 g)* unsalted butter

2 shallots, minced

1½ cups *(12 fl oz/375 ml)* heavy cream

Pinch of freshly grated nutmeg

Fine sea salt and freshly ground white pepper

⅓ cup *(1½ oz/45 g)* freshly grated Parmigiano-Reggiano cheese, plus more for serving

Kosher salt for cooking pasta

Make the pasta dough as directed, then roll out (pages 20–21 or 22) and cut into maltagliati as directed on page 23. Let dry for 30 minutes or up to 3 hours (see page 13).

Trim off the stems from the Swiss chard and discard, or reserve the stems for another use. Rinse the leaves thoroughly, and then place them in a saucepan with only the water clinging to the leaves. Cover, place over medium heat, and cook, stirring several times, until tender, 4–5 minutes. Remove from the heat and let cool. Squeeze out the excess water, then chop the leaves and set aside.

In a large pot, bring 5 qt (5 l) water to a rapid boil.

While the water is heating, make the sauce. In a frying pan large enough to accommodate the pasta later, melt the butter over medium heat. Add the shallots and sauté until translucent, about 3 minutes. Add the chard, stir to mix it with the shallots, and sauté for 1 minute longer. Add the cream, nutmeg, ½ teaspoon sea salt, and a few grinds of white pepper and bring the sauce to a simmer. Stir in the ⅓ cup (1½ oz/45 g) cheese, remove from the heat, and cover to keep warm.

Add 2 tablespoons kosher salt and the pasta to the boiling water and cover the pot. When the water returns to a boil, uncover, cook for about 5 seconds, and then drain. Add the pasta to the sauce in the pan and stir and toss until the pasta is well coated with the sauce. Transfer to a warmed large, shallow serving bowl or individual shallow bowls and serve right away. Pass the additional cheese at the table.

WHOLE-WHEAT PAPPARDELLE *with* MUSHROOMS

For the best flavor, use fresh wild mushrooms such as chanterelle or black trumpet, or flavorful cultivated mushrooms like shiitake or oyster. Or, for a variety of earthy nuances, use a combination. Avoid portobello or cremini mushrooms, which are too dry for this silky sauce.

FOR THE WHOLE-WHEAT PASTA

1½ cups (7½ oz/235 g) whole-wheat flour

½ cup (2½ oz/75 g) unbleached all-purpose flour, plus more for dusting

¼ teaspoon fine sea salt

3 large eggs, at room temperature

1 tablespoon olive or vegetable oil

1 cup (1 oz/30 g) dried porcini mushrooms, soaked in ½ cup (4 fl oz/125 ml) hot water for 30 minutes

¾ lb (375 g) fresh wild or cultivated mushrooms (see Note)

4 tablespoons (2 oz/60 g) unsalted butter

1 tablespoon extra-virgin olive oil

2 large shallots, minced

2 teaspoons chopped fresh thyme

Fine sea salt and freshly ground pepper

1 cup (8 fl oz/250 ml) heavy cream

Kosher salt for cooking pasta

To make the whole-wheat pasta, follow the method for Egg Pasta (page 16 or 18), but increase the kneading time to 12–14 minutes. Roll out the dough (pages 20–21 or 22) and cut into pappardelle as directed on page 23. Let dry for 30 minutes or up to 3 hours (see page 13).

Remove the porcini from the soaking water, and reserve the water. Rinse the porcini under cold running water to remove any sand or grit and squeeze dry. Using scissors, cut them into pieces about the size of your thumbnail. Line a fine-mesh sieve with cheesecloth or a paper towel, place over a cup, and strain the soaking water. Set the mushrooms and water aside separately.

Using a soft brush or clean kitchen towel, remove any dirt from the fresh mushrooms. Do not wash them, as water will adversely alter their texture. Separate the stems from the caps, discarding the stems if they are tough. Slice the caps and tender stems thinly.

In a large frying pan over medium-low heat, melt the butter with the olive oil. Add the shallots and thyme and sauté until the shallots are softened, about 5 minutes. Add the porcini and sauté for about 5 minutes to allow the flavors to blend. Add the fresh mushrooms and continue to sauté until they are tender, about 5 minutes. Add the mushroom soaking water, ½ teaspoon sea salt, and ¼ teaspoon pepper and simmer gently for 5 minutes, stirring occasionally. Add the cream and heat, stirring, until small bubbles begin to form around the edges of the pan. Do not let the cream boil. Remove from the heat and cover to keep warm.

In a large pot, bring 5 qt (5 l) water to a rapid boil. Add 2 tablespoons kosher salt and the pasta and cover the pot. When the water returns to a boil, uncover, cook for about 5 seconds, and then drain. Add the pasta to the sauce in the pan and toss until the pasta is well coated with the sauce. Transfer to a warmed large, shallow serving bowl or individual shallow bowls and serve right away.

TRENETTE *with* SAUSAGE, EGG, AND LEMON

This hearty sauce is from Umbria, a central Italian region famous for its sausages and pork products. Take care not to overcook the sausage, which will render it tough. Also, work quickly once you add the egg mixture to the pan so that the noodles are coated evenly and the dish is served piping hot.

Egg Pasta I *(page 16 or 18)*

1 large egg

¼ cup *(2 fl oz/60 ml)* heavy cream

Grated zest of 1 small lemon

Juice of ½ lemon

Pinch of freshly grated nutmeg

Freshly ground pepper

4 tablespoons *(2 fl oz/60 ml)* extra-virgin olive oil

2 oz *(60 g)* pancetta, finely diced

¼ lb *(125 g)* sweet Italian sausages (about 2), casings removed

Kosher salt for cooking pasta

Freshly grated Parmigiano-Reggiano cheese for serving

Make the pasta dough as directed, then roll out (pages 20–21 or 22) and cut into trenette as directed on page 23. Let dry for 30 minutes or up to 3 hours (see page 13).

In a bowl, lightly beat together the egg, cream, lemon zest and juice, nutmeg, and ⅛ teaspoon pepper. Set aside.

In a frying pan large enough to accommodate the pasta later, warm 1 tablespoon of the olive oil over medium heat. Add the pancetta and sauté until nicely colored, 4–5 minutes. Using a slotted spoon, transfer the pancetta to a bowl and set aside.

Add the sausage meat to the oil remaining in the pan and cook over medium heat, stirring to break up any clumps, until nicely colored and just cooked through, about 6 minutes. Remove the pan from the heat. Using the slotted spoon, transfer the sausage to the bowl with the pancetta. If only a small amount of fat is in the pan, leave it. If there is an excessive amount, drain off most of it. Add the remaining 3 tablespoons olive oil to the pan and set the pan aside.

In a large pot, bring 5 qt (5 l) water to a rapid boil. Add 2 tablespoons kosher salt and the pasta and cover the pot. When the water returns to a boil, uncover, cook for about 5 seconds, and then drain.

At the same time you add the pasta to the boiling water, return the frying pan to medium heat and warm the olive oil. Add the pancetta and sausage and heat through. Add the hot drained pasta to the pan and toss to mix well with the sausage and pancetta, then remove the pan from the heat. Immediately add the egg mixture and stir and toss vigorously to coat the strands well with the mixture (the egg will cook from the heat of the pasta). Transfer the pasta and sauce to a warmed large, shallow serving bowl or individual shallow bowls and serve right away. Pass the cheese at the table.

TAGLIATELLE *with* CILANTRO PESTO AND CHICKEN

This recipe for cilantro pesto, developed by food writer Rosa Ross, puts a spin on the classic combination of ribbon noodles tossed with basil pesto. The floral and citrus flavors of cilantro are brightened by an ample dose of lime juice, while the sauce is still anchored by familiar pine nuts.

Egg Pasta I *(page 16 or 18)*

FOR THE CILANTRO PESTO

2 cups *(2 oz/60 g)* loosely packed fresh cilantro leaves

2 cloves garlic, coarsely chopped

¼ cup *(1 oz/30 g)* pine nuts, lightly toasted

3 tablespoons extra-virgin olive oil

1 tablespoon fresh lime juice

Fine sea salt and freshly ground pepper

1 lb *(500 g)* skinless, boneless chicken breasts

Fine sea salt and freshly ground pepper

3 tablespoons extra-virgin olive oil

1 lime quarter

Kosher salt for cooking pasta

Make the pasta dough as directed, then roll out and cut into tagliatelle as directed on pages 20–21 or 22–23. Let dry for 30 minutes or up to 3 hours (see page 13).

To make the pesto, in a food processor, combine the cilantro, garlic, pine nuts, olive oil, lime juice, ½ teaspoon sea salt, and a few grinds of pepper and process to a paste, stopping occasionally to scrape down the sides of the work bowl. Be careful not to overprocess; the consistency of the pesto should be thick and fluid and have a slightly grainy texture. Transfer the pesto to a serving bowl large enough to accommodate the pasta later. Set aside.

Pat the chicken breasts dry with paper towels, then sprinkle on both sides with sea salt and pepper. In a large nonstick frying pan over medium-high heat, warm the olive oil until it is very hot but not smoking. Working in batches if needed to avoid crowding the pan, add the chicken and cook, turning once, until golden on both sides and just opaque in the center when cut into with a knife, about 2 minutes on each side. Transfer to a plate, tent loosely with aluminum foil, and set aside in a warm place. Just before you add the pasta to the boiling water, using a sharp chef's knife, cut each breast in half lengthwise, then cut the halves crosswise into thin slices. Squeeze the lime quarter over the chicken and re-cover to keep the chicken warm.

In a large pot, bring 5 qt (5 l) water to a rapid boil. Add 2 tablespoons kosher salt and the pasta and cover the pot. When the water returns to a boil, uncover, cook for about 5 seconds, and then drain, reserving about ½ cup (4 fl oz/125 ml) of the cooking water. Blend a few tablespoons of the cooking water with the pesto to make a creamy consistency, then add the pasta to the bowl and stir and toss with the pesto until the strands are well coated with the sauce, adding a little more of the cooking water if needed to loosen the sauce. Arrange the chicken slices on top of the pasta and serve right away.

BUCKWHEAT FETTUCCINE *with* SUMMER VEGETABLES

Buckwheat pasta, which has a mild, nutty flavor, is a specialty of Valtellina in the Lombardy province. Crumbles of goat cheese provide a welcome tang when tossed with sweet vegetables and herbs. Select young zucchini, which have more flavor and fewer seeds than mature squash.

FOR THE BUCKWHEAT PASTA

3 large eggs, at room temperature

1 tablespoon milk, heated to lukewarm

1 tablespoon olive oil

1½ cups *(7½ oz/235 g)* unbleached all-purpose flour, plus more for dusting

1 cup *(5 oz/155 g)* buckwheat flour

¼ teaspoon fine sea salt

FOR THE SAUCE

½ cup *(4 fl oz/125 ml)* extra-virgin olive oil

6 large cloves garlic, finely chopped

1 lb *(500 g)* small zucchini, trimmed and cut into julienne

1 red bell pepper, seeded and cut into julienne

Fine sea salt

¼ lb *(125 g)* fresh goat cheese, crumbled

Kosher salt for cooking pasta

Crumbled fresh goat cheese for serving

¼ cup *(⅓ oz/10 g)* small fresh flat-leaf parsley leaves

3 tablespoons torn fresh basil

To make the buckwheat pasta, follow the method for Egg Pasta (page 16 or 18), mixing the milk with the eggs and oil before combining with the flour and salt, and increasing the kneading time to 12–14 minutes. Roll out the dough and cut into fettuccine as directed on pages 20–21 or 22–23. Let dry for 30 minutes or up to 3 hours (see page 13).

In a large pot, bring 5 qt (5 l) water to a rapid boil.

While the water is heating, make the sauce. In a frying pan large enough to accommodate the pasta later, warm the olive oil over medium-low heat. Add the garlic and sauté until translucent, about 2 minutes. Raise the heat to high, add the zucchini and bell pepper, and sauté, tossing, until the vegetables are tender, about 10 minutes. Add ½ teaspoon sea salt and the goat cheese and toss together. The cheese will soften quickly in the heat of the pan. Remove from the heat and cover to keep warm.

Add 2 tablespoons kosher salt and the pasta to the boiling water and cover the pot. When the water returns to a boil, uncover, cook for about 5 seconds, and then drain, reserving about ½ cup (4 fl oz/125 ml) of the cooking water. Add the pasta to the sauce in the pan and and toss until well combined, adding some of the reserved cooking water if needed to moisten the sauce so that it coats the pasta nicely. Transfer the pasta to a warmed large, shallow serving bowl or individual shallow bowls and scatter the additional crumbled goat cheese and the parsley and basil over the top. Serve right away.

DRIED PASTA

ABOUT DRIED PASTA

A seemingly endless array of dried pasta shapes are available today, which can make choosing the right shape daunting. Most pastas belong to a family—for example, spaghetti, spaghettini, and capellini are all strand pastas—and each family is ideally paired with specific types of sauces. Once you learn some basic pairing guidelines, you can stray from the recipes, choosing which pasta shapes you like that marry well with the accompanying sauce.

DRIED VERSUS FRESH PASTA

Outside of Italy, dried pasta is widely perceived as being inferior to fresh pasta. Of course, as every Italian cook knows, such thinking is far from the truth. The difference between dried pasta and fresh pasta is not a question of quality, but of how the pasta is served. Factory-made dried pasta, which is available in myriad shapes and sizes, has a firmer consistency and more robust flavor than fresh pasta, which means that it must be paired with different kinds of sauces. For example, fresh pasta is often partnered with smooth, cream-based sauces, while most dried pasta is better suited to tomato sauces laced with chunky ingredients.

The best dried pastas are made in Italy from semolina flour, which is milled from high-protein durum (hard) wheat, and water (or occasionally egg). Their excellence is largely due to the fact that their production, in factories big and small, is regulated by national laws that ensure that only hard wheat is used. They will have also been cut and shaped with bronze dies (rather than plastic), which produce a slightly coarse texture perfect for absorbing sauce. You must be careful when buying imported artisanal pastas, however. Some small operations have not mastered the drying process fully, which causes the pasta to become too soft during cooking.

Good-quality dried pasta has an amber tint, a vaguely transparent quality, a clear, wheaty aroma and flavor and, when properly cooked, retains its elasticity. A final indicator of quality is the absence of excessive cloudiness in the cooking water.

COOKING AND SERVING

When properly cooked, dried pasta will have a tender, yet slightly chewy texture—in other words, it will be al dente, literally "to the tooth." If you cut into a piece, a fine white line should be visible at its core.

Despite the fact that much has been written about pasta in recent years, many people still believe that any type of dried pasta can be dressed with any type of sauce. Different pasta cuts absorb and combine with sauces based on their size, shape, and thickness. For example, short tubular cuts with ridged surfaces—their names include the word *rigate,* such as penne rigate—are designed to trap sauces in their ridges and holes, and concave and hollow pastas, such as orecchiette or ziti, cradle chunky sauces in their voids. Capellini, which is thin and relatively delicate, calls for a light, smooth sauce, and thick, dense bucatini mates well with heavier, chunkier sauces. Look to the chart on the opposite page for guidelines on pairing various cuts of dried pasta with suitable sauces.

In most cases, 1 pound (500 g) dried pasta will serve four to six people, unless the sauce is quite light and smooth. For soups to serve the same number of people or even more, you will need only a small amount of *pastina,* or soup pasta (thin strands, small shells)—usually no more than about 1 cup (4 oz/125g).

PAIRING DRIED PASTA AND SAUCE

In general, the taste and texture of dried pasta makes it well suited to robust and rustic sauces based on olive oil, pancetta, tomatoes, and combinations of vegetables, beans, olives, fish and shellfish, and meats. Tomato sauces and simple butter and cheese sauces combine easily with almost any type of pasta (including fresh pasta), except for the smallest varieties, which are designed for soups.

SAUCE OR DISH	IDEAL PASTA CUTS	PASTA NAME
baked dishes	thin strand pastas, short cut pastas, large hollow pastas, pasta sheets	cannelloni, capellini, conchiglioni, lasagne, lumaconi, manicotti, penne, perciatelli, rigatoni, ziti tagliati
butter sauces	thin strand pastas, short cut pastas	conchiglie, farfalle, lumache, vermicelli
cheese and cream sauces	strand pastas, short cut pastas, short shaped pastas	bucatini, cavatappi, farfalle, fusilli, gemelli, gnocchetti, mafalde, penne, pennette, radiatori, tagliatelle, vermicelli
chunky tomato sauces	short cut pastas, short shaped pastas	conchiglie, gnocchetti, linguine, lumache, penne
smooth tomato sauces	strand pastas, short cut pastas, short shaped pastas	bucatini, capellini, conchiglie, farfalle, gnocchetti, penne, pennette, rigatoni, spaghetti
meat sauces	short cut pastas, wide ribbon pastas, short shaped pastas, strand pastas	cavatappi, fusilli corti, fusilli lunghi, gemelli, lumache, mafalde, malloreddus, orecchiette, penne, pennette
oil-based sauces	short cut pastas, thin strand pastas	capellini, farfalle, linguine, lumache, spaghetti, spaghettini, ziti tagliati
pesto sauces	strand pastas	bucatini, linguine, spaghetti, spaghettini
seafood sauces	strand pastas, medium hollow pastas	linguine, spaghetti, spaghettini, ziti
soups	*pastina* (small pasta about the size of rice), thin strand pastas	acini di pepe, capellini, conchigliette, ditali, ditalini, egg noodles, farfallette, lumachine, orzo, stelline, tubettini
vegetable sauces	narrow ribbon pastas, short shaped pastas, strand pastas, medium hollow pastas	bucatini, cavatelli, conchiglie, ditalini, farfalle, gemelli, linguine, mafalde, orecchiette, penne, rigatoni, spaghetti, ziti, ziti tagliati

DRIED PASTA SHAPES

1 **SPAGHETTI** Long, cylindrical "small strings" about 1/12 inch (2 mm) thick and 10 inches (25 cm) long.

2 **ORECCHIETTE** "Small ears," these pasta are coin-sized with indentations to hold sauce.

3 **ZITI** Smooth-surfaced, medium-sized tube pasta often used in baked pasta dishes.

4 **MALLOREDDUS** Small, ridged, canoe-shaped pasta from Sardinia.

5 **RIGATONI** Large, ridged tube pasta that can range from 1¾ to 3¼ inches (4.5 to 8 cm) long.

6 **CAPELLINI** Also known as "angel hair," the delicate strands of this pasta are less than 1/16 inch (2 mm) thick.

7 **DITALINI** These "small thimbles" are short cylinders with either smooth or ridged surfaces.

8 **FUSILLI** Translated as "little spindles" but also commonly referred to as "corkscrews."

9 **FARFALLE** Scalloped and pinched, these pasta are often called "bow ties."

10 **SPAGHETTINI** Resembling spaghetti, but only 1/16 inch (2 mm) thick.

11 **CONCHIGLIE** Often called "shells," this conch shell–shaped pasta comes in many sizes.

12 **CAVATELLI** These bun-shaped pasta are formed from rounds that are rolled in on themselves.

13 **GEMELLI** These small, slender pasta are made up of two intertwined tubes, thus their name, which translates to "twins."

14 **BUCATINI** Long, thin, hollow tubes of pasta.

15 **PENNE** Short tubes cut on the diagonal, these "quills" are about ½ inch (12 mm) thick and 2 inches (5 cm) long, and can be found with smooth (*lisce*) or ridged (*rigate*) surfaces.

16 **LINGUINE** Somewhere between a narrow ribbon and flattened piece of spaghetti, with strands measuring about 1/8 inch (3 mm) wide and 10½ inches (26.5 cm) long.

BUCATINI *alla* CARBONARA

This recipe adheres to the authentic way of making a carbonara sauce, which, unlike many popular variations, includes no cream or wine. Beaten eggs and cheese cling to the strands of hot pasta, delivering the dish's signature silky consistency, and the sauce is accented with bits of crispy *guanciale*.

5 extra-large eggs

¾ cup *(3 oz/90 g)* equal parts freshly grated pecorino and Parmigiano-Reggiano cheese, plus more for serving

Fine sea salt and freshly ground pepper

Kosher salt for cooking pasta

1 lb *(500 g)* bucatini or spaghetti

¼ cup *(2 fl oz/60 ml)* extra-virgin olive oil

½ lb *(250 g)* guanciale or pancetta, finely diced

3 tablespoons minced fresh flat-leaf parsley

In a bowl, using a fork, beat the eggs until well blended. Stir in the ¾ cup (3 oz/90 g) cheese and season with sea salt and plenty of pepper.

Select a large, shallow serving bowl and warm it in a 200°F (95°C) oven.

In a large pot, bring 5 qt (5 l) water to a rapid boil. Check the package directions for the cooking time, then add 2 tablespoons kosher salt and the pasta to the boiling water, stir well, and cook, stirring occasionally, until the pasta is 2 minutes shy of being al dente.

Meanwhile, in a frying pan large enough to accommodate the pasta later, warm the olive oil over medium heat. Add the *guanciale* and sauté until nicely colored and crisp, about 4 minutes. Remove from the heat.

When the pasta is ready, drain it, reserving about 1 cup (8 fl oz/250 ml) of the cooking water. Add the pasta to the frying pan, place over low heat, and toss to coat the pasta with the oil. Add about ½ cup (4 fl oz/125 ml) of the cooking water to moisten, and simmer, continuing to toss, until the water is nearly evaporated, 1–2 minutes. Remove from the heat and transfer the contents of the pan to the warmed serving bowl. Add the egg mixture and parsley and toss vigorously to distribute the sauce evenly and to ensure that the eggs do not scramble. If the pasta seems dry, add more of the reserved cooking water to loosen it. Serve right away. Pass the pepper mill and the additional cheese at the table.

LINGUINE *with* CLAMS

This classic dish, rarely prepared well in restaurants, is easy to make at home. Its success relies on uncompromisingly fresh clams and fruity extra-virgin olive oil. For a beautiful presentation and fun eating, serve the clams in their shells, as the Italians do, and pick them up to eat with your hands.

Kosher salt for purging clams and cooking pasta

1 cup (5 oz/155 g) cornmeal

4 lb (2 kg) cockles or Manila clams, or 4 dozen small littleneck clams

½ cup (4 fl oz/125 ml) extra-virgin olive oil

5 large cloves garlic, minced

6 tablespoons (⅓ oz/10 g) chopped fresh flat-leaf parsley

¼ teaspoon red pepper flakes

½ cup (4 fl oz/125 ml) dry white wine

Fine sea salt

1 lb (500 g) thin linguine (labeled *linguine fini*) or spaghetti

In a large bowl or other large vessel, combine 4 qt (4 l) water and ⅓ cup (3 oz/90 g) kosher salt and stir until the salt dissolves, then stir in the cornmeal. Scrub the clams well with a stiff vegetable brush and add to the bowl. Add cold water to cover and let stand for 1–3 hours to purge the clams of any sand or grit. Drain well and rinse again, discarding any that do not close tightly to the touch.

In a deep frying pan large enough to accommodate the clams and pasta later, and with a tight-fitting lid, warm the olive oil over medium-low heat. Add the garlic, 4 tablespoons (¼ oz/7 g) of the parsley, and the red pepper flakes and cook gently, stirring occasionally, until the garlic is softened but not colored, 3–4 minutes. Add the clams, wine, and 1 teaspoon sea salt and immediately cover tightly. Raise the heat to medium and cook, occasionally shaking the pan for even cooking, until the clams open, about 10 minutes, depending on the type of clam used.

Uncover and use a spoon to toss the clams with the liquid in the pan. Lift out any empty shells and discard, and discard any clams that did not open. You can use the sauce with the clams in their shells or, if preferred, shell some or all of them. The sauce will be brothy and full of flavor.

While the clams are cooking, in a large pot, bring 5 qt (5 l) water to a rapid boil. Check the package directions for the cooking time, then add 2 tablespoons kosher salt and the pasta to the water, stir well, and cook, stirring occasionally, until the pasta is 1–2 minutes shy of being al dente.

Drain the pasta, add to the sauce in the pan, and place the pan over low heat. Add the remaining 2 tablespoons parsley and toss the pasta and clam sauce together for a minute or so. Some of the brothy sauce will be absorbed by the pasta, but plenty will remain, keeping the pasta very moist. Transfer to a warmed large, shallow serving bowl or individual shallow bowls and serve right away.

PENNE *alla* VODKA

Many stories account for the origin of this dish, ranging from a Neapolitan-born chef in a New York City restaurant to a Roman chef on the payroll of a vodka manufacturer to promote its product in Italy. The recipes vary widely as well; this interpretation includes prosciutto.

1 can *(28 oz/875 g)* San Marzano or other plum tomatoes

2 cups *(2 oz/60 g)* dried porcini mushrooms, soaked in hot water just to cover for 30 minutes

4 tablespoons *(2 oz/60 g)* unsalted butter

2 tablespoons extra-virgin olive oil

4 thin slices prosciutto, finely diced

2 shallots, chopped

1 small yellow onion, chopped

4 cloves garlic, chopped

½ cup *(4 fl oz/125 ml)* tomato sauce

10 large fresh basil leaves, cut crosswise into thin ribbons

Fine sea salt and freshly ground white pepper

½ cup *(4 fl oz/125 ml)* vodka

1 cup *(8 oz/250 g)* sour cream

Kosher salt for cooking pasta

1 lb *(500 g)* penne

2 oz *(60 g)* Asiago or grana padano cheese

Drain the tomatoes, reserving their juice. Strain the captured juice to hold back the seeds. Using your fingers, push out the excess seeds from the tomatoes. Place the tomatoes and their juice in a food processor and process until smooth. Drain the mushrooms, rinse under cold running water to remove any sand or grit, squeeze dry, and chop finely. Set the tomatoes and mushrooms aside separately.

In a large frying pan over medium heat, melt 2 tablespoons of the butter with the olive oil. Add the prosciutto and sauté until lightly colored, about 2 minutes. Add the mushrooms, shallots, onion, and garlic and sauté until softened, about 5 minutes. Add the puréed tomatoes, tomato sauce, and half of the basil. Cover partially and simmer, stirring occasionally, for about 10 minutes to allow the flavors to blend. Season with 1 teaspoon sea salt and ½ teaspoon pepper. Pour in the vodka, reduce the heat to medium-low, and simmer, uncovered, stirring occasionally, until the vodka evaporates and the sauce thickens, about 15 minutes. Taste and adjust the seasoning. Stir in the sour cream and the remaining 2 tablespoons butter and cook until heated through. Remove from the heat and cover to keep warm.

While the sauce is simmering, in a large pot, bring 5 qt (5 l) water to a rapid boil. Add 2 tablespoons kosher salt and the pasta, stir well, and cook, stirring occasionally, until al dente, according to package directions.

Drain the pasta, reserving about 1 cup (8 fl oz/250 ml) of the cooking water, and transfer the pasta to a warmed large, shallow serving bowl. Add the sauce and toss with the pasta until well combined. Add the cooking water, a little at a time, if needed to moisten the sauce so that it coats the pasta nicely. Using a vegetable peeler, shave the cheese over the top, then sprinkle with the remaining basil. Serve right away.

FRESH PEA SOUP *with* PAPPARDELLE

This soup is best in the springtime when fresh peas are sweet and prolific, but frozen peas can be substituted with good results. High-quality, flavorful chicken broth will make this soup shine. For a vegetarian version, omit the pancetta and use vegetable broth in place of the chicken broth.

Kosher salt for cooking pasta

¼ lb *(125 g)* pappardelle

2 tablespoons unsalted butter

2 oz *(60 g)* pancetta, chopped

1 small yellow onion, minced

3 tablespoons minced fresh flat-leaf parsley

1 lb *(500 g)* fresh English peas, shelled, or 1 package *(10 oz/315 g)* frozen English peas

6 cups *(48 fl oz/1.5 l)* low-sodium chicken broth

Fine sea salt and freshly ground white or black pepper

Freshly grated Parmigiano-Reggiano cheese for serving

In a large pot, bring 5 qt (5 l) water to a rapid boil. Check the package directions for the cooking time, then add 2 tablespoons kosher salt and the pasta to the boiling water, stir well, and cook, stirring occasionally, until the pasta is about 3 minutes shy of being al dente (it will continue to cook in the heat of the soup). Drain in a colander and rinse under cold running water until cool.

In a large saucepan over medium heat, melt the butter. Add the pancetta and sauté until lightly browned, about 2 minutes. Add the onion and parsley and sauté until the onion is translucent and softened, about 2 minutes. Add the peas and sauté for 2 minutes longer. Add the broth, stir to combine, and bring to a boil. Add the pasta and simmer until al dente, about 3 minutes.

Season to taste with sea salt and pepper. Ladle into warmed shallow bowls and serve right away. Pass the cheese at the table.

ORECCHIETTE *with* GRILLED ZUCCHINI AND LEEKS

While orecchiette are typically paired with broccoli rabe (see page 125) or tomato-based meat sauces, the sturdy shape is also ideal for carrying an amalgam of grilled summer vegetables. You can vary the vegetables used, just be sure to cut them into pieces that match the size of the pasta.

Kosher salt for blanching basil and cooking pasta

½ cup (½ oz/15 g) fresh basil leaves

¾ cup (6 fl oz/180 ml) extra-virgin olive oil

2 leeks, white and pale green parts, quartered lengthwise and thoroughly cleaned

1 lb (500 g) small zucchini, about 6 oz (185 g) each, trimmed and quartered lengthwise

Fine sea salt and freshly ground pepper

1 lb (500 g) orecchiette

3 oz (90 g) medium-aged sheep's milk cheese such as pecorino toscano or pecorino sardo (also called *fiore sardo*)

Prepare a hot fire in a charcoal or gas grill, or preheat the oven to 400°F (200°C).

Have ready a bowl of ice water. Bring a saucepan three-fourths full of water to a boil. Add 2 teaspoons kosher salt and the basil and blanch for 30 seconds. Drain, and then immerse the basil in the ice water. Drain again, pat dry with a paper towel, and chop. In a blender, combine ½ cup (4 fl oz/125 ml) of the olive oil and the basil and process until the basil is puréed. Set aside to let the basil infuse the oil.

If grilling the vegetables, in a large bowl, combine the leeks, zucchini, and the remaining ¼ cup (2 fl oz/60 ml) olive oil and toss to coat the vegetables evenly. Arrange the vegetables on the grill rack and grill, turning as needed, until nicely browned on both sides and tender, about 15 minutes. Remove the vegetables from the grill, let cool just until they can be handled, and then cut crosswise into ¼-inch (6-mm) pieces. Season with sea salt to taste while still hot. Cover to keep warm.

If roasting the vegetables, on a rimmed baking sheet, toss together the leeks, zucchini, and the remaining ¼ cup olive oil, then spread out in a single layer. Roast until golden brown and crispy on the edges, about 25 minutes. Remove the vegetables from the oven, let cool just until they can be handled, and then cut crosswise into ¼-inch (6-mm) pieces. Sprinkle with sea salt to taste while still hot. Cover to keep warm.

While the vegetables are cooking, in a large pot, bring 5 qt (5 l) water to a rapid boil. Add 2 tablespoons kosher salt and the pasta, stir well, and cook, stirring occasionally, until al dente, according to package directions.

Drain the pasta and transfer to a warmed large, shallow serving bowl. Add the basil oil, roasted vegetables, and pepper to taste and toss until well combined. Using a vegetable peeler, shave the cheese over the top. Serve right away.

BUCATINI *with* PORK AND FENNEL RAGÙ

Endless renditions of *ragù,* a thick meat sauce, are made throughout Italy. This chunky version is especially tasty because of the agreeable marriage of fennel and pork. The slender tubes called bucatini are ideal for supporting the hearty sauce, but short cut pastas will work well, too.

1 fennel bulb

4 tablespoons *(2 fl oz/60 ml)* extra-virgin olive oil

1 lb *(500 g)* sweet Italian sausages, casings removed

1 large red onion, chopped

2 large cloves garlic, chopped

½ teaspoon ground fennel

1 cup *(8 fl oz/250 ml)* dry red wine

3 tablespoons tomato paste

1½ cups *(9 oz/280 g)* drained canned crushed tomatoes

1 teaspoon minced fresh marjoram, or ½ teaspoon crumbled dried marjoram

Big pinch of saffron threads, soaked in 1 tablespoon hot chicken broth, or ⅛ teaspoon powdered saffron

About 1½ cups *(12 fl oz/ 375 ml)* low-sodium chicken broth

Fine sea salt and freshly ground pepper

Kosher salt for cooking pasta

1 lb *(500 g)* bucatini, rigatoni, gemelli, fusilli, or penne

Freshly grated Parmigiano-Reggiano cheese for serving

Cut off the stems and feathery tops and remove any bruised outer stalks from the fennel bulb. Reserve the tender, lighter green fronds for another use or for garnish. Slice off and discard the tough bottom of the bulb, then quarter the bulb lengthwise. Cut out and discard the tough core, and finely chop the bulb.

In a Dutch oven or large, deep frying pan over medium heat, warm 2 tablespoons of the olive oil. Add the sausage meat and cook until lightly browned but still pink inside, about 5 minutes. As the sausage cooks, use a wooden spoon to break it up a bit, but keep the texture chunky. Using a slotted spoon, transfer the sausage to a plate and set aside. Drain off the excess fat from the pan.

Add the remaining 2 tablespoons olive oil to the pan and warm over medium heat. Add the onion, garlic, chopped fennel bulb, and ground fennel and sauté until all the vegetables are softened, about 8 minutes. Return the sausage to the pan and stir in the wine and tomato paste. Sauté over medium heat until most of the alcohol has evaporated, about 3 minutes. Add the tomatoes, marjoram, and saffron with its broth and simmer for 5 minutes. Add the 1½ cups (12 fl oz/375 ml) broth, bring to a simmer, and simmer gently, uncovered, until the sauce becomes aromatic and all the ingredients are well married, about 45 minutes. Add more broth as needed if the sauce begins to dry out. Season to taste with sea salt and pepper. Reduce the heat to low and cover the pan to keep the sauce warm.

In a large pot, bring 5 qt (5 l) water to a rapid boil. Add 2 tablespoons kosher salt and the pasta, stir well, and cook, stirring occasionally, until al dente, according to package directions.

Drain the pasta and transfer to a warmed large, shallow serving bowl. Add the sauce and toss with the pasta until well combined. Serve right away. Pass the cheese at the table.

SPAGHETTI *with* SARDINIAN WALNUT SAUCE

This simple sauce comes together in the time it takes the pasta to cook. The ground nuts produce a creamy, unctuous mixture with a texture not unlike that of pesto. It needs a sturdy cut of pasta to support it; linguine or bucatini can be used, but do not substitute anything thinner than spaghetti.

½ cup *(2 oz/60 g)* chopped walnuts

⅓ cup *(3 fl oz/80 ml)* extra-virgin olive oil

2 large cloves garlic, finely chopped

1 tablespoon chopped fresh flat-leaf parsley

Kosher salt for cooking pasta

1 lb *(500 g)* spaghetti, linguine, or bucatini

1 cup *(4 oz/125 g)* shredded semisoft sheep's milk cheese, such as *fior di Sardegna* or Tuscan *caciotta*

Place the walnuts in a small food processor and pulse until fairly finely ground but not pasty. Be careful not to overgrind or the oil in the nuts will be released and it will affect the texture of the sauce.

In a frying pan large enough to accommodate the pasta later, combine the ground walnuts, olive oil, garlic, and parsley over medium-low heat and cook gently, stirring occasionally, until the garlic is softened but not colored, about 7 minutes. Remove from the heat and cover to keep warm.

Meanwhile, in a large pot, bring 5 qt (5 l) water to a rapid boil. Check the package directions for the cooking time, then add 2 tablespoons kosher salt and the pasta to the boiling water, stir well, and cook, stirring occasionally, until the pasta is about 1 minute shy of being al dente.

Drain the pasta, reserving about 1 cup (8 fl oz/250 ml) of the cooking water. Add the pasta to the sauce in the frying pan, place over low heat, and toss the pasta and sauce together for about 1 minute. Little by little, add just enough of the cooking water as needed to moisten the sauce. You will probably need no more than ½ cup (4 fl oz/125 ml). Add the cheese, toss until evenly distributed, and remove from the heat. Transfer to a warmed large, shallow serving bowl or individual shallow bowls and serve right away.

PENNE *alla* PUTTANESCA

Like Penne alla Vodka (page 70), the origin of this dish changes with the storyteller, and how it is made varies with each cook. One thing stays constant: It is always robust and zesty in the spirit of its name, which translates as "harlot's sauce." Use high-quality anchovies and olives for the best results.

1 can *(28 oz/875 g)* plum tomatoes

3 tablespoons extra-virgin olive oil

1 small red onion, minced

3 large cloves garlic, chopped

3 tablespoons chopped fresh flat-leaf parsley

1 teaspoon chopped fresh marjoram, or ½ teaspoon crumbled dried marjoram

3 olive oil–packed anchovy fillets, coarsely chopped, plus 1 tablespoon of the oil

¼ cup *(2 oz/60 g)* sharply flavored black olives such as Kalamata, pitted and coarsely chopped

½ teaspoon red pepper flakes

¼ cup *(1½ oz/45 g)* small (nonpareil) capers, drained

Fine sea salt, if needed

Kosher salt for cooking pasta

1 lb *(500 g)* penne

Drain the tomatoes, reserving their juice. Strain the captured juice to hold back the seeds. Using your fingers, push out the excess seeds from the tomatoes. Chop the tomatoes and set aside with the juice.

In a frying pan large enough to accommodate the pasta later, warm the olive oil over medium-low heat. Add the onion and garlic and cook gently, stirring occasionally, until the garlic has softened, 3–4 minutes. Add 2 tablespoons of the parsley and the marjoram and cook gently just until the herbs release their aroma, about 30 seconds. Add the anchovies and the 1 tablespoon anchovy oil and, using a wooden spoon, press the fillets into the pan bottom to mash them. When they are partially dissolved, after about 1 minute, add the tomatoes and their juice, the olives, red pepper flakes, and capers. Simmer, stirring frequently, until the sauce thickens, about 20 minutes. Stir in the remaining 1 tablespoon parsley. Taste and adjust the seasoning with sea salt, though none may be needed because of the anchovies and capers.

While the sauce is simmering, in a large pot, bring 5 qt (5 l) water to a rapid boil. Add 2 tablespoons kosher salt and the pasta, stir well, and cook, stirring occasionally, until al dente, according to package directions.

Drain the pasta, add to the sauce in the pan, and toss until well combined. Transfer to a warmed large, shallow serving bowl or individual shallow bowls and serve right away.

ZITI *with* LOBSTER, PEAS, AND TOMATOES

A reduced stock made from aromatic vegetables and fortified with lobster shells is the foundation for this rich lobster-and-tomato sauce scented with vermouth and saffron. You can use penne instead of ziti here, or try a strand pasta, such as linguine or spaghetti.

1 live lobster, 1½ lb *(750 g)*

1 small yellow onion, unpeeled

1 rib celery with leaves

½ carrot

2 fresh flat-leaf parsley sprigs

1 tablespoon extra-virgin olive oil

1 large or 2 medium cloves garlic, chopped

2 cups *(12 oz/375 g)* peeled, seeded, and finely chopped fresh or canned plum tomatoes, with juice

Fine sea salt and freshly ground pepper

2 tablespoons unsalted butter

1 cup *(5 oz/155 g)* fresh or frozen shelled English peas, blanched for 1 minute and drained if using fresh

¼ cup *(2 fl oz/60 ml)* dry vermouth

¼ teaspoon saffron threads

Kosher salt for cooking pasta

¾ lb *(375 g)* ziti, penne, linguine, or spaghetti

In a pot, bring 4 cups (32 fl oz/1 l) water to a boil. Drop in the lobster, head first, and cover the pot. When the water returns to a boil, cook until the lobster is red, about 5 minutes, then remove; reserve the cooking water. When the lobster is cool enough to handle, working over a bowl to catch any juices, twist off the tail, claws, and legs. Crack the claws and legs with a mallet and cut the tail in half lengthwise. Remove the meat from the claws and tail, cut into bite-size chunks, and set aside in a bowl. Discard the claw shells. Add the body (with tomalley, if present), legs, tail shells, any captured juices, the onion, celery, carrot, and parsley sprigs to the water in the pot, place over high heat, and bring to a boil. Reduce the heat to medium and simmer until reduced to ½ cup (4 fl oz/125 ml), about 45 minutes. Strain through a fine-mesh sieve placed over a bowl.

While the lobster stock is cooking, in a frying pan large enough to accommodate the pasta later, warm the olive oil over medium heat. Add the garlic and sauté until softened, about 1½ minutes. Add the tomatoes and their juice and cook over low heat until the sauce thickens, about 25 minutes. Season with sea salt and pepper.

In a sauté pan over medium-low heat, melt the butter. Add the lobster meat and peas and sauté for 2 minutes. Add the vermouth and simmer until it evaporates, about 2 minutes. Using a slotted spoon, transfer the lobster and peas to a plate. Add the lobster stock to the vermouth butter. In a small, dry frying pan over low heat, warm the saffron for 1 minute, then crush with your fingers into the stock mixture. Cook over medium heat for 5 minutes, then add the stock mixture to the tomato sauce. If the sauce is thin, simmer it over medium heat for several minutes. Add the lobster and peas, remove from the heat, and cover to keep warm.

In a large pot, bring 5 qt (5 l) water to a rapid boil. Add 2 tablespoons kosher salt and the pasta, stir well, and cook, stirring occasionally, until al dente, according to package directions. Drain the pasta, add to the sauce in the pan, and toss until well combined. Transfer to a warmed large, shallow serving bowl or individual shallow bowls and serve right away.

WHOLE-WHEAT SPAGHETTI *with* ROASTED SQUASH

Pleasantly firm to the bite, whole-wheat spaghetti, called *bigoli* in Italy, combines beautifully with a sauce of caramelized onions. A new twist on this classic flavor match is this topping of diced, roasted winter squash. Whole-wheat linguine can be used in place of the spaghetti.

9 tablespoons *(4½ fl oz/ 140 ml)* extra-virgin olive oil, plus more for coating squash

6 yellow onions, halved through the stem end and sliced lengthwise paper-thin

Fine sea salt and freshly ground pepper

1 piece butternut or calabaza squash, about 6 oz *(185 g),* peeled and cut into ½-inch *(12-mm)* dice

¼ cup *(1 oz/30 g)* fresh bread crumbs

Kosher salt for cooking pasta

1 lb *(500 g)* whole-wheat spaghetti or linguine

¼ cup *(1 oz/30 g)* freshly grated Parmigiano-Reggiano cheese

In a frying pan large enough to accommodate the pasta later, warm 6 tablespoons (3 fl oz/90 ml) of the olive oil over medium heat. Add the onions and sauté, stirring often to heat evenly and to prevent sticking, until lightly golden, soft, and creamy, about 45 minutes. Remove from the heat and season with sea salt and pepper. Cover to keep warm.

While the onions are cooking, preheat the oven to 450°F (230°C). On a rimmed baking sheet, toss the squash with just enough olive oil to coat lightly and spread it out in a single layer. Roast until golden brown outside and thoroughly tender inside, about 15 minutes. Set aside and cover to keep warm.

In a small frying pan over medium-low heat, warm the remaining 3 tablespoons olive oil. Add the bread crumbs and cook, stirring constantly, until golden and crunchy, about 2 minutes. Reduce the heat if the crumbs color too quickly. Remove from the heat and set aside.

Meanwhile, in a large pot, bring 5 qt (5 l) water to a rapid boil. Add 2 tablespoons kosher salt and the pasta, stir well, and cook, stirring occasionally, until al dente, according to package directions.

Drain the pasta and add it, still dripping wet, to the pan holding the caramelized onions. Add the cheese and toss until well combined. Taste and adjust for salt, then sprinkle liberally with pepper. Transfer the pasta to warmed individual shallow bowls. Top with the roasted squash and sprinkle with the crumbs. Serve right away.

BUCATINI *all'*ARRABBIATA

The name of this popular pasta dish—*arrabbiata* means "angry"—derives from the fiery chile added to the sauce. You can make the sauce up to the point at which the olive oil and parsley are added and store it tightly covered in the refrigerator for up to 5 days or in the freezer for up to 3 months.

1 can *(28 oz/875 g)* plum tomatoes, drained

6 tablespoons *(3 fl oz/90 ml)* extra-virgin olive oil

4 large cloves garlic, chopped

1 small yellow onion, minced

1 small dried hot chile, or ¼ teaspoon red pepper flakes, or to taste

2 tablespoons tomato paste

Fine sea salt

3 tablespoons minced fresh flat-leaf parsley

Kosher salt for cooking pasta

1 lb *(500 g)* bucatini

Using your fingers, push out the excess seeds from the tomatoes, and place the tomatoes in a bowl. With your hands, a fork, or a potato masher, crush the tomatoes well; set aside.

In a frying pan large enough to accommodate the pasta later, warm 4 tablespoons (2 fl oz/60 ml) of the olive oil over medium-low heat. Add the garlic, onion, and chile and heat gently, stirring occasionally, until the garlic is golden and the onion is translucent, about 4 minutes. Stir in the tomato paste, add the tomatoes and ½ teaspoon sea salt, and stir again. Simmer gently until the sauce is thickened and aromatic, about 20 minutes. Remove from the heat and stir in the parsley and the remaining 2 tablespoons olive oil. Taste and adjust the seasoning with sea salt. Cover and keep warm.

While the sauce is simmering, in a large pot, bring 5 qt (5 l) water to a rapid boil. Add 2 tablespoons kosher salt and the pasta, stir well, and cook, stirring occasionally, until al dente, according to package directions.

Drain the pasta, add to the sauce in the pan, and toss until the strands are well coated with the sauce. Transfer to a warmed large, shallow serving bowl or individual shallow bowls and serve right away.

Spaghettini *with* Tomato–Green Olive Pesto

Here is a pleasantly tart and tangy sauce for thin strand pasta, such as spaghettini, spaghetti, or thin or regular linguine. Chop the ingredients using a sharp chef's knife or a *mezzaluna* (half-moon) chopper to ensure the correct texture; a food processor will render the ingredients too pasty.

1 cup *(5 oz/155 g)* drained, oil-packed sun-dried tomatoes, or ⅔ cup *(2 oz/60 g)* dry-packed sun-dried tomatoes

½ cup *(2½ oz/75 g)* brine-cured green olives such as Sicilian or piccholine, pitted and chopped

1 large clove garlic, passed through a garlic press or finely chopped

1 teaspoon minced fresh thyme, or ½ teaspoon crumbled dried thyme

Fine sea salt

Pinch of red pepper flakes

½ cup *(4 fl oz/125 ml)* extra-virgin olive oil

Kosher salt for cooking pasta

1 lb *(500 g)* spaghettini, spaghetti, or thin linguine (labeled *linguine fini*)

¼ cup *(⅓ oz/10 g)* chopped fresh flat-leaf parsley

2 tablespoons freshly grated pecorino romano cheese

If using oil-packed tomatoes, using a sharp knife or scissors, cut them into small pieces, then finely chop with the knife. If using dry-packed tomatoes, place them in a small bowl with hot water just to cover and let stand until softened, about 20 minutes. Drain into a fine-mesh sieve set over a small bowl, then squeeze out the excess water, capturing it in the bowl. Reserve the soaking water. Finely chop the tomatoes.

In a bowl, combine the tomatoes, olives, garlic, thyme, ¼ teaspoon sea salt, and the red pepper flakes. Add the olive oil and stir to mix thoroughly without mashing the ingredients. Stir in ¼ cup (2 fl oz/60 ml) of the reserved tomato-soaking water, if used, or plain water. Taste and adjust the seasoning with salt. (At this point, the pesto can be transferred to a jar, topped with a film of olive oil, tightly covered, and refrigerated for up to 1 month. Bring to room temperature before using.)

In a large pot, bring 5 qt (5 l) water to a rapid boil. Add 2 tablespoons kosher salt and the pasta, stir well, and cook, stirring occasionally, until al dente, according to package directions.

Drain the pasta, reserving about 1 cup (8 fl oz/250 ml) of the cooking water, and transfer the pasta to a warmed large, shallow serving bowl. Add the parsley and cheese and toss to mix. Stir about 6 tablespoons (3 fl oz/90 ml) of the pasta water into the tomato pesto, mixing to a smooth consistency. Add the pesto to the pasta and toss together until well combined, loose, and moist, adding a little more of the cooking water if needed. Serve right away.

LINGUINE *with* CALAMARI SAUCE

The secret to a good calamari sauce is simple: the seafood must be fresh and cooked quickly to remain tender. Squid is often sold already cleaned, which saves a lot of preparation time. If cleaning the squid yourself, purchase ¼ lb (125 g) extra to account for waste.

¼ cup *(2 fl oz/60 ml)* extra-virgin olive oil

2 shallots, finely chopped

3 large cloves garlic, finely chopped

1 teaspoon minced fresh rosemary, or ½ teaspoon crumbled dried rosemary

¼ teaspoon red pepper flakes

¾ cup *(6 oz/185 g)* tomato paste

Fine sea salt

½ cup *(4 fl oz/125 ml)* dry red wine

1 cup *(8 fl oz/250 ml)* bottled clam juice

1 lb *(500 g)* cleaned small squid, cut into rings and tentacles

Kosher salt for cooking pasta

1 lb *(500 g)* linguine

2 tablespoons minced fresh flat-leaf parsley

In a frying pan large enough to accommodate the pasta later, warm the olive oil over medium-low heat. Add the shallots, garlic, rosemary, and red pepper flakes and cook gently, stirring occasionally, until the shallots and garlic are softened but not colored, about 5 minutes. Add the tomato paste and stir for about 2 minutes. Add ¼ teaspoon sea salt and the wine and simmer until most of the alcohol has evaporated, about 3 minutes. Add the clam juice and continue to simmer over medium-low heat until thickened and aromatic, about 20 minutes.

Add the squid and cook gently until tender, no more than 5 minutes. If the sauce becomes thin after cooking the squid, remove the squid with a slotted spoon to a bowl. Cook the sauce, always over gentle heat, until it once again thickens, then return the squid to the pan. Taste and adjust the seasoning. Remove from the heat and cover to keep warm.

In a large pot, bring 5 qt (5 l) water to a rapid boil. Check the package directions for the cooking time, then add 2 tablespoons kosher salt and the pasta to the boiling water, stir well, and cook, stirring occasionally, until the pasta is 1 minute shy of being al dente.

Drain the pasta, add to the sauce in the pan, and place the pan over low heat. Add the parsley and toss the pasta and sauce together for about 1 minute. Some of the sauce will be absorbed by the pasta, but plenty will remain, keeping the pasta moist. Transfer to a warmed large, shallow serving bowl or individual shallow bowls and serve right away.

PENNE *with* EGGPLANT, BASIL, AND MOZZARELLA

This dish is at its best at the height of summer, when you can taste that the tomatoes and eggplant have been ripening under the hot sun. Green peppercorns still contribute a pleasant bite, but they have a brighter, more herbal flavor than black pepper, which pairs well with the fresh vegetables.

1 eggplant, about 1 lb *(500 g)*

Fine sea salt and freshly ground black pepper

½ cup *(4 fl oz/125 ml)* extra-virgin olive oil

3 large cloves garlic, minced

½ teaspoon dry green peppercorns, finely ground in a spice grinder

1 cup *(8 fl oz/250 ml)* dry white wine

2 cups *(12 oz/375 g)* peeled, seeded, and chopped fresh or canned tomatoes

Kosher salt for cooking pasta

1 lb *(500 g)* penne rigate

⅓ cup *(1⅓ oz/40 g)* freshly grated Parmigiano-Reggiano cheese, plus more for serving

⅓ lb *(155 g)* fresh mozzarella cheese, torn or cut into small pieces

10 fresh basil leaves, torn into small pieces

Trim off the stem and blossom end of the eggplant but do not peel. Cut into ½-inch (12-mm) dice. Place the eggplant in a colander in the sink and sprinkle with 1 tablespoon sea salt, tossing the eggplant to distribute the salt evenly. Top with a flat plate, then with a heavy can, and let drain for 30 minutes. Rinse the eggplant and pat dry with paper towels.

In a large frying pan over medium-low heat, warm 6 tablespoons (3 fl oz/90 ml) of the olive oil. Add the garlic and sauté until softened, about 2 minutes. Add the eggplant and ground green peppercorns, stir well, cover tightly, and cook, lifting the lid to stir several times, until the eggplant is tender, 20–25 minutes. During the last 5 minutes, add the wine and continue to cook, uncovered, stirring often, until most of the alcohol has evaporated, 3–4 minutes. Season with sea salt and black pepper. At this point, the eggplant should be soft and creamy. Raise the heat to medium, add the tomatoes, and simmer, uncovered, until the tomatoes are tender, 12–15 minutes if using fresh tomatoes and about 25 minutes if using canned. Taste and adjust the seasoning. Remove from the heat and cover to keep warm.

Meanwhile, in a large pot, bring 5 qt (5 l) water to a rapid boil. Add 2 tablespoons kosher salt and the pasta, stir well, and cook, stirring occasionally, until al dente, according to package directions.

Drain the pasta and transfer it, still dripping wet, to a warmed large, shallow bowl. Add the remaining 2 tablespoons olive oil and the Parmigiano-Reggiano and toss well. Add the eggplant mixture, mozzarella, and basil and toss until well combined. Serve right away. Pass the additional Parmigiano-Reggiano at the table.

Spaghetti *with* Meatballs

Mixing three kinds of meat yields tender, flavorful meatballs, though you will also get good results using all beef. Soaking the bread in milk before combining it with the meat ensures the meatballs are light and fluffy, while the addition of fresh tomato keeps them moist during cooking.

FOR THE TOMATO SAUCE

2 cans *(28 oz/875 g each)* plum tomatoes, drained

Fine sea salt and freshly ground pepper

¼ cup *(⅓ oz/10 g)* chopped fresh basil

FOR THE MEATBALLS

¾ cup *(1½ oz/45 g)* crustless, day-old white bread cubes

⅓ cup *(3 fl oz/80 ml)* milk or low-sodium beef broth

1¼ lb *(625 g)* equal parts ground beef, veal, and pork or lean ground beef

2 oz *(60 g)* prosciutto, minced (optional)

1 yellow onion, grated on the large holes of a box grater

1 small, ripe but firm plum tomato, peeled, seeded, and minced

2 tablespoons minced fresh flat-leaf parsley

1 teaspoon chopped fresh marjoram, or ½ teaspoon dried marjoram

To make the tomato sauce, using your fingers, push out the excess seeds from the tomatoes, and place the tomatoes in a Dutch oven or similar pot large enough to accommodate the meatballs later. Using your hands, a fork, or a potato masher, crush the tomatoes well. Place the pot over medium-low heat and simmer, uncovered, stirring occasionally, until the crushed tomatoes have thickened, about 40 minutes.

Remove from the heat and let cool slightly. Pass the sauce through a food mill or fine-mesh sieve held over a bowl, forcing as much of the pulp through as possible. Return the purée to the pot, place over medium heat, and bring to a simmer. Season with sea salt and pepper and stir in the basil. Remove from the heat and set aside.

To make the meatballs, in a small bowl, combine the bread and milk and let stand for a few minutes until the bread is softened. Remove the bread and squeeze dry, capturing the milk in the bowl. Set the milk aside. In a separate bowl, combine the bread, ground meats, prosciutto (if using), onion, tomato, parsley, marjoram, cheese, egg, 1 teaspoon sea salt, and several grinds of pepper. Using your hands, mix thoroughly to distribute the ingredients evenly. To test for seasoning, fry a nugget of the meat mixture in a little olive oil, taste, and then adjust the mixture as needed with more salt and pepper.

To form each meatball, scoop up about 2 rounded teaspoons of the mixture and roll between your palms to form a ball the size of a walnut (about ¾ inch/2 cm in diameter). If the mixture seems a little dry, add some of the reserved milk to moisten.

¼ cup *(1 oz/30 g)* freshly grated Parmigiano-Reggiano cheese

1 extra-large egg, beaten

Fine sea salt and freshly ground pepper

Olive oil for frying

½ cup *(2½ oz/75 g)* unbleached all-purpose flour

Kosher salt for cooking pasta

1 lb *(500 g)* spaghetti

Freshly grated Parmigiano-Reggiano cheese for serving

Pour olive oil to a depth of ½ inch (12 mm) into a large frying pan and place over medium heat. While the oil is heating, spread the flour on a plate. Roll the meatballs in the flour, coating evenly and tapping off the excess. When the oil is shimmering and hot but not smoking, add the meatballs to the pan, reduce the heat to medium-low, and fry, turning as necessary, until golden brown all over but still pink on the inside, about 12 minutes (they will finish cooking in the sauce later). Using a slotted spoon, transfer to paper towels to drain. (At this point, the meatballs can be cooled, covered, and refrigerated for up to 4 days before continuing.) Pour off the oil from the pan and discard.

Ladle 1 cup (8 fl oz/250 ml) of the tomato sauce into the frying pan, place over medium-low heat, and stir to dislodge any bits of meat stuck to the bottom of the pan. Return to the pot of tomato sauce and add the meatballs. Place over medium-low heat, cover, and cook until the meatballs are cooked through, 15–20 minutes. (At this point, the meatballs and sauce can be cooled, covered, and refrigerated for up to 4 days or frozen for up to 3 months. Reheat gently before continuing.)

In a large pot, bring 5 qt (5 l) water to a rapid boil. Add 2 tablespoons kosher salt and the pasta, stir well, and cook, stirring occasionally, until al dente, according to package directions.

Drain the pasta and transfer to a warmed large, shallow serving bowl. Add the sauce and meatballs and toss until well combined. Serve right away. Pass the additional cheese at the table.

CAPELLINI *with* HEIRLOOM TOMATO SAUCE

Make this sauce when heirloom tomatoes are at their height in late summer. Swirling in extra-virgin olive oil at the last minute mellows the acidity of the tomatoes and gives the sauce a silky quality. Do not purée the sauce in a machine; only a food mill or fine-mesh sieve will create the proper texture.

3 lb *(1.5 kg)* heirloom tomatoes

¼ small red or yellow onion, finely sliced or chopped

1 cup *(1 oz/30 g)* firmly packed fresh basil leaves, roughly torn

Fine sea salt

Kosher salt for cooking pasta

1 lb *(500 g)* capellini

3 tablespoons extra-virgin olive oil

Freshly grated Parmigiano-Reggiano cheese for serving

Core the tomatoes and halve crosswise. Using your fingers, push out the excess seeds from the halves, then chop coarsely. In a large, heavy saucepan over medium-high heat, combine the tomatoes, onion, ¾ cup (¾ oz/20 g) of the basil, and ½ teaspoon sea salt. Bring to a boil, then reduce the heat to medium. Simmer, uncovered, for 20 minutes, stirring often to prevent the tomatoes from sticking to the bottom of the pan. At this point, the mixture should be fairly thick. If it is still watery, simmer for 5–10 minutes longer.

Remove from the heat and let cool slightly. Pass the sauce through a food mill or fine-mesh sieve held over a bowl, forcing as much of the pulp through as possible. Return the purée to the saucepan. You should have a light sauce, thick enough to coat a spoon. If the sauce is too thin, simmer it, uncovered, for about 10 minutes longer, or until it reaches the desired consistency. Taste and adjust the seasoning. Cover to keep warm.

In a large pot, bring 5 qt (5 l) water to a rapid boil. Add 2 tablespoons kosher salt and the pasta, stir well, and cook, stirring occasionally, until al dente, according to package directions.

Just before the pasta is ready, gently reheat the sauce over medium-low heat. When the sauce is hot, stir in the olive oil. Drain the pasta and transfer to a warmed large, shallow serving bowl. Add the sauce and toss until well combined. Sprinkle with the remaining ¼ cup (¼ oz/5 g) basil and serve right away. Pass the cheese at the table.

FARFALLE *with* SALMON AND ASPARAGUS

In Italy, pasta is served as a first course, or *primo*, with a protein course to follow as a *secondo*. Here is a modern treatment for pasta in which the two courses meet on the same plate at the same time. Farfalle are ideal for this dish; they are not only pretty, but capture the light sauce in their creases.

1 lb *(500 g)* asparagus, preferably pencil-thin

Kosher salt for cooking asparagus and pasta

6 tablespoons *(3 fl oz/90 ml)* extra-virgin olive oil, plus more for brushing

2 bunches green onions, including 3 inches *(7.5 cm)* of green tops, thinly sliced on the diagonal

Generous pinch of red pepper flakes

1 lb *(500 g)* center-cut, skin-on salmon fillet, trimmed of any fat and cut into 4–6 equal pieces

2 tablespoons Dijon mustard

Fine sea salt and freshly ground pepper

1 lb *(500 g)* farfalle

Position a rack in the lower third of the oven and preheat to 500°F (260°C).

Trim off the tough ends of the asparagus, then cut crosswise into 2 or 3 pieces, keeping the tips intact.

In a large pot, bring 5 qt (5 l) water to a boil. Add 2 tablespoons kosher salt and the asparagus and boil until almost tender, about 4 minutes. Just before the asparagus is done, in a frying pan large enough to accommodate the pasta later, warm the olive oil over medium heat. Stir in the green onions and red pepper flakes. Using a wire skimmer or sieve, scoop out the asparagus and add to the pan with the green onions. Toss the ingredients together and sauté until the asparagus pieces are tender, 1–2 minutes. They should not be crunchy. Remove from the heat and cover to keep warm. Reserve the water in the pot.

While the asparagus is cooking, place a baking sheet on the lower rack in the oven. Make 4 or 5 shallow slashes about 1 inch (2.5 cm) apart on the skin side of each salmon piece, being careful not to cut into the flesh. Pat the salmon dry with paper towels, then brush the flesh sides evenly with the mustard and then with olive oil. Season with sea salt and pepper.

Reduce the oven temperature to 375°F (190°C) and carefully place the salmon pieces, skin side down, on the baking sheet. Roast until the thickest part of each piece is opaque at the center when cut into with a paring knife, or until an instant-read thermometer inserted in the thickest part registers 125°F (52°C), 9–13 minutes.

While the salmon is cooking, return the reserved water to a rapid boil, add the pasta, and stir well. Cook, stirring occasionally, until al dente, according to package directions.

Drain the pasta, add to the sauce in the pan, and toss until well combined. Transfer to warmed individual shallow bowls and arrange a salmon piece on top of each portion. Serve right away.

CAVATELLI *with* BRUSSELS SPROUTS AND HAZELNUTS

This dish is best made with marble-sized Brussels sprouts, which have not yet developed the strong cabbage flavor of the mature vegetable. Once you have trimmed the Brussels sprouts and toasted and skinned the hazelnuts, this wintertime dish can be assembled quickly.

1 cup *(5 oz/155 g)* hazelnuts

1 lb *(500 g)* baby Brussels sprouts, ends trimmed

Kosher salt for cooking Brussels sprouts and pasta

½ cup *(4 oz/125 g)* unsalted butter, clarified (page 233)

Fine sea salt and freshly ground pepper

¾ lb *(375 g)* cavatelli

½ cup *(2 oz/60 g)* freshly grated Parmigiano-Reggiano cheese

1 cup *(8 oz/250 g)* whole-milk ricotta cheese

Preheat the oven to 350°F (180°C). Spread the hazelnuts on a rimmed baking sheet and toast in the oven until they are fragrant and have taken on color, about 10 minutes. Remove from the oven. While still warm, transfer the nuts to a coarse-textured kitchen towel and rub between your palms to remove the skins. Chop the nuts coarsely and set aside.

In a large pot, bring 5 qt (5 l) water to a rapid boil.

While the water is heating, trim off the tough base from each Brussels sprout. If the Brussels sprouts are large, cut them in half lengthwise.

Add 2 tablespoons kosher salt and the Brussels sprouts to the boiling water and boil until tender, about 10 minutes. The Brussels sprouts should not be crunchy. Using a wire skimmer or slotted spoon, transfer the Brussels sprouts to a bowl. Reserve the water in the pot.

In a frying pan large enough to accommodate the pasta later, warm the clarified butter over medium heat. When the butter is hot, add the hazelnuts and a sprinkle of sea salt and stir well. Add the Brussels sprouts and toss and stir until heated through, about 2 minutes. Remove from the heat and cover to keep warm.

Return the water to a rapid boil. Add the pasta, stir well, and cook, stirring occasionally, until al dente, according to package directions.

Drain the pasta, reserving about ½ cup (4 fl oz/125 ml) of the cooking water. Add the pasta to the sauce in the pan and toss until well combined, adding some of the reserved cooking water if needed to moisten the sauce so that it coats the pasta nicely. Season with sea salt and pepper. Transfer to a warmed large, shallow serving bowl or individual shallow bowls and top with the grated cheese. Serve right away. Pass the ricotta at the table for diners to dollop on top of their pasta.

Bucatini *with* Sausage and Porcini

This is an adaptation of a signature dish of Umbria called *spaghetti alla norcia*, named for the small town of Norcia near the foot of the Apennines. The town is famous for its pork products and sausage, such as the sweet variety used here, which mingles with earthy mushrooms in the sauce.

2 cups *(2 oz/60 g)* dried porcini mushrooms, soaked in 1 cup *(8 fl oz/250 ml)* hot water for 30 minutes

5 tablespoons *(3 fl oz/80 ml)* extra-virgin olive oil or *(2½ oz/75 g)* unsalted butter, or a mixture

2 yellow onions, minced

1 lb *(500 g)* sweet Italian sausages, casings removed

1 teaspoon ground fennel

Pinch of red pepper flakes

Pinch of freshly grated nutmeg

½ cup *(4 fl oz/125 ml)* heavy cream

Fine sea salt

Kosher salt for cooking pasta

1 lb *(500 g)* bucatini

Remove the mushrooms from the water and reserve the water. Rinse the mushrooms under cold running water to remove any sand or grit and squeeze dry. Chop the mushrooms. Line a fine-mesh sieve with cheesecloth or a paper towel, place over a cup, and strain the soaking water. Set the mushrooms and water aside separately.

In a large frying pan, warm 2 tablespoons of the olive oil over medium-low heat. Add the onions and mushrooms and sauté until the onions are well softened but not browned, about 7 minutes. Meanwhile, in another frying pan over medium-low heat, warm the remaining 3 tablespoons olive oil. Add the sausage meat and cook, stirring to break up any clumps, until nicely colored and just cooked through, about 8 minutes. Stir in the fennel.

Add the sausage to the onion mixture along with the red pepper flakes and stir well. Raise the heat to medium, add the mushroom soaking liquid, and simmer until the liquid has evaporated, about 5 minutes. Stir in the nutmeg and cream and cook, stirring occasionally, until the sauce has thickened, about 3 minutes. Season with sea salt.

Meanwhile, in a large pot, bring 5 qt (5 l) water to a rapid boil. Add 2 tablespoons kosher salt and the pasta, stir well, and cook, stirring occasionally, until al dente, according to package directions.

Drain the pasta and transfer to a warmed large, shallow serving bowl. Add the sauce and toss with the pasta until well combined. Divide among individual shallow bowls and serve right away.

SPAGHETTI *with* TOMATOES AND HERBED RICOTTA

Sauces made from sugary sweet, vine-ripened cherry tomatoes are among the most appealing of all tomato sauces; cooking them briefly over high heat produces a light, chunky sauce. Dollops of creamy ricotta flavored with fresh herbs complete the light but satisfying dish.

⅓ cup *(3 fl oz/80 ml)* extra-virgin olive oil

6 cloves garlic, bruised *(see page 233)*

2½ lb *(1.25 kg)* grape or cherry tomatoes

Fine sea salt and freshly ground pepper

1 cup *(8 oz/250 g)* whole-milk ricotta cheese

3 tablespoons fresh basil leaves, cut crosswise into thin ribbons

1 tablespoon chopped fresh flat-leaf parsley

Kosher salt for cooking pasta

1 lb *(500 g)* spaghetti

In a frying pan large enough to accommodate the pasta later, warm the olive oil over medium heat. Add the garlic and sauté, pressing on the garlic with the back of a wooden spoon to release its juices. When the garlic turns a rich gold but is not yet brown, 1–2 minutes, remove and discard it and immediately add the tomatoes and ½ teaspoon sea salt. Raise the heat to high and cook, tossing, until the tomatoes are tender and beginning to burst open but have not fully collapsed, about 5 minutes. Remove from the heat and season with sea salt and pepper. Cover the pan to keep warm.

While the tomatoes are cooking, in a bowl, stir together the cheese, 2½ tablespoons of the basil, and the parsley and set aside.

In a large pot, bring 5 qt (5 l) water to a rapid boil. Add 2 tablespoons kosher salt and the pasta, stir well, and cook, stirring occasionally, until al dente, according to package directions.

Drain the pasta, add to the sauce in the pan, sprinkle with the remaining ½ tablespoon basil, and toss until well combined. Transfer to warmed individual shallow bowls and top each portion with dollops of the herbed cheese. Serve right away.

MINESTRONE

There are countless ways to make minestrone, but all successful versions use fresh vegetables, good extra-virgin olive oil, and authentic Parmigiano-Reggiano cheese. This rendition gets extra heft from ham. Serve with crusty bread and pass extra-virgin olive oil at the table for drizzling on top.

1 large rib celery

3 tablespoons extra-virgin olive oil

3 canned plum tomatoes, seeded and chopped, plus ¼ cup *(2 fl oz/60 ml)* of their juice

1 large yellow onion, coarsely chopped

1 potato, peeled and diced

¾ lb *(375 g)* butternut squash, peeled and diced

1 large carrot, peeled and diced

½ lb *(250 g)* green cabbage, finely shredded

3 tablespoons plus 1 teaspoon minced fresh rosemary

6 tablespoons *(½ oz/15 g)* finely chopped fresh flat-leaf parsley

Fine sea salt and freshly ground pepper

1 cup *(7 oz/220 g)* drained cooked cannellini beans, well rinsed

¼ lb *(125 g)* green beans, cut into 1-inch *(2.5-cm)* lengths

2 small zucchini, trimmed and diced

1½ cups *(3 oz/90 g)* cauliflower florets

¾ lb *(375 g)* ham steak, diced

Kosher salt for cooking pasta

1 cup *(4 oz/125 g)* ditalini

Freshly grated Parmigiano-Reggiano cheese for serving

Cut the celery rib into thin slices and chop the leaves. In a large pot, combine the olive oil, celery and chopped leaves, tomatoes and their juice, onion, potato, butternut squash, carrot, cabbage, the 1 teaspoon rosemary, 3 tablespoons of the parsley, and 10 cups *(2½ qt/2.5 l)* water. Season with sea salt and pepper, cover, and bring to a boil over high heat. Immediately reduce the heat to medium-low, cover partially, and simmer for 40 minutes.

Add the cannellini beans, green beans, zucchini, cauliflower, and ham, re-cover partially, and cook until the vegetables are tender but not mushy, about 8 minutes. Stir in the 3 tablespoons rosemary and the remaining 3 tablespoons parsley.

Meanwhile, in a saucepan, bring 2 qt *(2 l)* water to a boil. Check the package directions for the cooking time, then add 1 tablespoon kosher salt and the pasta to the boiling water, stir well, and cook, stirring occasionally, until the pasta is half-cooked. Drain and add to the soup.

Continue cooking the soup, uncovered, over medium heat until the pasta is just shy of al dente, about 2 minutes. (It will continue to cook in the heat of the soup.) Taste and adjust the seasoning with sea salt and pepper. Ladle into warmed shallow bowls and sprinkle with the cheese. Serve right away.

LINGUINE *with* GARLICKY SHRIMP

Chervil is an herb the French love for its suggestion of fennel and tarragon. It lends a fresh, easy variation on the classic shrimp-parsley union, but if you cannot find it, use flat-leaf parsley. Serve good crusty Italian bread with this dish for soaking up the flavorful, brothy sauce.

2 lb *(1 kg)* large shrimp, preferably South American white, peeled and deveined

6 tablespoons *(3 fl oz/90 ml)* extra-virgin olive oil

4 large cloves garlic, finely chopped

¼ teaspoon red pepper flakes

2 small tomatoes, peeled, seeded, and coarsely chopped, or 2 canned plum tomatoes, seeded and coarsely chopped

Fine sea salt

½ cup *(4 fl oz/125 ml)* dry white wine

4 tablespoons *(⅓ oz/10 g)* chopped fresh chervil or flat-leaf parsley, or a combination

Kosher salt for cooking pasta

1 lb *(500 g)* linguine

Make a deep cut along the back of each shrimp, so it can be opened flat like a book. Use paper towels to pat the shrimp dry.

In a large pot, bring 5 qt (5 l) water to a boil. While the water is heating, make the sauce. In a frying pan large enough to accommodate the pasta later, warm the olive oil over medium-low heat. Add the garlic and red pepper flakes and cook gently, stirring occasionally, until the garlic is softened but not browned, about 2 minutes.

Add the shrimp to the pan, placing them opened-side down in the pan so they do not curl too much. Sauté the shrimp, turning once, until opaque, about 2 minutes on each side. Add the tomatoes, season with ½ teaspoon sea salt, and stir to mix. Stir in the wine and cook until most of the alcohol has evaporated, about 3 minutes. Sprinkle with 2 tablespoons of the chervil, and taste and adjust the seasoning. Remove from the heat and cover to keep warm.

When the water is boiling, check the package directions for the cooking time, then add 2 tablespoons kosher salt and the pasta to the boiling water, stir well, and cook, stirring occasionally, until the pasta is just shy of being al dente.

Return the sauce to low heat. Drain the pasta, add to the sauce in the pan, and toss until the strands are well coated with the sauce. Transfer to a warmed large, shallow serving bowl or individual shallow bowls, top with the remaining 2 tablespoons chervil, and serve right away.

SPAGHETTINI *with* MUSSELS AND WHITE WINE

Here is a classic way of cooking mussels that works nicely with a variety of strand pastas—the shellfish throw off plenty of delicious broth that easily coats the whole length of the noodles. Look for small mussels, which will be the sweetest and most tender, for this aromatic dish.

6 lb *(3 kg)* mussels

6 tablespoons *(3 fl oz/90 ml)* extra-virgin olive oil

½ cup *(2 oz/60 g)* chopped yellow onion

3 large cloves garlic, chopped

½ cup *(¾ oz/20 g)* plus 3 tablespoons chopped fresh flat-leaf parsley

2 teaspoons chopped fresh oregano, or 1 teaspoon crumbled dried oregano

1½ cups *(12 fl oz/375 ml)* dry white wine

¼ teaspoon red pepper flakes

Kosher salt for cooking pasta

1 lb *(500 g)* spaghettini, spaghetti, or linguine

Scrub the mussels with a stiff vegetable brush under cold running water, then place in a large bowl. Add cold water to cover and let stand for 1–3 hours to rid them of any sand or grit. Drain well and rinse again, discarding any that do not close tightly to the touch.

In a heavy Dutch oven large enough to accommodate the mussels easily, warm the olive oil over medium heat. Add the onion and sauté until wilted, about 4 minutes. Add the garlic, the 3 tablespoons parsley, and the oregano and continue to sauté until the onion is lightly colored but not browned, about 3 minutes. Add the mussels and toss together all the ingredients. Add the wine and red pepper flakes, raise the heat to medium-high, cover, and bring to a boil. Reduce the heat to medium and cook, covered, until the mussels open, 2–3 minutes longer. Remove from the heat and discard any unopened mussels.

When the mussels have cooled somewhat, remove most of them from their shells, keeping a couple dozen or so intact for serving. Return the mussels to their broth and cover to keep warm.

In a large pot, bring 5 qt (5 l) water to a rapid boil. Add 2 tablespoons kosher salt and the pasta, stir well, and cook, stirring occasionally, until al dente, according to package directions.

Drain the pasta and divide among warmed individual shallow bowls. Using a large spoon or ladle, spoon some of the mussels and broth over each serving, trying not to stir up the bottom of the pot where stray grains of sand might have fallen. Scatter the ½ cup (¾ oz/20 g) parsley on top and serve right away.

RIGATONI *with* BROCCOLI RABE AND CHICKPEAS

Many cooks outside of Italy have at last discovered broccoli rabe—a vegetable with tender leaves and small, broccoli-like florets—but it is rarely cooked properly. The secret is to boil the greens briefly in salted water before sautéing to mellow their bitter edge and tenderize the stalks.

2 lb *(1 kg)* broccoli rabe

Kosher salt for cooking broccoli rabe and pasta

½ cup *(4 fl oz/125 ml)* extra-virgin olive oil

5 large cloves garlic, thickly sliced lengthwise

2 small dried chiles, or pinch of red pepper flakes

1 cup *(7 oz/220 g)* drained cooked chickpeas, well rinsed

Fine sea salt

¾ lb *(375 g)* rigatoni

Using a small, sharp knife or vegetable peeler, peel away the thick skin from the tough lower stalks of the broccoli rabe (most of the bottom stalk portion). Cut crosswise into 3-inch (7.5-cm) lengths. Place in a bowl, add cold water to cover, and let stand for 1 hour.

Fill a saucepan three-fourths full of water and bring to a boil. Drain the greens and add to the boiling water along with 1 tablespoon kosher salt. Cover partially and cook for 5 minutes after the water returns to a boil.

While the broccoli rabe is cooking, in a frying pan large enough to accommodate the pasta later, warm the olive oil over medium heat. Add the garlic and chiles, reduce the heat to medium-low, and sauté gently until the garlic colors, about 5 minutes. Drain the greens and add them, still dripping wet, to the frying pan. Raise the heat to medium, stir well, and sauté for 2 minutes. Add the chickpeas, reduce the heat to medium-low, cover, and cook gently, stirring occasionally, until the chickpeas are heated through and the greens are tender, about 5 minutes longer. Season with sea salt to taste. Remove from the heat and cover to keep warm.

While the sauce is cooking, in a large pot, bring 5 qt (5 l) water to a rapid boil. Add 2 tablespoons kosher salt and the pasta, stir, and cook, stirring occasionally, until al dente, according to package directions.

Drain the pasta, reserving about ½ cup (4 fl oz/125 ml) of the cooking water. Add the pasta to the sauce in the pan and toss to combine, adding up to a few tablespoons of the cooking water if needed to moisten the sauce so that it coats the pasta nicely. Transfer to a warmed large, shallow serving bowl or individual shallow bowls and serve right away.

Gemelli *with* Tomatoes, Arugula, and Burrata

Burrata, which means "buttered," is a luscious, creamy fresh cheese made by mixing together cream and unspun mozzarella curds. When the cheese hits the hot pasta, it melts with the juicy tomatoes and olive oil, forming an irresistible sauce that works its way into the grooves of the twisted noodles.

1 large clove garlic, minced or passed through a garlic press

¼ cup *(2 fl oz/60 ml)* extra-virgin olive oil, plus more for drizzling

1 lb *(500 g)* small cherry or Sweet 100 tomatoes, halved

Fine sea salt and freshly ground pepper

1 cup *(1 oz/30 g)* firmly packed baby arugula leaves

Kosher salt for cooking pasta

1 lb *(500 g)* gemelli

½ lb *(250 g)* burrata cheese, roughly torn

In a small bowl, combine the garlic and the ¼ cup (2 fl oz/60 ml) olive oil and let stand for about 20 minutes, until the garlic infuses the olive oil with its flavor.

Strain the infused oil through a fine-mesh sieve held over a large, shallow serving bowl, and discard the garlic. Add the tomatoes, ¼ teaspoon sea salt, and several grinds of pepper to the oil. Set aside.

Rinse the arugula in several changes of cold water to be sure there is no trace of sand, then dry thoroughly with kitchen towels or in a salad spinner. Add the arugula to the serving bowl with the other ingredients. Toss to mix well. Cover the sauce and let stand at room temperature for at least 30 minutes or up to 4 hours before using. Taste and adjust the seasoning just before using.

In a large pot, bring 5 qt (5 l) water to a rapid boil. Add 2 tablespoons kosher salt and the pasta, stir well, and cook, stirring occasionally, until al dente, according to package directions.

Drain the pasta, reserving about ½ cup (4 fl oz/125 ml) of the cooking water, and transfer the pasta to the bowl holding the sauce. Toss well, adding up to a few tablespoons of the cooking water if needed to moisten the sauce so that it coats the pasta nicely. Divide the pasta among warmed individual serving bowls. Top with the cheese, dividing it evenly, and drizzle with olive oil. Serve right away.

DITALINI *with* ESCAROLE AND WHITE BEANS

The happy marriage of pasta and beans *(pasta e fagioli)* enjoys many forms in the Italian kitchen—in soups, salads, or main-course dishes like this one. This recipe can be made with or without pancetta, as the generous quantity of garlic provides plenty of flavor on its own.

1 large head escarole, about 1½ lb *(750 g)*

6 tablespoons *(3 fl oz/90 ml)* extra-virgin olive oil, plus more for serving

6 large cloves garlic, chopped

2 oz *(60 g)* pancetta or lean bacon, diced (optional)

1 dried chile, seeded, or a generous pinch of red pepper flakes

2 cups *(14 oz/440 g)* drained cooked cannellini beans, well rinsed

Kosher salt for cooking pasta

½ lb *(250 g)* ditalini

Fine sea salt

Remove any yellow or wilted leaves from the escarole, cut out the core, and cut the leaves crosswise into ribbons 2 inches (5 cm) wide. Set aside.

In a frying pan large enough to accommodate the pasta later, warm the olive oil over medium-low heat. Add the garlic, pancetta (if using), and chile and sauté until the garlic and pancetta are lightly colored, about 5 minutes. Raise the heat to medium, add the escarole, and sauté, tossing and stirring often, until the escarole is wilted, about 5 minutes. Reduce the heat to low, add the beans, cover, and cook for 5 minutes to heat the beans through and allow the flavors to blend.

In a large pot, bring 4 qt (4 l) water to a rapid boil. Add 1½ tablespoons kosher salt and the pasta, stir well, and cook, stirring occasionally, until al dente, according to package directions.

Drain the pasta, add to the sauce in the pan, and toss until well combined. Taste and adjust the seasoning with sea salt. Transfer to a warmed large, shallow serving bowl and serve right away.

BUCATINI *all'*AMATRICIANA

This dish is traditionally made with *guanciale* (cured pig's jowl), which is a delicacy, although pancetta can be used instead. For layers of flavor, pecorino cheese is added in three stages: while the sauce is cooking, when the pasta and sauce are tossed together, and at the table when served.

1 can *(28 oz/875 g)* plum tomatoes

2 tablespoons extra-virgin olive oil

½ small yellow onion, finely chopped

3 oz *(90 g) guanciale* or lean pancetta, thickly sliced and cut into julienne

⅛ teaspoon red pepper flakes, or to taste

2 tablespoons tomato paste

Fine sea salt

2 tablespoons freshly grated aged pecorino romano cheese, plus more for serving

Kosher salt for cooking pasta

1 lb *(500 g)* bucatini

Drain the tomatoes, reserving their juice. Strain the captured juice to hold back the seeds. Using your fingers, push out the excess seeds from the tomatoes. Coarsely chop the tomatoes and set aside.

In a frying pan large enough to accommodate the pasta later, warm the olive oil over medium-low heat. Add the onion and *guanciale* and sauté until the onion is golden but not browned, about 6 minutes. Stir in the red pepper flakes and tomato paste. Add the tomatoes and their juice and ½ teaspoon sea salt and simmer, uncovered, stirring occasionally, until thickened, about 30 minutes. Stir in 1 tablespoon of the cheese, remove from the heat, and cover to keep warm.

In a large pot, bring 5 qt (5 l) water to a rapid boil. Add 2 tablespoons kosher salt and the pasta, stir well, and cook, stirring occasionally, until al dente, according to package directions.

Drain the pasta, add to the sauce in the pan, and toss to mix. Sprinkle another 1 tablespoon cheese and toss until the strands are well coated with the sauce. Transfer to a warmed large, shallow serving bowl or individual shallow bowls and serve right away. Pass additional cheese at the table.

LINGUINE *with* ASPARAGUS, PEAS, AND HERBS

Here is a true springtime dish, made with the season's early harvest of asparagus and peas. The vegetables are meant to be tender, not crunchy and firm, so don't be tempted to undercook them. If freshly picked peas are not available, substitute frozen baby peas, also called petite peas.

1 lb *(500 g)* asparagus

Kosher salt for cooking vegetables and pasta

1 cup *(5 oz/155 g)* fresh shelled English peas or frozen baby peas

3 tablespoons unsalted butter

3 tablespoons extra-virgin olive oil

6 green onions, including 3 inches *(7.5 cm)* of green tops, thinly sliced on the diagonal

2 yellow onions, chopped

6 oz *(185 g)* baby spinach, coarsely chopped

Fine sea salt and freshly ground pepper

½ cup *(4 fl oz/125 ml)* heavy cream

2 tablespoons minced fresh mint

¼ cup *(⅓ oz/10 g)* minced fresh flat-leaf parsley

1 lb *(500 g)* linguine

Freshly grated Parmigiano-Reggiano cheese for serving

In a large pot, bring 5 qt (5 l) water to a rapid boil.

While the water is heating, snap off the tough ends of the asparagus. Using a vegetable peeler, peel away the thick skin to within about 2 inches (5 cm) of the tips. Cut the spears crosswise into 1-inch (2.5-cm) pieces, leaving the tips intact. Add 2 tablespoons kosher salt and the asparagus to the boiling water and cook until tender, about 6 minutes. The asparagus must not be crunchy. Using a wire skimmer or slotted spoon, transfer the asparagus to a bowl. Add the peas to the boiling water and cook for 1 minute. Drain and add to the bowl holding the asparagus. Set aside. Reserve the water in the pot.

Meanwhile, in a frying pan large enough to accommodate the pasta later, melt the butter with the olive oil over medium-low heat, Add the green onions and yellow onions and sauté until translucent, about 5 minutes. Stir in the spinach, ½ teaspoon sea salt, and several grinds of pepper and sauté, tossing often, until the spinach is wilted, about 3 minutes. Add the asparagus and peas, then stir in the cream and heat until hot, about 1 minute. Add the mint and parsley and stir well. Taste and adjust the seasonings. Remove from the heat and cover to keep warm.

Return the water to a rapid boil. Add 2 tablespoons kosher salt and the pasta to the boiling water, stir well, and cook, stirring occasionally, until al dente, according to package directions.

Just before the pasta is ready, if the sauce has cooled, return it to medium-low heat to warm, then remove from the heat. Drain the pasta, add to the sauce in the pan, and toss until the strands are well coated with the sauce. Transfer to a warmed large, shallow serving bowl or individual shallow bowls and serve right away. Pass the cheese at the table.

TOASTED VERMICELLI NOODLE SOUP

For this soup, use the Mexican noodles labeled *fideo,* which are sometimes sold already broken into short pieces, if you can find them. Otherwise, vermicelli or angel hair noodles also work well. Toasting the noodles partially cooks them, but retains their crunch in the hot, rich broth.

2 cups *(12 oz/375 g)* peeled, seeded, and chopped fresh or canned plum tomatoes

4 cloves garlic, coarsely chopped

1 large red onion, coarsely chopped

½ teaspoon chopped chipotle chile in adobo sauce

Fine sea salt

6 cups *(48 fl oz/1.5 l)* low-sodium chicken broth

6 tablespoons *(3 fl oz/90 ml)* extra-virgin olive oil

¼ lb *(125 g)* fideo, vermicelli, or angel hair pasta

1 avocado, pitted, peeled, and diced

¼ cup *(⅓ oz/10 g)* fresh cilantro leaves, roughly chopped

1 lime, cut into 4 wedges

In a food processor or blender, combine the tomatoes, garlic, onion, chipotle chile, and 1 teaspoon sea salt and process until well blended and smooth. Transfer to a saucepan. Add the broth to the saucepan, stir well, and bring to a simmer over medium-low heat. Simmer for about 5 minutes to allow the flavors to blend.

While the soup is simmering, in a small sauté pan over medium heat, warm the olive oil. Break the pasta into 1-inch (2.5-cm) lengths. Add to the oil and sauté, tossing to color evenly, until golden brown, about 2 minutes. Remove from the heat and cover to keep warm.

When the soup is ready, ladle it into warmed individual shallow bowls. Top with the hot, crisp noodles. Distribute the avocado and cilantro among the bowls and serve right away, passing lime wedges at the table for seasoning the soup.

LINGUINE *with* TUNA AND TOMATOES

Italians use premium canned belly tuna packed in olive oil, labeled *ventresca di tonno*, for many types of sauces. The tuna is rich, moist, and smooth, and produces a first-rate sauce for thin strand pastas. In Italy, grated cheese is traditionally not served with seafood pastas, which holds true here.

1 can *(28 oz/875 g)* plum tomatoes

3 tablespoons extra-virgin olive oil

4 large cloves garlic, bruised *(see page 233)*

3 tablespoons tomato paste

Pinch of red pepper flakes

3 fresh basil leaves

1 teaspoon chopped fresh oregano, or ½ teaspoon crumbled dried oregano

Fine sea salt

1 can *(6½ oz/200 g)* Italian tuna belly in olive oil, drained and finely flaked

Kosher salt for cooking pasta

1 lb *(500 g)* linguine or spaghetti

2 tablespoons chopped fresh flat-leaf parsley

Drain the tomatoes, reserving their juice. Strain the captured juice to hold back the seeds. Using your fingers, push out the excess seeds from the tomatoes, and place the tomatoes in a bowl. Using your hands, a fork, or a potato masher, crush the tomatoes well. Set the juice and tomatoes aside separately.

In a frying pan large enough to accommodate the pasta later, warm the olive oil over medium-low heat. Add the garlic and heat gently, stirring occasionally, until lightly browned, about 3 minutes. Stir in the tomato paste, then add the crushed tomatoes and simmer for 2 minutes. Stir in the reserved tomato juice, red pepper flakes, basil, and oregano and season with sea salt. Simmer gently for 10 minutes to allow the flavors to blend, then stir in the tuna. Cover partially and continue to simmer gently until the sauce is thickened, about 20 minutes. Remove and discard the garlic cloves and basil leaves, if desired. Remove from the heat and cover the pan to keep warm.

In a large pot, bring 5 qt (5 l) water to a rapid boil. Add 2 tablespoons kosher salt and the pasta, stir well, and cook, stirring occasionally, until al dente, according to package directions.

Drain the pasta and add to the sauce in the pan. Add the parsley and toss until the strands are well coated with the sauce. Transfer to a warmed large, shallow serving bowl or individual shallow bowls and serve right away.

Chicken Noodle Soup

The secret to making a good chicken soup is in the broth: Use a high proportion of chicken to water, and strike a harmonious balance of aromatic vegetables. To keep the broth as clear as possible, do not allow it to boil rapidly, and skim the foam from the surface often.

1 whole chicken, about 3½ lb *(1.75 kg)*

4 fresh flat-leaf parsley sprigs, plus 3 tablespoons chopped

1 celery root, peeled and finely diced to measure 1 cup *(5 oz/155 g)*

1 large rib celery, including leaves, rib chopped and leaves minced

1 large carrot, peeled and chopped

1 yellow onion, chopped

1 fresh tomato, peeled, seeded, and chopped, or 2 canned plum tomatoes, seeded and chopped

2 bay leaves

Fine sea salt and freshly ground white pepper

4 green onions, white and light green parts, minced

½ cup *(2 oz/60 g)* dried egg noodles, or spaghetti broken into 2-inch *(5-cm)* lengths

In a large pot, combine the chicken, parsley sprigs, celery root, celery, carrot, onion, tomato, bay leaves, 2 teaspoons sea salt, and 2 qt (2 l) water. Bring just to a boil over medium-high heat and then immediately reduce the heat to medium-low. The liquid should be at a gentle but steady simmer. Cook, uncovered, skimming off any foam that forms on the surface, until the chicken is cooked through, about 45 minutes or until an instant-read thermometer inserted into the thickest part of the thigh away from bone registers 160°F (71°C).

Remove from the heat and transfer the chicken to a platter. When cool enough to handle, remove the skin and pull the meat off the bones. Cut the meat into bite-size pieces. Strain the broth through a fine-mesh sieve into a clean saucepan. Place the broth over high heat and bring to a boil. Add the green onions and the noodles and cook until the noodles are al dente, according to package directions.

Reduce the heat to low, add the chicken and chopped parsley, and heat through. Season with sea salt and white pepper. Ladle into warmed shallow bowls and serve right away.

Spaghetti *with* Radicchio and Bacon

The original version of this dish, developed by Venetian writer and gondola restorer Paolo Lanapoppi, is meatless, but this recipe includes bacon; its sweet, smoky flavor pairs so well with the pleasantly bitter radicchio and a generous dusting of freshly ground pepper.

7 tablespoons *(3½ fl oz/ 105 ml)* extra-virgin olive oil

5 large cloves garlic, roughly chopped

¼ lb *(125 g)* sliced bacon, cut into into strips 1 inch *(2.5 cm)* long and ½ inch *(12 mm)* wide

1 large red onion, finely chopped

¾ lb *(375 g)* Treviso radicchio, roughly chopped

Fine sea salt and freshly ground pepper

Kosher salt for cooking pasta

1 lb *(500 g)* spaghetti

2 tablespoons chopped fresh flat-leaf parsley

In a frying pan large enough to accommodate the pasta later, warm 2 tablespoons of the olive oil over medium-low heat. Add the garlic and sauté until lightly browned, 3–4 minutes. Add the bacon and sauté until nicely colored and crisp, about 6 minutes. Using a slotted spoon, transfer the garlic and bacon to paper towels to drain.

Discard all but 2 tablespoons of the fat from the pan, return the pan to medium-low heat, and add the remaining 5 tablespoons (2½ fl oz/75 ml) olive oil. Add the onion and sauté until softened and lightly colored, about 6 minutes. Add the radicchio and stir and toss to coat to it evenly with the oil. Add ¾ cup (6 fl oz/180 ml) hot water and toss to combine. Cover and continue to cook over medium-low heat, stirring occasionally, until the radicchio is tender, 10–12 minutes. Add ½ teaspoon sea salt, re-cover, remove from the heat, and set aside.

In a large pot, bring 5 qt (5 l) water to a rapid boil. Check the package directions for the cooking time, then add 2 tablespoons kosher salt and the pasta to the boiling water, stir well, and cook, stirring occasionally, until the pasta is 1 minute shy of being al dente.

Drain the pasta, reserving about 1 cup (8 fl oz/250 ml) of the cooking water. Add the pasta to the pan with the sauce, place over high heat, and toss the pasta and the sauce together for about 1 minute to distribute all the ingredients evenly, adding a little of the cooking water if needed to moisten the sauce. Transfer to warmed individual shallow bowls and top with the bacon, garlic, parsley, and plenty of pepper. Serve right away.

FUSILLI *with* GORGONZOLA SAUCE

This is a classic sauce from the northern region of Lombardy, where Gorgonzola is made. As simple as it is, its success depends on using young, very mild Gorgonzola, also known as *fior di latte* (flower of the milk), *Gorgonzola dolce,* or *dolcelatte*. Do not use aged Gorgonzola; it will overpower the sauce.

4 tablespoons *(2 oz/60 g)* **unsalted butter**

6 oz *(185 g)* **young Gorgonzola cheese** *(see Note)*, **crumbled**

1 cup *(8 fl oz/250 ml)* **heavy cream**

¾ cup *(3 oz/90 g)* **freshly grated Parmigiano-Reggiano cheese, plus more for serving**

Fine sea salt and freshly ground pepper

Kosher salt for cooking pasta

1 lb *(500 g)* **fusilli**

In a frying pan large enough to accommodate the pasta later, melt the butter over medium-low heat. Stir in the Gorgonzola, mashing it with a spoon to blend it well. Add the cream and bring to a gentle simmer, stirring occasionally. Immediately reduce the heat to low, never permitting it to simmer beyond the gentlest and occasional bubble. Continue to simmer gently until the sauce is thick enough to coat a spoon, about 3 minutes. Remove from the heat and stir in the Parmigiano-Reggiano and sea salt and pepper to taste. Cover to keep warm.

In a large pot, bring 5 qt (5 l) water to a rapid boil. Add 2 tablespoons kosher salt and the pasta, stir well, and cook, stirring occasionally, until al dente, according to package directions.

Just before the pasta is ready, if the sauce has cooled, return it to medium-low heat to reheat, then remove from the heat. Drain the pasta, reserving about ½ cup (4 fl oz/125 ml) of the cooking water. Add the pasta to the sauce in the pan and toss until well combined, adding some of the reserved cooking water if needed to moisten the sauce so that it coats the pasta nicely. Transfer to a warmed large, shallow serving bowl or individual shallow bowls and serve right away. Pass the additional Parmigiano-Reggiano at the table.

SPAGHETTI *with* BLACK OLIVE–CAPER PESTO

Small, meaty Gaeta olives, named for a town that lies between Rome and Naples, are ideal for using in this flavor-packed pesto. Greece's fleshy Kalamata olives are a good second choice. The pesto can be made up to 3 weeks in advance and stored, tightly capped, in the refrigerator.

2 cups *(10 oz/315 g)* pitted black olives such as Gaeta or Kalamata

2 tablespoons capers, drained

2 teaspoons chopped fresh flat-leaf parsley

1 teaspoon fresh minced marjoram, or ½ teaspoon crumbled dried marjoram

1 large clove garlic, roughly chopped

2 tablespoons chopped red onion

1 olive oil–packed anchovy fillet, chopped, or 1 teaspoon anchovy paste

Grated zest of 1 lemon

¼ cup *(2 fl oz/60 ml)* extra-virgin olive oil

Freshly ground pepper

Kosher salt for cooking pasta

1 lb *(500 g)* spaghetti, spaghettini, or capellini

In a food processor, combine the olives, capers, parsley, marjoram, garlic, onion, anchovy, lemon zest, and olive oil. Pulse briefly to grind. The resulting mixture should have some texture. Avoid overgrinding, which will make the mixture too pasty and smooth. Season with pepper.

In a large pot, bring 5 qt (5 l) water to a rapid boil. Add 2 tablespoons kosher salt and the pasta, stir well, and cook, stirring occasionally, until al dente, according to package directions.

Drain the pasta, reserving about 1 cup (8 fl oz/250 ml) of the cooking water. Transfer the pasta to a warmed large, shallow serving bowl, add the pesto, and toss, adding as much of the reserved cooking water as needed to loosen the pesto so that the strands are well coated with the sauce. Serve right away.

ORECCHIETTE *with* CAULIFLOWER AND LEEKS

In this recipe, leeks and garlic are roasted until nicely browned and sweet, and then tossed with small cauliflower florets and tangy goat cheese to make an unctuous cheese sauce. Small, sturdy, cap-shaped "little ears," orecchiette are the perfect pasta to carry the chunky sauce.

¼ lb *(125 g)* fresh goat cheese, cut into 4 pieces

4 leeks

5 tablespoons *(3 fl oz/80 ml)* extra-virgin olive oil

12 large cloves garlic, peeled but left whole

Fine sea salt and freshly ground pepper

Kosher salt for cooking pasta

¾ lb *(375 g)* orecchiette

1 small head cauliflower, trimmed and cut into small florets to measure 4 cups *(8 oz/250 g)*

¼ cup *(1½ oz/45 g)* Gaeta or Niçoise olives, pitted and cut in half lengthwise

Preheat the oven to 400°F (200°C). Select a large, shallow serving bowl for the pasta, place the cheese in the bowl, and set aside.

Cut off and discard the dark green tops from each leek, leaving the pale green portion intact, and trim away the root end. Cut each leek in half lengthwise and clean thoroughly under cold running water. Use 1 tablespoon of the olive oil to oil a rimmed baking sheet. Brush the leeks and garlic cloves all over with the remaining 4 tablespoons (2 fl oz/60 ml) olive oil and arrange in a single layer on the prepared baking sheet. Season with sea salt.

Roast until the vegetables are nicely browned and thoroughly softened, about 20 minutes. When cool enough to handle, chop the leeks into ½-inch (12-mm) pieces, and cut the garlic cloves into quarters. Set aside.

While the vegetables are roasting, in a large pot, bring 5 qt (5 l) water to a rapid boil. Add 2 tablespoons kosher salt and the pasta and cook for 5 minutes. Add the cauliflower and continue to cook until the cauliflower is tender and the pasta is al dente, according to package directions.

Just before the pasta is ready, add 2 tablespoons of the cooking water to the bowl with the goat cheese and whisk until creamy. Drain the pasta and cauliflower, reserving about 1 cup (8 fl oz/250 ml) of the cooking water, transfer the pasta and cauliflower to the serving bowl, and toss with the cheese sauce to coat the pasta. Add the leeks, garlic, and olives and season with pepper. Toss to combine well, adding some of the cooking water if needed to moisten the sauce so that it coats the pasta nicely. Serve right away.

Conchiglie *with* Roasted Tomatoes

Here is a dish to make in the summer when you can find grape, cherry, or pear tomatoes that are especially sweet, such as Sun Gold, and in a variety of colors, from red to yellow. Briefly roasting the tomatoes with some olive oil and salt releases just enough juices to make a full-flavored sauce.

½ cup *(4 fl oz/125 ml)* extra-virgin olive oil, plus more for baking sheet

Fine sea salt

1 lb *(500 g)* cherry or pear tomatoes, halved

¼ lb *(125 g)* fresh goat cheese, crumbled

2 tablespoons chopped fresh basil

½ teaspoon red pepper flakes

Kosher salt for cooking pasta

1 lb *(500 g)* conchiglie (medium pasta shells)

1 teaspoon fresh marjoram leaves

Preheat the oven to 425°F (220°C).

Oil a rimmed baking sheet with olive oil and sprinkle the surface lightly with sea salt. Place the tomatoes, cut sides down, on the pan. Roast the tomatoes until liquid forms on the bottom of the pan, no more than 10 minutes. The tomatoes should just soften, not actually cook.

In a large, shallow bowl in which you will serve the pasta, combine the tomatoes and their juices, the ½ cup (4 fl oz/125 ml) olive oil, the cheese, basil, red pepper flakes, and sea salt to taste and stir to mix.

In a large pot, bring 5 qt (5 l) water to a rapid boil. Add 2 tablespoons kosher salt and the pasta, stir well, and cook, stirring occasionally, until al dente, according to package directions. Drain the pasta, reserving about ½ cup (4 fl oz/125 ml) of the cooking water. Transfer the pasta to the serving bowl with the sauce and toss until well combined, adding up to a few tablespoons of the reserved cooking water if necessary to moisten and coat the pasta nicely. Sprinkle with the marjoram leaves and serve right away.

Malloreddus *with* Lamb Ragù

This dish combines the specialties of two regions: malloreddus, canoe-shaped pasta that is a specialty of Sardinia, and lamb *ragù*, a signature dish of Puglia. The *ragù* can be stored, with the shanks immersed in the sauce, in the refrigerator for up to 5 days or in the freezer for 3 months.

2 cans *(28 oz/875 g each)* plus 1 can *(14 oz/440 g)* plum tomatoes

½ cup *(4 fl oz/125 ml)* extra-virgin olive oil

4 meaty lamb shanks, about 1 lb *(500 g)* total

4 cloves garlic, bruised *(see page 233)*

1 large yellow onion, chopped

¾ cup *(6 fl oz/180 ml)* dry red wine

¾ cup *(6 oz/185 g)* tomato paste

Pinch of red pepper flakes

Fine sea salt

5 large fresh basil leaves

Kosher salt for cooking pasta

1 lb *(500 g)* malloreddus, cavatelli, or gnocchetti

Freshly grated pecorino romano cheese for serving

Pass the tomatoes and their juice through a food mill or fine-mesh sieve set over a pot large enough to accommodate the shanks later. Bring to a boil over medium-high heat, then reduce the heat to low and keep the tomatoes at a gentle simmer.

In a frying pan large enough to accommodate the lamb shanks, warm the olive oil over medium-high heat. When the oil is hot, add the shanks to the pan and brown on all sides, turning as needed, about 15 minutes total. Transfer the shanks to the pot with the tomatoes. Pour off all but ⅓ cup *(3 fl oz/80 ml)* of the oil from the pan and place over medium-low heat. Add the garlic and sauté until golden, 1–2 minutes. Scoop out the garlic cloves and add them to the tomatoes. Add the onion to the pan and sauté over medium-low heat until softened and golden, 10–15 minutes. Raise the heat to medium, pour in the wine, and simmer until most of the alcohol has evaporated, about 3 minutes. Add the tomato paste and stir to scrape up any browned bits stuck to the bottom of the pan. Sauté for 5 minutes to allow the flavors to blend.

Add the onion mixture and red pepper flakes to the simmering tomatoes and lamb, season with sea salt, and stir well. Cover partially and simmer over low heat, stirring occasionally, until the meat is tender and falling off the bones, 2–2½ hours. Keep an eye on the heat to be sure the sauce bubbles gently and steadily as it simmers; it should not bubble vigorously. Stir in the basil. Taste and adjust the seasoning with sea salt.

In a large pot, bring 5 qt (5 l) water to a rapid boil. Add 2 tablespoons kosher salt and the pasta, stir well, and cook, stirring occasionally, until al dente, according to package directions.

Just before the pasta is ready, transfer the lamb shanks to a work surface and remove the meat from the bones. Using two forks, shred the meat, then stir it into the tomato sauce. When the pasta is ready, drain it and transfer to a warmed large, shallow serving bowl. Add the sauce, toss well to combine, and sprinkle with some of the cheese. Serve right away, and pass the additional cheese at the table.

Farfalle *alla* Primavera

The tender, pencil-thin asparagus of early spring is ideal for this recipe. If the asparagus is sweet and nutty, it is better to enhance the flavor with high-quality olive oil or a second pinch of red pepper flakes than to serve with grated cheese, which detracts from the clean and simple appeal of the dish.

1 lb *(500 g)* asparagus, preferably pencil-thin

Kosher salt for cooking vegetables and pasta

½ cup *(2½ oz/75 g)* fresh or frozen shelled English peas

6 tablespoons *(3 fl oz/90 ml)* extra-virgin olive oil, plus more for drizzling

4 green onions, including 3 inches *(7.5 cm)* of dark green tops, thinly sliced on the diagonal

Generous pinch of red pepper flakes

1 lb *(500 g)* farfalle

Fine sea salt

Trim off the tough ends of the asparagus. If the spears are not pencil-thin, using a vegetable peeler, peel away the thick skin to within about 2 inches (5 cm) of the tips. Cut crosswise on the diagonal into 2-inch pieces, keeping the tips intact.

In a large pot, bring 5 qt (5 l) water to a boil. Add 2 tablespoons kosher salt and the asparagus and cook for 3 minutes. Add the peas and continue to cook for 2 minutes longer. Just before the asparagus and peas are ready, in a frying pan large enough to accommodate the pasta later, warm the olive oil over medium heat. Add the green onions and red pepper flakes. Using a wire skimmer or slotted spoon, scoop out the asparagus and peas, reserving the water in the pot, and add to the pan with the green onions. Toss the ingredients together and then sauté until the asparagus pieces are sweet and tender, 1–2 minutes. They must not be crunchy. Remove from the heat and cover to keep warm.

Return the water to a rapid boil, add the pasta, and stir well. Cook, stirring occasionally, until al dente, according to package directions.

Drain the pasta, add to the sauce in the pan, and toss until well combined. Taste and adjust the seasoning with sea salt. Drizzle in several tablespoons of olive oil, toss again, and transfer to a warmed large, shallow serving bowl or individual shallow bowls. Serve right away.

ORECCHIETTE *with* SAUSAGE AND BROCCOLI RABE

Orecchiette, or "little ears," serve as cups for the morsels of sausage and bits of greens in this typical Puglian sauce, but other short pastas with grooves or divots work well, too. You can use spicy Italian sausage instead of the sweet sausage called for in the recipe if you prefer more of a kick.

2 lb *(1 kg)* broccoli rabe

Kosher salt for cooking broccoli rabe and pasta

6 tablespoons *(3 fl oz/90 ml)* extra-virgin olive oil

¾ lb *(375 g)* sweet Italian sausages, casings removed

4 cloves garlic, minced

Pinch of red pepper flakes

1 lb *(500 g)* orecchiette, cavatelli, or gnocchetti

Fine sea salt

Using a small, sharp knife or vegetable peeler, peel away the thick skin from the tough lower stalks of the broccoli rabe (most of the bottom stalk portion). Cut crosswise into about 1-inch (2.5-cm) lengths. Place in a bowl, add cold water to cover, and let stand for 1 hour.

In a large pot, bring 5 qt (5 l) water to a boil. Add 2 tablespoons kosher salt and the broccoli rabe, cover partially, and cook for 1 minute after the water returns to a boil. Using a wire skimmer or a sieve, transfer the broccoli rabe to a bowl and set aside. Scoop out and reserve ½ cup (4 fl oz/125 ml) of the cooking water and set aside. Reserve the water remaining in the pot.

In a deep frying pan large enough to accommodate the pasta later, warm 2 tablespoons of the olive oil over medium-low heat. Add the sausage meat and cook, stirring to break up any clumps and to color evenly, until browned, about 10 minutes. Add the garlic and pepper flakes and cook, stirring occasionally, until the garlic is softened, about 3 minutes. Add the broccoli rabe and the reserved ½ cup water and toss to mix. Cover and cook, stirring occasionally, until the greens are tender, 8–10 minutes.

While the sausage–broccoli rabe mixture is cooking, return the water in the pot to a rapid boil. Add the pasta, stir well, and cook, stirring occasionally, until al dente, according to package directions.

Drain the pasta and add to the sauce in the pan. Add the remaining 4 tablespoons (2 fl oz/60 ml) olive oil and toss to coat the pasta. Season with sea salt and transfer to a warmed large, shallow serving bowl or individual shallow bowls. Serve right away.

RED LENTIL SOUP *with* FARFALLETTE

Miniature bow-tie pasta or shells add a fanciful twist to basic lentil soup, yielding a chunky, brothy mix that is popular with both children and adults. You can double the recipe, as the soup freezes well and is nice to have on hand for quick weeknight suppers. Thaw in the refrigerator and reheat gently.

2¼ cups *(1 lb/500 g)* red lentils

6 tablespoons *(3 fl oz/90 ml)* extra-virgin olive oil

2 large yellow onions, minced

2 large carrots, peeled and finely chopped

6 tablespoons *(½ oz/15 g)* chopped fresh flat-leaf parsley or cilantro

1 teaspoon ground fennel

¼ teaspoon cayenne pepper, or to taste

3 qt *(3 l)* low-sodium vegetable or chicken broth

Fine sea salt

Kosher salt for cooking pasta

1 cup *(3½ oz/105 g)* farfallette, conchigliette, or anellini

Pick over the lentils, discarding any grit or misshapen lentils. Rinse well and set aside.

In a Dutch oven or wide soup pot over medium-low heat, warm the olive oil. Add the onions, carrots, 3 tablespoons of the parsley, the fennel, and the cayenne. Cover and cook, stirring occasionally, until the vegetables are well softened, about 10 minutes. Add the lentils and stir to mix well. Add the broth and 2 teaspoons sea salt, raise the heat to high, and bring to a boil. Reduce the heat to medium-low and simmer, uncovered, until the lentils are tender, about 35 minutes.

While the lentils are cooking, in a saucepan, bring 4 cups (32 fl oz/1 l) water to a rapid boil. Check the package directions for the cooking time, then add 2 teaspoons kosher salt and the pasta to the boiling water, stir well, and cook, stirring occasionally, until about 3 minutes shy of being al dente. Drain in a colander and rinse under cold running water.

Add the pasta to the soup about 3 minutes before it is ready. Taste and adjust the seasoning. Ladle into warmed bowls, sprinkle with the remaining parsley, dividing it evenly, and serve right away.

Capellini *with* Garlic and Anchovies

This typical Italian sauce is simple, but packed with flavor. The garlic, anchovies, and red pepper flakes are sautéd briefly in hot oil to form a sauce that evenly coats the fine strands of capellini. The anchovies impart a natural saltiness to the dish, so be sure to taste before seasoning with salt.

Kosher salt for cooking pasta

1 lb *(500 g)* capellini

¼ cup *(6 fl oz/180 ml)* extra-virgin olive oil

12 large cloves garlic, chopped

½ teaspoon red pepper flakes

5 olive oil–packed anchovy fillets, chopped

Fine sea salt, if needed

In a large pot, bring 5 qt (5 l) water to a rapid boil. Add 2 tablespoons kosher salt and the pasta, stir well, and cook, stirring occasionally, until al dente, according to package directions.

Meanwhile, in a frying pan large enough to accommodate the pasta later, warm the olive oil over medium-low heat. Add the garlic and sauté until softened, about 1 minute; do not let it brown. Add the red pepper flakes and anchovies and sauté until the garlic is evenly golden, about 4 minutes longer. Immediately remove from the heat. Taste and season with sea salt if needed. Cover and keep warm.

Drain the pasta, reserving about 1 cup (8 fl oz/250 ml) of the cooking water, and add the pasta to the sauce in the pan. Toss well, adding some of the reserved cooking water if needed to moisten the sauce so that it coats the pasta nicely. Transfer to a warmed large, shallow serving bowl or individual shallow bowls and serve right away.

CONCHIGLIE *with* KALE AND WHITE BEANS

This is a rustic and satisfying southern Italian dish that can be made with various hearty greens, including Tuscan kale, escarole, or parboiled broccoli rabe. Pancetta or smoky bacon adds rich flavor, but can be omitted for a vegetarian option. Red pepper flakes deliver a terrific kick.

1½ lb *(750 g)* Tuscan kale

6 tablespoons *(3 fl oz/90 ml)* extra-virgin olive oil

6 large cloves garlic, bruised *(see page 233)*

2 oz *(60 g)* sliced pancetta or bacon, finely diced

Fine sea salt

¼ teaspoon red pepper flakes

2 cups *(14 oz/440 g)* drained cooked cannellini beans, well rinsed

Kosher salt for cooking pasta

½ lb *(250 g)* conchiglie (medium pasta shells)

Using a long, sharp knife, cut off the tough stems from the kale, then fold each leaf in half lengthwise and slice off the tough central rib. Cut crosswise into ribbons 2 inches (5 cm) wide.

In a frying pan large enough to accommodate the pasta later, warm the olive oil over medium heat. Add the garlic and pancetta and sauté until both are lightly colored, about 5 minutes. Add the kale, toss to coat it with the oil and seasonings, and sauté until wilted, about 7 minutes. Add ¾ cup (6 fl oz/180 ml) water, a scant ½ teaspoon sea salt, and the red pepper flakes; mix well, cover, and cook until the kale is nearly tender, about 5 minutes. Add the beans, re-cover, reduce the heat to low, and cook until the beans are heated through, about 5 minutes. Remove from the heat and cover to keep warm.

While the sauce is cooking, in a large pot, bring 4 qt (4 l) water to a rapid boil. Add 1½ tablespoons kosher salt and the pasta, stir, and cook, stirring occasionally, until al dente, according to package directions.

Drain the pasta, add to the sauce in the pan, and toss well to combine. Taste and adjust the seasoning with sea salt. Transfer to a warmed large, shallow serving bowl or individual shallow bowls and serve right away.

STUFFED AND BAKED PASTA

ABOUT STUFFED AND BAKED PASTA

A variety of stuffed pastas are sold fresh or frozen in supermarkets, but they cannot compare to the delicate pasta pillows you can make at home. The best stuffed pastas are fashioned from paper-thin dough, then filled with a mixture of harmonious ingredients. Baked pastas, often made with short cut pasta or wide, flat noodles, are the busy home cook's best friend: they can be assembled in advance and then baked at dinnertime.

SHAPES FOR STUFFED PASTA

The Italian region of Emilia-Romagna, which is famous for its silky fresh egg pasta, is also renowned for its stuffed pastas. But Italian cooks all over the country fashion stuffed pastas in dozens of shapes with names like anolini, cannelloni, cappellacci, cappelletti, ravioli, ravioletti, tortelli, tortellini, and tortelloni. Sometimes the same shape has two different names, such as anolini and tortelli, depending on the region in which it is made. Cappelletti and tortellini are also two names for the same little meat- or cheese-filled pasta envelopes, with just one difference: tortellini start with circles of pasta, which give them a navel-like shape, and cappelletti start with squares, which give them a peak-shaped top when formed. Fazzoletti (handkerchiefs), made from a batter rather than a dough, are members of the stuffed pasta family as well. Also known as manicotti or crespelle, they are wrapped around delicate fillings of seafood, meat, or vegetables.

FILLINGS FOR STUFFED PASTA

The fillings for stuffed pasta are as varied as the shapes. The classic cheese filling for ravioli is a blend of ricotta, Parmigiano-Reggiano cheese, egg yolk, and nutmeg (see page 147). Meat fillings are usually reserved for smaller stuffed pastas, such as the celebrated tortellini of Emilia-Romagna, which traditionally conceal a mixture of prosciutto, mortadella, veal, pork, and Parmigiano-Reggiano. As with other Italian dishes, no codified formula exists for fillings. From town to town and cook to cook, the recipes vary with longtime customs, family tradition, and locally produced meats and/or cheeses. In this chapter, you will find fillings defined by region, such as the potato and mint ravioli of Sardinia (page 164) or the pumpkin ravioli (page 138) of Emilia-Romagna. You will also discover recipes that are what the Italians call *alla fantasia,* or completely original, such as open-faced ravioli (pages 159 and 167). These are squares of fresh pasta stacked in layers with a filling between them.

SEALING STUFFED PASTA

Stuffed pastas must be sealed perfectly to cook properly. First, using a pastry brush or your finger, lightly paint water, milk, beaten egg, or egg yolk mixed with a little water on the pasta around the filling. Then cover the filling with pasta (usually by folding pasta over the top) and press out all the air as you seal the dough firmly around the filling. Trapped air will cause the pasta to inflate in the cooking pot, which means it will float on the surface, rather than cook fully submerged in the water. If the seal is not secure, the pasta can also break open in the pot and lose its filling.

COOKING AND SERVING STUFFED PASTA

You will usually need to cook stuffed pasta in two batches to avoid reducing the water temperature too much. First, depending on the recipe, bring broth or salted water to a rapid boil, then gently slip in the pasta. Cover the pot until the water returns to a boil, then uncover and cook, gently stirring occasionally to prevent sticking, for 3–5 minutes. Do not let the water boil too hard, or the pastas may knock against one another and break.

Most stuffed pastas are done when they float to the surface, but a simple test is a better indication: using a wire skimmer or slotted spoon, transfer a single pasta piece to a cutting board. Cut off a corner with a paring knife. If the pasta looks cooked through and the corner tastes tender, the pasta is done. Use the skimmer or slotted spoon to transfer the remaining pasta to a warmed serving dish.

Some stuffed pastas are eaten in broth. Others are eaten with a simple sauce and sometimes a little grated cheese, with just butter and cheese, or with a light cream sauce and cheese. Never use a heavy sauce with a stuffed pasta, as it can easily overwhelm its natural delicacy.

BAKED PASTA

Called *pasticci* or *pasta al forno,* Italian baked pastas are wildly varied and often hearty. Classic ingredients, such as sausages, meats, eggplant, cauliflower, or mushrooms, are cooked separately and combined or arranged in layers with pasta and one or two sauces, and then baked in the oven. The sauces, which range from béchamel to tomato to a meat-laced *ragù,* moisten and bind the various components, and one or two cheeses typically add flavor and richness. The most famous member of this large family is lasagne, which boasts scores of variations, including the type of pasta used: some recipes call for pale yellow egg pasta, others call for emerald green spinach pasta, and still others use alternating layers of both colors.

Macaroni-based baked dishes, such as the penne mixed with lamb and eggplant on page 153, must always be made with good-quality imported Italian pasta, which will hold up to being cooked twice: once on the stove top in boiling water and then in the oven. Such cuts as penne, ziti, and cavatappi (corkscrews) are good choices for these dishes, because they trap sauce in their hollows and grooves and retain their firm texture during baking. Macaroni-based dishes and layered pasta dishes are substantial main courses that need only the addition of salad or a vegetable to complete the menu.

COOKING PASTA IN BATCHES

When preparing lasagne, open ravioli, or cannelloni, you need to cook the pasta rectangles or squares in boiling water in batches before you layer them with the filling. Have ready a large bowl of ice water near the stove for cooling the cooked noodles. Lay out damp kitchen towels on a nearby work surface, and have more damp towels and some dry towels nearby. Bring a large pot of salted water to a boil and add 2 or 3 pasta rectangles or 4 or 5 squares. Cover and cook for a total of 1 minute (the pasta will cook more in the oven), then retrieve the pasta pieces with a slotted spoon or wire skimmer and immediately immerse them in the ice-water bath. Lift the pasta pieces out of the water and arrange them, not touching, on a damp kitchen towel, and then cover with a second damp towel. Repeat until all the pasta is cooked, then pat the pasta with a dry kitchen towel to absorb the excess moisture.

STORING STUFFED AND BAKED PASTA

Stuffed pasta can be frozen for future use. Arrange the ravioli or other shape, not touching, on rimmed baking sheets and freeze until firm, about 1 hour. Transfer to resealable plastic freezer bags and freeze for up to 3 months, then cook directly from the freezer. Baked pastas can be fully assembled, well wrapped with a double layer of plastic wrap, and refrigerated for up to 24 hours or frozen for up to 3 months. Allow the frozen dish to thaw in the refrigerator before baking. You may need to add 10–15 minutes to the cooking time for these previously frozen pastas.

STUFFED AND BAKED SHAPES

1 **ANOLINI** Half-moon–shaped dumplings made from disks of fresh pasta 2 inches (5 cm) in diameter.

2 **HANDKERCHIEFS** Similar to cannelloni in shape and use, these pasta are made from a crepelike batter.

3 **RAVIOLETTI** Miniature versions of ravioli made from 1½-inch (4-cm) squares of pasta.

4 **CONCHIGLIONI** The large version of conchiglie or "shells," these conch shell–shaped pasta are used for stuffing.

5 **CANNELLONI** Thin sheets of pasta cut in to 3½-by-4½-inch (9-by-11.5-cm) rectangles. Rolled around filling, they resemble large tubes.

6 **TORTELLINI** Made by forming 2-inch (5-cm) rounds of dough into tight little rings.

7 **RAVIOLI** 2–2½-inch (5–6-cm) squares of fresh pastas containing a variety of fillings. Can be cut with a straight or fluted edge.

8 **TORTELLONI** Resembling tortellini but made with 3-inch (7.5-cm) squares and folded to make a peak at the top.

9 **LASAGNE** Dried or fresh noodles that are about 4 by 5 inches (10 by 13 cm) and usually layered with filling and baked.

MAKING RAVIOLI

I MARK THE CENTER

Lay 1 section of pasta flat on a lightly floured work surface. Fold the dough in half lengthwise to mark the center, then unfold it so it lies flat again.

2 ADD THE FILLING

Beginning about 2 inches (5 cm) from one of the short ends, place teaspoonfuls of the filling at 2-inch intervals down the center of one side of the fold.

3 BRUSH THE DOUGH

Dip a pastry brush in cool water and lightly brush around the filling; this acts as a glue that keeps the filling tightly sealed inside the pasta. Fold the dough over the filling.

4 SEAL THE RAVIOLI

Using your fingers, mold the dough around the filling to eliminate any air pockets (these could cause the ravioli to burst). Press the edges of the dough firmly together to seal.

5 CUT THE RAVIOLI

Using a fluted or straight pasta cutter or a chef's knife, trim off about ⅛ inch (3 mm) from all sides of the pasta strip. Cut evenly between the mounds to make 2 to 2½-inch (5 to 6-cm) square ravioli.

6 SET THE RAVIOLI ASIDE

Place the ravioli in a single layer on a floured rimmed baking sheet. Turn every few minutes to prevent the ravioli from sticking. Do not let them sit too long or the filling will seep through the dough.

MAKING ANOLINI AND TORTELLINI

ANOLINI

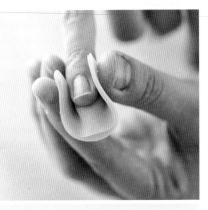

1 CUT OUT DISKS

Using a round cookie cutter or biscuit cutter with a 2-inch (5-cm) diameter, cut the pasta sections into disks.

2 FILL THE DISKS

Place 1 teaspoon filling in the center of each disk. Paint the area around the filling with beaten egg or milk.

3 SEAL THE EDGES

Fold the disk in half over the filling and press around the filling mound to make a secure seal with your fingers, working out any air pockets. Place on a floured rimmed baking sheet.

TORTELLINI

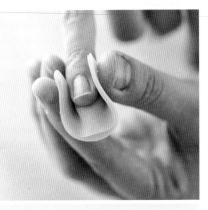

1 FILL THE DISKS

Follow steps 1 and 2 above to cut out dough disks, but use ½ teaspoon filling for each. Paint the area around the filling with beaten egg or milk.

2 SEAL THE FILLING

To seal, fold the dough disk in half, but so that one edge lines up sightly below the other. Press around the filling mound to make a secure seal, working out any air pockets.

3 WRAP AROUND FINGER

Wrap the half-moon around the tip of your pinky finger, keeping the rounded end pointing up. Slightly overlap the two corners and pinch them together. Place on floured rimmed baking sheets.

PUMPKIN RAVIOLI *with* SAGE BUTTER

Here is the classic ravioli of the city of Ferrara, in Emilia-Romagna, although the city of Mantua, in Lombardy, also claims the dish. It is best served with a simple sauce of lightly browned butter and fresh sage, which heightens and contrasts with the sweetness of the pumpkin in the filling.

FOR THE FILLING

1-lb *(500-g)* piece Cheese or Sugar Pie pumpkin, calabaza, or butternut squash, seeds and strings removed

1 large egg yolk, lightly beaten

2 tablespoons freshly grated Parmigiano-Reggiano or grana padano cheese

¼ teaspoon freshly grated nutmeg

Fine sea salt

1–2 tablespoons dried bread crumbs

Egg Pasta II *(page 16 or 18)*

5 tablespoons *(2½ oz/75 g)* unsalted butter, clarified *(see page 233)*

12 large fresh sage leaves

Kosher salt for cooking ravioli

Freshly grated Parmigiano-Reggiano cheese for serving

To make the filling, preheat the oven to 400°F (200°C). Prick the pumpkin with a fork before roasting to help evaporate the moisture. Place directly on the oven rack and roast until tender when pierced with the tip of a knife, 45–50 minutes.

When cool enough to handle, scrape the pumpkin flesh from the peel; transfer to a food processor and process until smooth.

Transfer the pumpkin purée to a bowl. Add the beaten egg yolk to the pumpkin along with the cheese, nutmeg, and ¼ teaspoon sea salt. Mix well, adding the bread crumbs as needed to bind the ingredients into a cohesive mixture. Cover and set aside.

Make the pasta dough as directed, then roll out the dough as directed for stuffed pastas on pages 20–21 or 22. Follow the instructions on page 136 to assemble the ravioli.

Pour the clarified butter into a small frying pan and place over low heat. Add the sage leaves to the pan and warm until the butter is saturated with the flavor of the sage, 3–4 minutes. Remove from the heat and cover to keep warm.

In a large pot, bring 5 qt (5 l) water to a rapid boil. Add 2 tablespoons kosher salt and gently drop in half of the ravioli, then cover the pot. When the water returns to a boil, uncover and cook, stirring gently occasionally and reducing the heat as needed to prevent the ravioli from knocking against one another and breaking. The total cooking time should be 3–5 minutes. Test a raviolo for doneness (see page 133), then lift out the ravioli with a large slotted spoon, allowing a little of the water to cling to them so they remain moist, and transfer to a warmed large, shallow serving bowl; cover the bowl to keep the ravioli warm. Repeat to cook the remaining ravioli. Drizzle the sage butter over the ravioli and serve right away. Pass the cheese at the table.

SPINACH LASAGNE *alla* BOLOGNESE

Many variations of this classic dish, called *lasagne verde* in Italian, exist, including one made with alternating layers of plain egg pasta and spinach egg pasta for a lovely contrasting effect. Two sauces are traditionally used, a *ragù* (here, *ragù alla bolognese)* and *salsa besciamella* (béchamel sauce).

Bolognese Sauce *(page 24)*

3 cups *(24 fl oz/750 ml)*
Béchamel Sauce *(page 232)*

FOR THE SPINACH PASTA

¼ lb *(125 g)* spinach,
tough stems removed

Kosher salt for cooking
spinach and pasta

Egg Pasta I *(page 16 or 18)*

Unbleached all-purpose
flour as needed

Unsalted butter for
baking dish

1 cup *(4 oz/125 g)* freshly
grated Parmigiano-Reggiano
cheese

First, make the Bolognese Sauce. Remove the sauce from the heat, cover, and set aside. While the Bolognese Sauce is cooking, make the Béchamel Sauce, remove from the heat, cover, and set aside.

To make the spinach pasta, bring a saucepan three-fourths full of water to a boil and add the spinach and 1 teaspoon kosher salt. Cook, stirring, just until tender, about 2 minutes. Drain into a colander and let stand until cool. Squeeze the spinach to remove excess moisture, then wring it in a dry kitchen towel to make it as dry as possible. Chop finely by hand or, preferably, in a food processor. Proceed as directed to make the egg pasta, but omitting 1 of the eggs and mixing the spinach in with the egg mixture before adding it to the flour. If the dough is very sticky, work in up to ½ cup (2 oz/60 g) more flour. Cover with an inverted bowl or slightly damp kitchen towel and let rest for 20 minutes, then roll out as directed for lasagne on pages 20–21 or 22. Using a pastry wheel or knife, cut the pasta sheets into 4-by-6-inch (10-by-15-cm) rectangles.

In a large pot, bring 5 qt (5 l) water to a rapid boil. Add 2 tablespoons kosher salt and the pasta rectangles, in batches, and cook for 1 minute (see page 133). Drain and dry flat on clean, damp kitchen towels.

Position a rack in the upper third of the oven and preheat to 350°F (180°C). Select a 9-by-13 inch (23-by-33-cm) baking dish and butter it generously. Spread a thin layer of the Bolognese Sauce on the bottom. Arrange a layer of pasta rectangles over the sauce so they almost touch. Spread a layer of the Bolognese Sauce over the pasta, and top with a layer of the Béchamel Sauce, smoothing it with the back of a wooden spoon. Sprinkle a little of the cheese over the Béchamel Sauce. Repeat the layers, starting with the pasta and ending with the cheese, until all of the ingredients are used up. You should have about 10 pasta layers.

Bake until the layers are heated through and the surface is bubbling and golden, about 30 minutes. If the lasagne is bubbling but the surface has not colored, turn the oven to broil and broil until golden. Let stand for 10 minutes before serving.

BAKED PENNE *with* COMTÉ AND MUSHROOMS

Think of this dish, created by chef and author Rick Rodgers, as French-style macaroni and cheese. Comté, a mild, nutty cheese, melts quickly into the warmed milk–crème fraîche mixture to form a sophisticated cheese sauce. Japanese bread crumbs, known as *panko,* form a crunchy top crust.

5 tablespoons *(2½ oz/75 g)* unsalted butter, plus more for the baking dish

2 tablespoons olive oil

1 lb *(500 g)* fresh cremini mushrooms, brushed cleaned, trimmed, and quartered

Fine sea salt and freshly ground pepper

Kosher salt for cooking pasta

1 lb *(500 g)* short tubular pasta such as penne, ziti, or cavatappi

¼ cup *(1½ oz/45 g)* unbleached all-purpose flour

2 cups *(16 fl oz/500 ml)* milk, heated

1 cup *(8 fl oz/250 ml)* crème fraîche

3 cups *(12 oz/375 g)* shredded Comté or Gruyère cheese

½ cup *(2 oz/60 g)* panko bread crumbs or coarse dried bread crumbs

Preheat the oven to 350°F (180°C). Lightly butter a shallow 9-by-13-inch (23-by-33-cm) baking dish.

In a large frying pan over medium-high heat, warm the olive oil. Add the mushrooms and cook, stirring occasionally, until lightly browned, about 10 minutes. Season with sea salt and pepper, remove from the heat, and set aside.

Meanwhile, in a large pot, bring 5 qt (5 l) water to a rapid boil. Check the package directions for the cooking time, then add 2 tablespoons kosher salt and the pasta, stir well, and cook, stirring occasionally, until the pasta is 1–2 minutes shy of being al dente. Drain in a colander, refresh under cold running water to prevent the pasta from sticking together, and drain again.

Return the pasta pot to medium heat and add 4 tablespoons (2 oz/60 g) of the butter. When the butter has melted, whisk in the flour, reduce the heat to low, and cook and stir for 1 minute. Do not let the flour-and-butter paste brown. Gradually whisk in the hot milk and then the crème fraîche, raise the heat to high, and continue to whisk until the mixture comes to a boil and thickens enough to coat the back of a wooden spoon. Add the cheese, stir until melted, and remove from the heat. Stir in the pasta and mushrooms and season with salt and pepper. Transfer to the prepared baking dish and sprinkle evenly with the bread crumbs. Cut the remaining 1 tablespoon butter into tiny cubes, and dot the cubes over the bread crumbs.

Bake until the surface is bubbling and the topping is crisp, about 25 minutes. Let stand for 5 minutes before serving.

CONCHIGLIONI *with* RICOTTA AND SPINACH

Here, classic stuffed shells are topped with a flavorful, smooth sauce made by slowly simmering tomatoes with just a handful of ingredients, and then passing the mixture through a food mill. Adding an egg to the ricotta mixture ensures that the filling remains cohesive and firm during baking.

FOR THE SAUCE

1 can *(28 oz/875 g)* plum tomatoes

1 small carrot, peeled and cut in half

½ small yellow onion, roughly chopped

4 large fresh basil leaves, minced

2 tablespoons extra-virgin olive oil

Fine sea salt and freshly ground pepper

FOR THE FILLING

3½ cups *(1¾ lb/875 g)* whole-milk ricotta cheese

1¼ lb *(625 g)* spinach, tough stems removed

Kosher salt for cooking spinach

1 large egg, lightly beaten

½ cup *(2 oz/60 g)* freshly grated Parmigiano-Reggiano cheese

Scant ⅛ teaspoon freshly grated nutmeg

Fine sea salt and freshly ground pepper

Kosher salt for cooking pasta

½ lb *(250 g)* conchiglioni

¼ cup *(1 oz/30 g)* freshly grated Parmigiano-Reggiano cheese

To make the sauce, drain the tomatoes, reserving half of their juice. In a saucepan, combine the tomatoes and reserved juice, the carrot, and the onion. Place over medium-high heat and bring to a boil. Immediately reduce the heat to medium-low, cover partially, and cook, stirring occasionally, for 45 minutes. Remove from the heat, stir in the basil, and let cool slightly, then pass the chunky mixture through a food mill or a medium-mesh sieve. Stir in the olive oil, season with sea salt and pepper, and set aside.

While the sauce is cooking, ready the ricotta and spinach for the filling. Place the ricotta in a fine-mesh sieve set over a bowl and set aside to drain for about 30 minutes. Bring a saucepan three-fourths full of water to a boil and add the spinach and a scant ¼ teaspoon kosher salt. Cook just until tender, about 2 minutes. Drain well, reserving the cooking water. Squeeze out excess moisture from the spinach, then chop it finely.

Measure the spinach water, pour into a large pot, add more water to total 5 qt (5 l), and bring to a rapid boil. Check the package directions for the cooking time, then add 2 tablespoons kosher salt and the pasta, stir well, and cook, stirring occasionally, until the pasta is 1–2 minutes shy of being al dente. Drain in a colander, refresh under cold running water, and drain again.

To finish the filling, transfer the ricotta to a bowl and beat in the egg until smooth. Add the spinach, the ½ cup (2 oz/60 g) grated cheese, the nutmeg, ¼ teaspoon sea salt, and a few grinds of pepper and mix well.

Preheat the oven to 375°F (190°C). Smear the bottom of a 9-by-13-inch (23-by-33-cm) baking dish with 2–3 tablespoons of the sauce. Using a teaspoon, stuff the conchiglioni with the filling. They should be generously filled but not so stuffed that they are wide open. Place the stuffed conchiglioni, side by side and open side up, in the prepared dish. Drizzle the remaining sauce evenly over the top and sprinkle with the ¼ cup (1 oz/30 g) grated cheese. Cover with aluminum foil and bake until the sauce is bubbling, about 25 minutes. Let stand for 10 minutes before serving.

Shrimp-and-Mushroom-Filled Handkerchiefs

Fazzoletti, literally "handkerchiefs," are Italian crêpes made from an egg-and-flour batter. The same term is sometimes used for egg pasta sheets that are cut and filled the same way. The handkerchiefs can be filled with a variety of seafood, meat, cheese, or vegetables.

1 cup *(8 fl oz/250 ml)* Béchamel Sauce *(page 232),* thinned with ¼ cup *(2 fl oz/60 ml)* warm milk

FOR THE FILLING

3 tablespoons unsalted butter

3 shallots, finely chopped

1 small celery heart, minced

1½ lb *(750 g)* shrimp, peeled, deveined, and coarsely chopped

4 oz *(125 g)* fresh white mushrooms, brushed clean, quartered, and thinly sliced

2 tablespoons chopped fresh flat-leaf parsley

Fine sea salt and freshly ground pepper

FOR THE CRÊPES

2 extra-large eggs

Fine sea salt

1 cup *(8 fl oz/250 ml)* milk

3 tablespoons unsalted butter, melted

¾ cup *(4 oz/125 g)* plus 1 tablespoon unbleached all-purpose flour

Unsalted butter for baking dish

⅓ cup *(1½ oz/45 g)* freshly grated Parmigiano-Reggiano cheese

Make the Béchamel Sauce as directed and set aside.

To make the filling, in a frying pan over medium heat, melt the butter. Add the shallots and celery heart and sauté until softened but not colored, about 6 minutes. Raise the heat to medium-high, add the shrimp, and sauté, stirring to cook evenly, for 1 minute. Add the mushrooms and sauté until just tender, about 1 minute. If the pan seems too dry, add a teaspoon or two of water to moisten. Stir in the parsley and season with sea salt and pepper to taste. Stir in 1–2 tablespoons of the Béchamel Sauce, then remove from the heat and set aside.

To make the crêpes, in a bowl, beat the eggs with a fork until blended, then mix in a pinch of sea salt. Add the milk, a little at a time, while continuing to beat, then stir in 1 tablespoon of the melted butter. Sift the flour directly into the bowl, beating steadily until all of the flour has been incorporated into the liquid and the batter is smooth. Place an 8-inch (20-cm) frying pan or crêpe pan over medium heat. When the pan is hot, brush it lightly with a little of the remaining melted butter. Add 2 tablespoons of the batter and tilt the pan to cover the surface evenly. Cook until golden, 1–2 minutes. Using a spatula, flip the crêpe and cook for about 2 minutes longer. Transfer to a plate. Repeat with the remaining batter, lightly brushing the pan with more butter if the crêpes begin to stick. You should have 16–20 crêpes total.

Position a rack in the upper third of the oven and preheat to 450°F (230°C). Gently reheat the Béchamel Sauce, then pass it through a fine-mesh sieve if lumps have formed. Butter a large, shallow baking dish. Spread a heaping tablespoon of the filling onto a crêpe, roll it into a cylinder, and place it in the baking dish. Repeat until all of the filling is used up, placing the rolls side by side in a single layer. Pour the warm béchamel evenly over the rolls, and sprinkle evenly with the cheese.

Bake until the filling is heated through and the sauce is bubbling and golden, about 15 minutes. Let stand for 10 minutes before serving.

Cheese Ravioli *with* Tomato-Basil Sauce

What makes homemade ravioli so good is the thinness of the pasta envelopes, which no machine can produce. These cheese ravioli are the way this often imitated but rarely duplicated classic should taste. A quickly assembled sauce of tomatoes and basil complements the delicacy of the filling.

FOR THE FILLING

2 cups *(1 lb/500 g)* ricotta cheese

¾ cup *(3 oz/90 g)* freshly grated Parmigiano-Reggiano cheese

2 large egg yolks

¼–½ teaspoon freshly grated nutmeg

Fine sea salt and freshly ground white pepper

Egg Pasta II *(page 16 or 18)*

Simple Tomato Sauce *(page 232)*

Generous handful of fresh basil leaves, chopped

Fine sea salt and freshly ground black pepper

Kosher salt for cooking pasta

Freshly grated Parmigiano-Reggiano cheese for serving

To make the filling, place the ricotta in a fine-mesh sieve set over a bowl. Refrigerate for 3–4 hours to drain off as much excess moisture as possible. Discard the liquid and transfer the ricotta to a bowl. Add the grated cheese, egg yolks, nutmeg to taste, ¼ teaspoon sea salt, and ⅛ teaspoon white pepper and mix until well blended and smooth. Cover and refrigerate until ready to use.

Make the pasta dough as directed, then roll out the dough as directed for stuffed pastas on pages 20–21 or 22. Follow the instructions on page 136 to assemble the ravioli.

In a large pot, bring 5 qt (5 l) water to a rapid boil.

Meanwhile, make the tomato sauce as directed, stirring in the basil as the last ingredient. Season with sea salt and black pepper. Remove from the heat and cover to keep warm.

Add 2 tablespoons kosher salt to the boiling water and gently drop in half of the ravioli, then cover the pot. When the water returns to a boil, uncover and cook, stirring gently occasionally and reducing the heat as needed to prevent the ravioli from knocking against one another and breaking. The total cooking time should be 3–5 minutes. Test a raviolo for doneness (see page 133), then lift out the ravioli with a large slotted spoon, allowing a little of the water to cling to them so they remain moist, and transfer to a warmed large, shallow serving bowl; cover the bowl with aluminum foil to keep the ravioli warm. Repeat to cook the remaining ravioli. Spoon the tomato sauce over the ravioli and sprinkle with a little cheese. Serve right away. Pass the additional grated cheese at the table.

CHEESE AND ARUGULA RAVIOLI *with* WALNUT SAUCE

These cheese and arugula ravioli are a variation on the classic cheese and spinach combination, with the usual tomato-based sauce replaced by a creamy concoction of walnuts and crème fraîche. Use baby arugula, which has a mild, sweet flavor; the mature greens can be quite spicy and bitter.

FOR THE FILLING

2¼ cups (1½ lb/750 g) ricotta cheese

1½ lb (750 g) baby arugula, stems removed

2 egg yolks, lightly beaten

½ cup (2 oz/60 g) freshly grated Parmigiano-Reggiano cheese

Fine sea salt and freshly ground white or black pepper

FOR THE SAUCE

1 slice two-day-old white bread, crust removed

⅓ cup (3 fl oz/80 ml) milk

½ cup (2 oz/60 g) walnuts, lightly toasted and chopped

¾ cup (6 fl oz/180 ml) crème fraîche

Fine sea salt and freshly ground white or black pepper

3 tablespoons freshly grated Parmigiano-Reggiano cheese

Egg Pasta II (page 16 or 18)

Kosher salt for cooking ravioli

Freshly grated Parmigiano-Reggiano cheese for serving

To make the filling, place the ricotta in a fine-mesh sieve set over a bowl. Refrigerate for 3–4 hours to drain off as much excess moisture as possible. Discard the liquid and transfer the ricotta to a bowl.

Place the arugula, with the rinsing water still clinging to the leaves, in a large, deep frying pan over medium-high heat. Cook, tossing often, until wilted and tender, about 5 minutes. Remove from the heat and let cool. Squeeze out the excess water and then mince the leaves.

Add the arugula, egg yolks, grated cheese, ½ teaspoon sea salt, and ¼ teaspoon pepper to the ricotta and mix until smooth. Cover and refrigerate.

To make the sauce, soak the bread in the milk until soft, then squeeze dry. In a food processor, combine the bread and walnuts and pulse until finely ground. Do not grind to a paste. Transfer the mixture to a bowl, add the crème fraîche and salt and pepper to taste, and beat with a spoon until well mixed. Cover and set aside. Reserve the 3 tablespoons grated cheese for adding later.

Make the pasta dough as directed, then roll out the dough as directed for stuffed pastas on pages 20–21 or 22. Follow the instructions on page 136 to assemble the ravioli.

In a large pot, bring 5 qt (5 l) water to a rapid boil. Add 2 tablespoons kosher salt to the boiling water and gently drop in half of the ravioli, then cover the pot. When the water returns to a boil, uncover and cook, stirring gently occasionally and reducing the heat as needed to prevent the ravioli from knocking against one another and breaking. The total cooking time should be 3–5 minutes. Test a raviolo for doneness (see page 133), then lift out the ravioli with a large slotted spoon, allowing a little of the water to cling to them so they remain moist, and transfer to a large, shallow serving bowl; cover the bowl to keep the ravioli warm. Repeat to cook the remaining ravioli. Add a few tablespoons of the cooking water to the walnut mixture to thin it to a saucy consistency, then stir in the 3 tablespoons grated cheese. Spoon the sauce over the ravioli. Serve right away and pass the additional grated cheese at the table.

SAUSAGE, MOZZARELLA, AND BASIL LASAGNE

Here is a robust, southern Italian–style lasagne made with cooked dried noodles layered with ricotta and mozzarella in the Neapolitan fashion. The hot Italian sausage and peppery salami give it some fire, and a generous amount of basil provides a sweet foil to the heat of the sausage.

Kosher salt for cooking pasta

1 lb *(500 g)* dried
lasagne noodles

1 can *(28 oz/875 g)*
plum tomatoes in purée

¾ cup *(6 oz/185 g)*
tomato paste

5 tablespoons *(3 fl oz/80 ml)*
extra-virgin olive oil

1 small yellow onion, minced

1 large clove garlic, minced

2 tablespoons chopped
fresh basil

1 teaspoon minced fresh
oregano, or ½ teaspoon
crumbled dried oregano

Fine sea salt

1½ lb *(750 g)* hot Italian
sausages, casings removed

2 oz *(60 g)* Italian salami,
finely diced

2 cups *(1 lb/500 g)*
whole-milk ricotta cheese

⅛ teaspoon freshly
grated nutmeg

½ lb *(250 g)* fresh mozzarella
cheese, shredded

¼ cup *(1 oz/30 g)* freshly
grated Parmigiano-Reggiano
cheese

In a large pot, bring 5 qt (5 l) water to a rapid boil. Check the package directions for the cooking time, then add 2 tablespoons kosher salt and the noodles to the boiling water, stir, and cook, stirring occasionally, until the pasta is half-cooked. Drain the noodles in a colander, reserving ¼ cup (2 fl oz/60 ml) of the cooking water. Rinse the noodles under cold running water until cool, then let dry on clean, damp kitchen towels.

In a blender, combine the tomatoes and their purée, tomato paste, and 1 cup (8 fl oz/250 ml) water and pulse for about 5 seconds to liquefy. In a saucepan over medium heat, warm 4 tablespoons (2 fl oz/60 ml) of the olive oil. Add the onion and garlic and sauté until softened, about 4 minutes. Add the tomato mixture, basil, oregano, and ¾ teaspoon sea salt and stir well. Simmer gently, uncovered, until thickened, about 30 minutes. Remove from the heat.

While the tomato sauce is cooking, in a frying pan over medium heat, warm the remaining 1 tablespoon olive oil. Add the sausage meat and salami and sauté, stirring to break up any clumps of sausage and to color evenly, until lightly browned, about 10 minutes. Remove from the heat, drain off the excess fat, and set aside.

When the tomato sauce is almost ready, preheat the oven to 400°F (200°C). In a bowl, combine the ricotta, nutmeg, and the reserved ¼ cup cooking water and stir to mix well. Spread a thin layer of the tomato sauce on the bottom of a 9-by-13-inch (23-by-33-cm) baking dish. Arrange a layer of noodles over the sauce so they almost touch. Spread a layer of the tomato sauce over the noodles, and top evenly with one-third each of the sausage and ricotta mixtures, mozzarella, and Parmigiano-Reggiano, in that order. Repeat the layering twice, ending with a layer of Parmigiano-Reggiano. Cover with aluminum foil and bake for 25 minutes. Remove the foil and continue to bake until the surface is browned and bubbling, 5–10 minutes longer. Let stand for 10 minutes before serving.

GOAT CHEESE TORTELLONI *with* ASPARAGUS

Tortelloni can be round, square, or triangular, as they are here. The dough is cut into squares, and then filled and folded in the same "little hat" fashion as tortellini but with pointed peaks. The asparagus must be cooked until tender, not crisp, to meld with the silky cream sauce.

FOR THE FILLING

1 cup *(8 oz/250 g)* whole-milk ricotta cheese

½ lb *(250 g)* fresh goat cheese

2 large egg yolks

¾ cup *(3 oz/90 g)* freshly grated Parmigiano-Reggiano, grana padano, or aged Asiago cheese

Fine sea salt and freshly ground pepper

Egg Pasta I *(page 16 or 18)*

FOR THE SAUCE

1 lb *(500 g)* asparagus, tough ends removed

Fine sea salt and freshly ground pepper

4 tablespoons *(2 oz/60 g)* unsalted butter

1 cup *(8 fl oz/250 ml)* heavy cream

2 oz *(60 g)* fresh goat cheese, crumbled

¼ cup *(1 oz/30 g)* freshly grated Parmigiano-Reggiano cheese

Kosher salt for cooking pasta

Freshly grated Parmigiano-Reggiano cheese for serving

To make the filling, place the ricotta in a fine-mesh sieve set over a bowl. Refrigerate for 3–4 hours to drain off as much excess moisture as possible. Discard the liquid and transfer the ricotta to a bowl. Add the goat cheese and egg yolks and mix well. Stir in the Parmigiano-Reggiano, ¼ teaspoon sea salt, and ⅛ teaspoon pepper. Cover and refrigerate.

Make the pasta dough as directed to yield 1 lb (500 g), cut into quarters, and roll out 2 quarters as directed for stuffed pastas on pages 20–21 or 22. (Reserve the remaining dough for another use.) Cut the dough sheets into 3-inch (7.5-cm) squares and assemble the tortelloni as directed for tortellini on page 137, but folding the squares in half to make triangles before wrapping them around your finger.

To make the sauce, in a frying pan, combine the asparagus with water to cover and ½ teaspoon sea salt and bring to a boil. Cover and cook until just tender, about 8 minutes. Drain and cut into 2-inch (5-cm) lengths. In a frying pan over low heat, melt the butter. Add the cream and goat cheese, and season with ¼ teaspoon sea salt and a few grinds of pepper. Add the asparagus and cook, stirring, until heated through and the cheese has melted, about 5 minutes. Add the Parmigiano-Reggiano and taste and adjust the seasoning. Remove from the heat; cover to keep warm.

In a large pot, bring 5 qt (5 l) water to a rapid boil. Meanwhile, smear a thin layer of the sauce on the bottom of a warmed large, shallow serving bowl. Add 2 tablespoons kosher salt to the boiling water and gently drop in half of the tortelloni, then cover the pot. When the water returns to a boil, uncover and cook, stirring occasionally and reducing the heat as needed to prevent the tortelloni from knocking against one another. The total cooking time should be 3–5 minutes. Test a tortellono for doneness (see page 133), then lift out the tortelloni with a large slotted spoon, allowing a little of the water to cling to them, and transfer to the serving bowl. Pour half of the sauce evenly over them and cover the bowl to keep warm. Cook the remaining tortelloni and top with the remaining sauce. Serve right away. Pass the additional Parmigiano-Reggiano at the table.

Baked Penne *with* Lamb, Eggplant, and Fontina

Too many baked pasta dishes turn out dry because the sauce lacks a creamy, binding consistency. This recipe answers that dilemma by dressing the pasta generously in béchamel sauce before layering with eggplant and a savory lamb *ragù*. The fontina cheese melts and forms a golden crust on top.

2 eggplants, about 1 lb *(500 g)* each, peeled and cut into ½-inch *(12-mm)* dice

Fine sea salt and freshly ground pepper

5 tablespoons *(3 fl oz/80 ml)* extra-virgin olive oil, plus more for greasing

1 large yellow onion, chopped

2 large cloves garlic, minced

2 teaspoons minced fresh rosemary, or 1 teaspoon crumbled dried rosemary

3 tablespoons chopped fresh flat-leaf parsley

1 lb *(500 g)* ground lamb

½ cup *(4 fl oz/125 ml)* dry red or white wine

3 tablespoons tomato paste

2 cups *(12 oz/375 g)* peeled, seeded, and chopped fresh or canned plum tomatoes, with juice

½ cup *(4 fl oz/125 ml)* low-sodium beef broth

1 cup *(8 fl oz/250 ml)* Béchamel Sauce *(page 232)*

¼ lb *(125 g)* fontina cheese, shredded

Kosher salt for cooking pasta

¾ lb *(375 g)* penne

Place the eggplant in a colander in the sink and toss with 2 tablespoons sea salt. Top with a flat plate, then with a heavy can, and let drain for about 40 minutes. Rinse and pat dry with paper towels. Preheat the oven to 400°F (200°C). In a large bowl, toss the eggplant with 2 tablespoons of the olive oil, then divide between 2 rimmed baking sheets. Roast until the eggplant is soft and nicely colored, about 15 minutes. Remove from the oven, sprinkle with sea salt, and set aside. Leave the oven on.

While the eggplant is roasting, in a large saucepan over medium heat, warm the remaining 3 tablespoons oil. Add the onion, garlic, rosemary, and parsley and sauté until the onion is tender, about 5 minutes. Add the lamb and continue to sauté, stirring to break up any clumps, until nicely colored on the outside but still a little pink on the inside, about 12 minutes. Drain off the excess fat from the pan and return to medium heat. Add the wine and sauté until evaporated, about 3 minutes. Stir in the tomato paste, add the tomatoes and their juice, and season with sea salt and pepper. Simmer, uncovered, for about 1 hour, adding the broth as needed to prevent the sauce from drying out. Remove from the heat.

While the sauce is cooking, make the Béchamel Sauce. Remove from the heat and stir in all but 3 tablespoons of the cheese. Cover and set aside. In a large pot, bring 4 qt (4 l) water to a rapid boil. Check the package directions for the cooking time, and then add 2 tablespoons kosher salt and the pasta to the boiling water, stir, and cook, stirring occasionally, until the pasta is half-cooked. Drain and rinse, then return to the pot. Add the béchamel, toss to coat evenly, and set aside.

Lightly oil a 9-by-13-inch (23-by-33-cm) baking dish. Smear about one-third of the lamb sauce over the bottom of the dish, and layer with half of the pasta and half of the eggplant. Top with half of the remaining sauce. Layer with the remaining pasta and eggplant, and top with the remaining sauce. Scatter the reserved cheese over the top. Cover the dish with aluminum foil, place in the oven, and bake for 20 minutes. Uncover and continue to bake until the surface is nicely colored and bubbling, about 5 minutes. Let stand for 10–15 minutes before serving.

MEAT TORTELLINI *with* BUTTER SAUCE

This recipe, from the Emilian town of Modena, yields about 100 tortellini. If you don't want to cook all of them at once, freeze on baking sheets, then transfer to resealable freezer bags and freeze for up to 3 months. Cook directly from the freezer, increasing the cooking time to 5–7 minutes.

FOR THE FILLING

2 tablespoons unsalted butter

2 oz *(60 g)* boneless veal, cut into 1-inch *(2.5-cm)* dice

2 oz *(60 g)* boneless pork loin, cut into 1-inch *(2.5-cm)* dice

3 thin slices prosciutto, finely chopped

2 oz *(60 g)* mortadella, finely chopped

⅓ cup *(1½ oz/45 g)* freshly grated Parmigiano-Reggiano cheese

⅛ teaspoon freshly grated nutmeg

1 large egg, beaten

Fine sea salt and freshly ground pepper

Egg Pasta II *(page 16 or 18)*

6 tablespoons *(3 oz/90 g)* unsalted butter, melted

Kosher salt for cooking pasta

½ cup *(2 oz/60 g)* freshly grated Parmigiano-Reggiano cheese

To make the filling, in a frying pan over medium heat, melt the butter. Add the veal and cook gently, turning occasionally, until it loses its pink color, about 8 minutes. Do not let it brown and get hard; the meat should remain soft, inside and out. Using a slotted spoon, transfer the veal to a cutting board. Add the pork to the same pan over medium heat and sauté in the same manner until it loses its pink color, about 10 minutes. Transfer to a cutting board. Using a chef's knife, chop the veal and pork very finely. (Alternatively, pulse the meat in a food processor, being careful not to grind it to a paste.)

In a bowl, stir together the veal, pork, prosciutto, and mortadella. Add the cheese, nutmeg, egg, ½ teaspoon sea salt, and several grinds of pepper and mix well with a wooden spoon. Cover and refrigerate until ready to use.

Make the pasta dough as directed, then roll out the dough as directed for stuffed pastas on pages 20–21 or 22. Follow the instructions on page 137 to assemble the tortellini. Do not let the tortellini stand for more than 3 hours before cooking.

In a large pot, bring 5 qt (5 l) water to a rapid boil. Meanwhile, smear some of the melted butter on the bottom of a warmed large, shallow serving bowl or platter and keep in a warm place. Add 2 tablespoons kosher salt to the boiling water and gently drop in half of the tortellini, then cover the pot. When the water returns to a boil, uncover and cook, stirring gently occasionally and reducing the heat as needed to prevent the tortellini from knocking against one another and breaking. The total cooking time should be 2–3 minutes. Test a tortellino for doneness (see page 133), then lift the tortellini out with a large slotted spoon, allowing a little of the water to cling to them so they remain moist, and transfer to the serving bowl; drizzle with a little of the melted butter. Cover the bowl to keep the tortellini warm. Repeat to cook the remaining tortellini. Drizzle with the remaining butter, sprinkle with the ½ cup (2 oz/60 g) cheese, and serve right away.

BAKED ZITI *with* CAULIFLOWER AND GRUYÈRE

Here is a merging of the all-American macaroni and cheese and one of Britain's favorite comfort foods, "cauliflower cheese," a succulent treatment of creamed cauliflower baked until bubbling and golden on the top. It is so delicious that even avowed cauliflower haters are known to love it.

FOR THE SAUCE

3¼ cups *(26 fl oz/810 ml)* milk

4 tablespoons *(2 oz/60 g)* unsalted butter

3 tablespoons unbleached all-purpose flour

Fine sea salt and freshly ground white pepper

6 oz *(185 g)* Gruyère cheese, shredded

¼ cup *(1 oz/30 g)* freshly grated Parmigiano-Reggiano cheese

2 tablespoons unsalted butter

¼ cup *(1 oz/30 g)* fine dried bread crumbs

Kosher salt for cooking pasta and vegetables

1 lb *(500 g)* ziti

1 large head cauliflower, trimmed and cut into florets

To make the sauce, in a saucepan over medium heat, warm the milk until small bubbles appear around the edges of the pan, then remove from the heat. While the milk is heating, in a heavy saucepan over low heat, melt the 4 tablespoons (2 oz/60 g) butter. Add the flour and stir vigorously with a wooden spoon to remove any lumps. Cook, stirring often, for about 4 minutes. Gradually add the hot milk while stirring constantly, then continue to cook, stirring often, until the sauce is smooth and thick enough to coat the back of a spoon, about 15 minutes. Add ½ teaspoon sea salt, a few grinds of pepper, and the Gruyère, and stir until the cheese is melted, about 2 minutes. Stir in the Parmigiano-Reggiano, remove from the heat, and cover to keep warm.

Preheat the broiler. Position an oven rack 8 inches (20 cm) from the heat source. In a small frying pan, melt the 2 tablespoons butter over medium heat. Add the bread crumbs and stir and toss to coat evenly. Remove from the heat and set aside.

In a large pot, bring 6 qt (6 l) water to a rapid boil. Add 2 tablespoons kosher salt, the pasta, and the cauliflower and stir well. Cook, stirring occasionally, until the pasta is al dente, according to package directions. Drain the pasta and cauliflower and return them to the pot. Add the cheese sauce and toss to coat evenly. Taste and adjust the seasoning with sea salt and white pepper. Transfer the sauced mixture to a flameproof baking dish just large enough to accommodate it. Sprinkle the buttered crumbs evenly over the top.

Place the baking dish in the broiler and broil until the surface is bubbling and golden, about 5 minutes. Serve right away.

SWISS CHARD ANOLINI *with* CREAMY TOMATO SAUCE

These tantalizing crescent-shaped pasta pillows are served all over Italy, usually accompanied by a simple tomato sauce. A touch of crème fraîche or cream, as used here, makes the sauce silky and pink. The anolini can be stuffed with kale or spinach instead of the Swiss chard.

FOR THE FILLING

2 cups *(1 lb/500 g)* whole-milk ricotta cheese

2 lb *(1 kg)* Swiss chard (about 2 bunches), tough stems removed

Fine sea salt and freshly ground pepper

2 large egg yolks, lightly beaten

¼ teaspoon freshly grated nutmeg

½ cup *(2 oz/60 g)* freshly grated Parmigiano-Reggiano cheese

Egg Pasta II *(page 16 or 18)*

Creamy Tomato Sauce *(page 232)*

Kosher salt for cooking pasta

To make the filling, place the ricotta in a fine-mesh sieve set over a bowl. Refrigerate for 3–4 hours to drain off as much excess moisture as possible. Discard the liquid and transfer the ricotta to a bowl.

Wash the chard leaves and drain. Remove any discolored leaves and discard. Fold the leaves in half and cut away the tough central spines; discard, or reserve them for another use. Put the leaves with the water still clinging to them in a saucepan, add ¼ teaspoon sea salt, cover, and cook over medium heat until tender, about 12 minutes, depending on the freshness of the chard. Drain well and squeeze out as much moisture from the chard as possible, then mince finely. Add the chard, egg yolks, nutmeg, grated cheese, a scant ½ teaspoon sea salt, and a few grinds of pepper to the ricotta and mix with a wooden spoon until a smooth paste forms. Cover and refrigerate until ready to use.

Make the pasta dough as directed, then roll out the dough as directed for stuffed pastas on pages 20–21 or 22. Follow the instructions on page 137 to assemble the anolini.

Make the Creamy Tomato Sauce as directed and cover to keep warm.

In a large pot, bring 5 qt (5 l) water to a rapid boil. Meanwhile, smear a thin layer of the sauce on the bottom of a warmed large, shallow serving bowl. Add 2 tablespoons kosher salt to the boiling water and gently drop in half of the anolini, then cover the pot. When the water returns to a boil, uncover and cook, stirring gently occasionally and reducing the heat as needed to prevent the anolini from knocking against one another and breaking. The total cooking time should be about 3 minutes. Test an anolino for doneness (see page 133), then lift the anolini out of the water with a large slotted spoon, allowing a little of the water to cling to them so they remain moist, and transfer to the serving bowl. Pour half of the sauce over the anolini, coating them evenly. Cover the bowl to keep the anolini warm. Repeat with the remaining anolini, cooking them and topping them with the remaining sauce. Serve right away.

Artichoke Ravioli *with* Mint Butter

The meaty, earthy, herbal flavors of artichoke hearts are showcased in this elegant alternative to the usual ricotta-filled ravioli. The butter sauce, infused and brightened with fresh mint and parsley, echoes the natural flavors of the artichokes, but you can also substitute a light tomato sauce.

FOR THE FILLING

4 tablespoons *(2 oz/60 g)* unsalted butter

2 shallots, minced

14 oz *(440 g)* frozen artichoke hearts, thawed and patted dry

¼ lb *(125 g)* baby spinach leaves, stems removed

2 teaspoons minced fresh marjoram, or 1 teaspoon crumbled dried marjoram

½ cup *(2 oz/60 g)* freshly grated Parmigiano-Reggiano cheese

1 large egg

¼ teaspoon freshly grated nutmeg

Fine sea salt and freshly ground pepper

Egg Pasta II *(page 16 or 18)*

½ cup *(4 oz/125 g)* unsalted butter, clarified *(see page 233)*

¼ cup *(⅓ oz/10 g)* minced fresh mint

2 tablespoons minced fresh flat-leaf parsley

Freshly ground pepper

Kosher salt for cooking pasta

Freshly grated Parmigiano-Reggiano cheese for serving

To make the filling, in a saucepan over medium heat, melt 3 tablespoons of the butter. Add the shallots and sauté until tender, about 3 minutes. Add the artichoke hearts and sauté for 3 minutes. Stir in ¼ cup (2 fl oz/60 ml) water, cover, reduce the heat to low, and cook until the artichokes are tender, about 20 minutes.

While the artichokes are cooking, in a saucepan over medium heat, melt the remaining 1 tablespoon butter. Add the spinach with only the rinsing water clinging to the leaves and sauté, tossing often, until wilted, about 2 minutes. Drain, then chop and set aside. Remove the artichokes from the heat and let cool slightly. Transfer to a food processor and add the spinach, marjoram, cheese, egg, nutmeg, and ¼ teaspoon each sea salt and pepper. Pulse to blend evenly.

Make the pasta dough as directed, then roll out the dough as directed for stuffed pastas on pages 20–21 or 22. Follow the instructions on page 137 to assemble the ravioli.

Add the clarified butter to a small saucepan and whisk in the mint, parsley, and pepper to taste. Remove from the heat and cover to keep warm.

In a large pot, bring 5 qt (5 l) water to a rapid boil. Meanwhile, smear a tablespoon of the mint butter on the bottom of a warmed large, shallow serving bowl. Add 2 tablespoons kosher salt to the boiling water and gently drop in half of the ravioli, then cover the pot. When the water returns to a boil, uncover and cook, stirring gently occasionally and reducing the heat as needed to prevent the ravioli from knocking against one another and breaking. The total cooking time should be 3–5 minutes. Test a raviolo for doneness (see page 133), then lift out the ravioli with a large slotted spoon, allowing a little of the water to cling to them so they remain moist, and transfer to the serving bowl. Cover to keep warm. Repeat to cook the remaining ravioli. Spoon the mint butter over the ravioli and serve right away. Pass the additional cheese at the table.

OPEN TARRAGON RAVIOLI *with* CRAB AND LEMON

This beautiful pasta is made by arranging tarragon leaves between pasta sheets, then rolling
out the dough again. The resulting herb-patterned dough is cut into squares, then stacked
with the creamy, lemon-laced crab mixture in a stunning "open" ravioli.

Egg Pasta I *(page 16 or 18)*

1 cup *(1 oz/30 g)*
tarragon leaves

FOR THE FILLING

5 tablespoons *(2½ oz/75 g)*
unsalted butter

2 tablespoons extra-virgin
olive oil

2 shallots, finely chopped

Grated zest of 2 lemons

3 tablespoons minced
fresh flat-leaf parsley

⅓ cup *(3 fl oz/80 ml)*
dry white wine

¼ cup *(2 fl oz/60 ml)*
fresh lemon juice

¾ lb *(375 g)* lump crabmeat,
picked over for shell
fragments and cartilage

6 tablespoons *(3 fl oz/90 ml)*
crème fraîche

Fine sea salt and freshly
ground white pepper

Kosher salt for cooking pasta

To make the herb pasta, make the pasta dough as directed to yield 1 lb
(500 g), cut into quarters, and roll out 2 quarters as directed for stuffed
pastas on pages 20–21 or 22. (Reserve the remaining dough for another
use.) Cut each of the 2 pasta sheets into two 24-inch (60-cm) lengths.
Arrange ¼ cup (¼ oz/7 g) of the tarragon leaves on a 12-inch (30-cm) half
of each length, then fold the other halves over to cover. Press the sheets
together with your hands or a rolling pin to seal. Pass the herb-filled
sheet through the rollers of a pasta machine, working from the middle
setting to the second-to-last setting, or roll out by hand to about 1/16 inch
(2 mm) thick. Cut the pasta sheets into squares the width of the sheets,
about 4 inches (10 cm). You should have 24 squares.

To make the filling, in a frying pan over medium heat, melt the butter
with the olive oil. Remove 2 tablespoons of the butter-oil mixture
and set aside in a warm place. Add the shallots to the pan and sauté until
translucent and tender, about 4 minutes. Add the lemon zest and parsley
and sauté, stirring, for 1 minute. Add the wine and lemon juice, reduce
the heat to low, and simmer for 1 minute. Fold in the crabmeat and the
crème fraîche and warm over low heat until the crabmeat is heated through,
about 2 minutes. Remove from the heat, season with sea salt and white
pepper, and cover to keep warm.

In a large pot, bring 5 qt (5 l) water to a rapid boil. Add 2 tablespoons
kosher salt and the pasta squares, in batches, and cook for 1 minute
(see page 133). Drain and dry flat on clean, damp kitchen towels.

To serve, place 2 pasta squares on each of 6 warmed individual plates.
Top the squares with half of the filling, dividing it evenly. Place another
pasta square on top of each filled square, then top with the remaining
filling, dividing it evenly. Top with the remaining pasta squares. Drizzle
the servings evenly with the reserved butter-oil mixture. Serve right away.

CANNELLONI *with* CHICKEN SAUSAGE AND SPINACH

In this recipe, adapted from one by the Bologna-based chef Franco Rossi, small rectangles of fresh pasta dough are wrapped around a filling of chicken sausage. You can also use purchased dry cannelloni tubes; cook them in salted water, then stuff and bake as directed in the recipe.

FOR THE FILLING

2 teaspoons extra-virgin olive oil

¾ lb *(375 g)* spinach, tough stems removed

Fine sea salt and freshly ground white pepper

3 tablespoons unsalted butter

2 oz *(60 g)* pancetta, cut into small dice

1 cup *(6 oz/185 g)* minced shallots

1 lb *(500 g)* sweet Italian-style chicken sausages, casings removed

½ teaspoon ground fennel

½ lb *(250 g)* fresh white mushrooms, brushed clean, quartered, and sliced thinly

½ cup *(2 oz/60 g)* freshly grated Parmigiano-Reggiano cheese

Egg Pasta I *(page 16 or 18)*

Kosher salt for cooking pasta

Extra-virgin olive oil for greasing

Simple Tomato Sauce *(page 232)*

Béchamel Sauce *(page 232)*

½ cup *(2 oz/60 g)* freshly grated Parmigiano-Reggiano cheese

To make the filling, in a large frying pan over medium heat, warm the olive oil. Add the spinach and cook until wilted, about 4 minutes. Season lightly with sea salt and remove from the heat. Let cool, and then squeeze out as much moisture as possible. Chop and set aside.

Rinse the pan, return it to medium heat, and melt the butter. Add the pancetta and sauté until nicely colored, about 5 minutes. Using a slotted spoon, transfer to a plate and set aside. Add the shallots to the pan and sauté until tender, about 4 minutes. Reduce the heat to medium-low and add the sausage meat, 1 teaspoon sea salt, ¼ teaspoon pepper, and the fennel. Sauté, stirring to break up any clumps, until the sausage meat is lightly colored on the outside and just barely pink on the inside, about 5 minutes. Add the mushrooms and sauté until tender, about 4 minutes. Add the spinach and sauté for 4 minutes. Remove from the heat and stir in the pancetta and the cheese. Set aside.

Make the pasta dough as directed, then roll out the dough as directed for stuffed pasta on pages 20–21 or 22. Cut the pasta sheets into about twenty-four 3½-by-4½-inch (9-by-11.5-cm) rectangles. In a large pot, bring 5 qt (5 l) water to a rapid boil. Add 2 tablespoons kosher salt and the pasta rectangles, in batches, and cook for 1 minute (see page 133).

Preheat the oven to 400°F (200°C). Grease two or more baking dishes each large enough to hold 12 cannelloni. Reheat the tomato and béchamel sauces. Smear a layer of tomato sauce on the bottom of each baking dish. To fill the cannelloni, put a generous tablespoon of the filling along a short end of 1 rectangle and roll it up, making a small, secure bundle. Transfer the bundle, seam side up, to 1 of the prepared baking dishes. Repeat to assemble the remaining cannelloni. When all of the cannelloni are in the baking dishes, smear with a generous layer of tomato sauce and top with the same amount of béchamel. Sprinkle evenly with the cheese. Cover the dishes with aluminum foil and bake for 15 minutes to heat through. Remove the foil and continue to bake until the béchamel forms a golden crust, about 5 minutes. Let stand for 10 minutes before serving.

TORTELLINI *in* BRODO

Here is a delicious version of a traditional Italian soup, in which the classic meat tortellini of Emilia-Romagna are served in a rich mixed meat broth. This recipe allows for 15 to 20 pieces of tortellini per person; you can make fewer tortellini for a brothier soup, if desired.

FOR THE BROTH

3 lb *(1.5 kg)* chicken legs, thighs, and/or backs

2 lb *(1 kg)* beef chuck, short ribs, or shank, in one piece

2 lb *(1 kg)* veal neck bones

1 yellow onion, unpeeled

1 carrot

1 large rib celery, including leaves

2 fresh or canned plum tomatoes, quartered

Large handful of fresh flat-leaf parsley sprigs

2 fresh thyme sprigs (optional)

1 bay leaf

½ teaspoon peppercorns

90–100 Meat Tortellini *(see page 154),* uncooked

Fine sea salt

Freshly grated Parmigiano-Reggiano cheese for serving

To make the broth, skin the chicken pieces and remove any excess fat. Trim any excess fat from the beef. Place the chicken and beef in a large, deep pot and add the veal bones, onion, carrot, celery, tomatoes, parsley, thyme sprigs (if using), bay leaf, peppercorns, and 2½ qt (2.5 l) water. Place over medium-high heat and bring to a boil, skimming any foam that forms on the surface. Reduce the heat to medium-low, cover partially, and simmer gently, skimming occasionally to remove any foam or fat that forms on the surface, until full bodied and flavorful, about 3 hours.

While the broth is cooking, make the tortellini as directed and set aside.

When the broth is ready, remove from the heat. Using a large slotted spoon, lift out the chicken, beef, and veal. Discard the chicken parts and veal bones, and reserve the beef for another use. Pour the broth through a fine-mesh sieve lined with cheesecloth into a clean pot. Let stand for a few minutes, then, using a large spoon, scoop off and discard any fat from the surface. (If making the broth in advance, transfer it to a container, let cool, cover, and refrigerate until well chilled. The fat will have solidified on surface and can be easy lifted and discarded.)

Season the broth with sea salt, place over high heat, and bring to a rapid boil. Gently drop in the tortellini and cover the pot. When the broth returns to a boil, uncover and cook, stirring gently occasionally and reducing the heat as needed to prevent the tortellini from knocking against one another and breaking. The total cooking time should be 2–3 minutes.

Ladle the tortellini and broth into warmed shallow bowls and serve right away. Pass the cheese at the table.

POTATO, GOAT CHEESE, AND MINT RAVIOLI

In Sardinia, ravioli are called *culingionis,* and their filling varies depending on where they are made on the island. Among the classic varieties are Swiss chard and pecorino; seasoned meats; herb-laced ricotta; and the mint-scented potato filling enriched with fresh goat cheese as in this recipe.

FOR THE FILLING

1 lb *(500 g)* Yukon gold potatoes, unpeeled

3 tablespoons extra-virgin olive oil

1 yellow onion, minced

1 large clove garlic, minced

2 tablespoons finely chopped fresh mint

2 oz *(60 g)* fresh goat cheese, crumbled

6 tablespoons *(1½ oz/45 g)* freshly grated pecorino sardo or pecorino romano cheese

Fine sea salt and freshly ground pepper

Egg Pasta II *(page 16 or 18)*

Simple Tomato Sauce *(page 232)*

2 tablespoons chopped mixed fresh basil and mint

Kosher salt for cooking ravioli

Freshly grated pecorino sardo or pecorino romano for serving

To make the filling, in a saucepan, combine the potatoes with water to cover, bring to a boil over high heat, reduce the heat to medium, and cook until the potatoes are tender when pierced with a knife, about 25 minutes. Drain the potatoes and, when cool enough to handle, peel them and pass them through a potato ricer into a bowl. (Alternatively, mash them very finely with a potato masher.)

In a small frying pan over medium-low heat, warm the olive oil. Add the onion and garlic and cook gently, stirring occasionally, until softened but not colored, about 6 minutes. Add to the potato along with the mint, goat cheese, pecorino, 1 teaspoon sea salt, and ¼ teaspoon pepper. Using your hands or a wooden spoon, work the mixture well to distribute the ingredients evenly. Taste and adjust with sea salt and pepper.

Make the pasta dough as directed, then roll out the dough as directed for stuffed pastas on pages 20–21 or 22. Follow the instructions on page 136 to assemble the ravioli.

Make the tomato sauce as directed, stirring in the herbs during the last minute of cooking. Cover and keep warm.

In a large pot, bring 5 qt (5 l) water to a rapid boil. Add 2 tablespoons kosher salt to the boiling water and gently drop in half of the ravioli, then cover the pot. When the water returns to a boil, uncover and cook, stirring gently occasionally and reducing the heat as needed to prevent the ravioli from knocking against one another and breaking. The total cooking time should be 3–5 minutes. Test a raviolo for doneness (see page 133), then lift out the ravioli with a large slotted spoon, allowing a little of the water to cling to them so they remain moist, and transfer to a warmed, large shallow serving bowl. Cover the bowl to keep the ravioli warm. Repeat to cook the remaining ravioli. Spoon the tomato sauce over the ravioli. Serve right away, and pass the additional pecorino at the table.

SERVES 4–6

PESTO RAVIOLETTI *with* CREAMY TOMATO SAUCE

These diminutive ravioli, with their pastel green filling of basil pesto and topping of rosy sauce, are a lovely sight on any dinner table. Ravioletti can also be cooked and served in a subtle vegetable broth or rich meat broth (see page 162), and offered with crusty bread as a soup course.

FOR THE FILLING

1 lb *(500 g)* whole-milk ricotta cheese

¼ cup *(2 oz/60 g)* Basil Pesto *(page 29)*

1 large egg yolk

Fine sea salt and freshly ground pepper

Creamy Tomato Sauce *(page 232)*

Egg Pasta II *(page 16 or 18)*

Kosher salt for cooking pasta

To make the filling, place the ricotta in a fine-mesh sieve set over a bowl. Refrigerate for 3–4 hours to drain off as much excess moisture as possible. Discard the liquid and transfer the ricotta to a bowl.

Add the pesto, egg yolk, ¼ teaspoon sea salt, and ⅛ teaspoon pepper to the ricotta and mix with a wooden spoon until a smooth paste forms. Cover and refrigerate until ready to use.

Make the tomato sauce as directed and cover to keep warm.

Make the pasta dough as directed, then roll out the dough as directed for stuffed pastas on pages 20–21 or 22. Cut the pasta sheets lengthwise to create sheets that are about 1½ inches (4 cm) wide. Follow the instructions for assembling ravioli on page 136, cutting crosswise at about 1½-inch (4-cm) intervals to create square ravioletti.

In a large pot, bring 5 qt (5 l) water to a rapid boil. Meanwhile, smear a thin layer of the tomato sauce on the bottom of a warmed large, shallow serving bowl. Add 2 tablespoons kosher salt to the boiling water and gently drop in half of the ravioletti, then cover the pot. When the water returns to a boil, uncover and cook, stirring gently occasionally and reducing the heat as needed to prevent the ravioletti from knocking against one another and breaking. The total cooking time should be about 3 minutes. Test a ravioletto for doneness (see page 133), then lift the ravioletti out with a large slotted spoon, allowing a little of the water to cling to them so they remain moist, and transfer to the serving bowl. Pour half of the sauce over them, coating evenly. Cover the bowl to keep the ravioletti warm. Repeat to cook the remaining ravioletti and top with the remaining sauce. Serve right away.

OPEN CILANTRO RAVIOLI *with* PORK AND CARROTS

Here is an East-meets-West fusion that is as beautiful as it is delicious. Fresh pasta is rolled with cilantro leaves nestled between the sheets to create a dough marbled with green. The dough is then cut into squares, cooked, and piled into layers with an Asian-flavored pork filling.

Egg Pasta I *(page 16 or 18)*

1 cup *(1 oz/30 g)* fresh cilantro leaves

FOR THE MARINADE

½ cup *(4 fl oz/125 ml)* light soy sauce

¼ cup *(2 fl oz/60 ml)* dry sherry

1 tablespoon Asian sesame oil

1 teaspoon rice vinegar

1 tablespoon sugar

1 clove garlic, minced

2 green onions, minced

1 lb *(500 g)* boneless pork loin, partially frozen

6 tablespoons *(3 fl oz/90 ml)* peanut oil

1 large carrot, peeled and cut into julienne

6 slices fresh ginger

1 yellow onion, chopped

1 large clove garlic, minced

5 oz *(155 g)* mixed enoki and shiitake mushrooms

Kosher salt for cooking pasta

Soy-Ginger Sauce *(page 232)*

1 tablespoon toasted sesame seeds

Cilantro leaves for serving

To make the herb pasta, make the pasta dough as directed to yield 1 lb (500 g), cut into quarters, and roll out 2 quarters as directed for stuffed pastas on pages 20–21 or 22. (Reserve the remaining dough for another use.) Cut each of the 2 pasta sheets into two 24-inch (60-cm) lengths. Arrange ¼ cup (¼ oz/7 g) of the cilantro leaves on a 12-inch (30-cm) half of each length, fold the other halves over to cover, and press to seal. Pass the sheets through the rollers of a pasta machine, working from the middle setting to the second-to-last setting, or roll out by hand to about 1⁄16 inch (2 mm) thick. Cut into 4-inch (10-cm) squares. You should have 24 squares.

To make the marinade, in a bowl, combine all of the ingredients and mix well. Using a sharp knife, thinly slice the pork against the grain, then cut into thin strips. Add the pork to the marinade, stir well to coat evenly, and cover and refrigerate for at least 30 minutes or up to 1 hour.

In a wok or large nonstick frying pan over medium heat, warm 1 tablespoon of the peanut oil. Add the carrot and 2 of the ginger slices and toss and stir until the carrot is tender, about 5 minutes. Transfer the carrot to a plate and cover to keep warm. Raise the heat to high and add 3 tablespoons of the peanut oil to the pan. Add the pork and its marinade and toss and stir until cooked through, about 5 minutes. Transfer to the plate with the carrot and cover to keep warm. Add the remaining 2 tablespoons peanut oil to the pan over medium heat. Add the remaining 4 ginger slices, the onion, and garlic and sauté until tender, about 3 minutes. Add the mushrooms and sauté until tender, about 3 minutes. Transfer the mushroom mixture to a separate plate and cover. Discard the ginger slices.

In a large pot, bring 4 qt (4 l) water to a rapid boil. Add 1 tablespoon kosher salt and the pasta squares, in batches, and cook for 1 minute (see page 133). Place 2 pasta squares on each of 6 warmed plates. Top the squares with half each of the mushroom and pork mixtures, dividing evenly, and place another pasta square on top. Top with the remaining mushroom and pork mixtures, dividing evenly, and then with the remaining pasta squares. Drizzle all of the servings evenly with the Soy-Ginger Sauce, sprinkle with the sesame seeds and cilantro, and serve right away.

White Vegetarian Lasagne

Cooked dried lasagne noodles are layered with an assortment of mushrooms and spinach for a meatless baked pasta dish that departs from the common tomato-cheese combination. As in most baked pasta dishes, a creamy sauce plays a crucial role in binding the ingredients together and keeping the pasta moist.

Kosher salt for cooking pasta

9–12 dried lasagne noodles

2 teaspoons extra-virgin olive oil

2 cups *(16 fl oz/500 ml)* milk

6 tablespoons *(3 oz/90 g)* unsalted butter

¼ cup *(1½ oz/45 g)* unbleached all-purpose flour

Fine sea salt

4 cups *(32 fl oz/1 l)* low-sodium vegetable broth

4 large carrots, peeled and shredded *(about 4 cups/14 oz/440 g)*

10 oz *(315 g)* assorted fresh mushrooms, such as oyster, shiitake, and chanterelle, brushed clean, tough stems removed, and chopped

2 tablespoons minced fresh thyme

10 oz *(315 g)* baby spinach

1½ cups *(1½ oz/45 g)* fresh basil leaves

1 lb *(500 g)* fresh mozzarella cheese, shredded

1 cup *(4 oz/125 g)* freshly grated Parmigiano-Reggiano cheese

In a large pot, bring 5 qt (5 l) water to a rapid boil. Check the package directions for the cooking time, then add 2 tablespoons kosher salt and the pasta to the boiling water, stir well, and cook, stirring occasionally, until the pasta is half-cooked. Drain and rinse under cold running water. Toss the noodles with the olive oil to prevent them from sticking together and set aside on clean, damp kitchen towels.

To make the sauce, in a saucepan over medium heat, warm the milk until small bubbles appear around the edges of the pan, then remove from the heat. While the milk is heating, in a heavy saucepan over low heat, melt 4 tablespoons (2 oz/60 g) of the butter. Add the flour and ½ teaspoon sea salt and stir vigorously with a wooden spoon to remove any lumps. Cook, stirring often, for about 4 minutes. Gradually add the hot milk while stirring constantly, then continue cooking, stirring often, until the sauce is smooth and thick enough to coat the back of a spoon, about 5 minutes. Add 2 cups (16 fl oz/500 ml) of the broth and cook, stirring, until well mixed and heated through. Remove from the heat and cover to keep warm.

While the sauce is cooking, in a saucepan over high heat, bring the remaining 2 cups (16 fl oz/500 ml) broth to a boil. Add the carrots, cover, and cook until just tender, about 4 minutes. Drain well over a bowl, reserving the carrots and broth separately.

In a large frying pan over medium heat, melt the remaining 2 tablespoons butter. Add the mushrooms and sauté until lightly colored and nearly tender, 2–3 minutes. Stir in the thyme, remove from the heat, set aside.

Try substituting other fresh
vegetables for the mushrooms
in this recipe. Roasted summer
squash slices, parboiled artichoke
hearts, or roasted eggplant slices
are all wonderful additions
to this lasagne.

Gently reheat the sauce over low heat. Preheat the oven to 350°F (180°C).
Ladle ¼ cup (2 fl oz/60 ml) of the sauce onto the bottom of a 9-by-13-inch
(23-by-33-cm) baking dish. Lay 3 or 4 noodles, side by side but not
overlapping, on top of the sauce. Scatter half of the spinach evenly over
the noodles. Top evenly with half of the basil leaves. Distribute half of the
carrots evenly over the basil. Arrange another layer of noodles over
the carrots. Distribute the mushroom mixture evenly over the noodles.
Ladle a scant 2 cups (16 fl oz/500 ml) of the sauce over the mushrooms.
Top evenly with half of the mozzarella, and then with half of the
Parmigiano-Reggiano. Arrange another layer of the noodles on top of
the cheese, and top with the remaining spinach and then the remaining
basil. Distribute the remaining carrots evenly over the basil. Ladle the
remaining sauce evenly over the top, and then sprinkle with the remaining
mozzarella, followed by the remaining Parmigiano-Reggiano. Pour the
reserved 2 cups broth evenly along the sides of the dish, being careful not
to disturb the topping.

Bake until the topping is browned and bubbling, 40–45 minutes.
Let stand for 15 minutes before serving.

DUMPLINGS

ABOUT DUMPLINGS

Whether dropped, rolled, or filled, dumplings are a universal pleasure, found in nearly every cuisine. They take various forms: roughly shaped balls of dough, bundles of meat or vegetables enclosed in thin noodle wrappers, mixtures of bread, potatoes, cheese, or vegetables bound with egg and cooked in broth. In this chapter, you will find a selection of recipes from the three most prolific dumpling cultures: Italy, eastern Europe, and Asia.

GNOCCHI

Gnocchi are among the easiest pasta dishes to prepare at home. The secret to making them particularly light is simple: the drier the potato, the less flour you will need to form the dough, and the more delicate the result. Keep in mind that while gnocchi need to be dry enough to hold their shape, the more flour you add to the dough, the heavier and denser the dumplings will be. Some recipes call for adding beaten egg or egg white to the dough to help hold the mixture together. But these additions produce gnocchi that are firmer and somewhat bouncy when cooked, qualities that detract from their lightness. As long as you use a relatively dry-fleshed potato such as Yukon gold or russet, you should be able to form a dough that will hold together.

Once you have mixed the dough, but before you have formed it into ropes and cut the gnocchi (see page 177), check the consistency of the dough: Pinch off a few ½–¾-inch (12-mm–2-cm) pieces and drop them into boiling water. The pieces should retain their shape and float to the surface. If they fall apart, add more flour to the dough, a tablespoon at a time, and test again. If they are still not holding together, add a lightly beaten egg or egg white to the dough, which should give the dough the proper consistency.

Once you cut the ropes into small pieces, it is important to imprint them with a characteristic ribbed or dimpled look. This creates hollows in the dumplings which is key to ensure that they are light and tender. Various surfaces can be used to mark the dough. You can gently press the tines of a fork into each piece to create shallow ridges, or you can run each piece lightly over a ridged wooden butter paddle or over the medium-sized holes of a box grater.

GNUDI AND SPOON GNOCCHI

The "dough" used for *gnudi* (naked gnocchi), which resemble ravioli without the pasta wrapper, and for spoon gnocchi is a moist mixture that is shaped with two spoons and then dropped into boiling salted water. As with classic potato gnocchi, these dropped dumplings should incorporate only as much flour as necessary to keep them from disintegrating in the water. Always test one or two before you cook the whole batch.

SPAETZLE

A number of countries claim to have originated the classic dumplings known as spaetzle, and today they are enjoyed in Germany, Austria, Hungary, and the German-speaking parts of France and Switzerland, under a variety of names. Unlike most dumpling doughs, spaetzle dough is thick but fluid, so that it will pass through the holes of a spaetzle maker, a tool that combines a flat, perforated panel topped with a movable hopper. Alternatively, you can push the dough through a colander, food mill, or potato ricer (see page 179).

ASIAN DUMPLINGS

Chinese-style dumplings, such as Chicken Dumplings with Soy-Ginger Sauce (page 189) and Shrimp and Pork Shumai (page 194), are made with purchased round dumpling wrappers. These wrappers are surprisingly thin and delicate and allow you to make delicious dumplings at home without having to make the dough from scratch. If you can find only square wonton wrappers, use a round cookie cutter to cut them into circles. Look for round dumpling wrappers or wonton wrappers in the refrigerated section of most supermarkets and in Asian groceries.

To shape the open-topped Chinese steamed dumplings *(shumai)* in this chapter, place a small amount of filling in the center of a wrapper, bring the sides up around the filling, and then pleat the top edge (see page 179). The shaped dumpling is then lightly tapped on the bottom to flatten, so it will stand upright in the steamer.

Japanese *gyoza,* which are similar to Chinese pot stickers and are panfried rather than steamed, are also made with round wrappers, usually labeled "gyoza wrappers." (As with the Chinese dumplings, if you are unable to find round wrappers, purchase wonton wrappers and cut them into circles.) As with any stuffed pasta, you must use only a modest amount of filling for each wrapper to leave room for expansion as the dumpling cooks; a teaspoonful of filling is generally plenty. To shape *gyoza,* place a spoonful of the filling on the center of the wrapper, fold the wrapper in half to create a half-moon, and seal the edge with a series of pleats (see page 179).

Asian dumplings should be cooked immediately after they are shaped, or the dough will draw moisture from the filling and lose its texture. Or you can arrange the dumplings, not touching, on rimmed baking sheets and freeze them until firm, about 1 hour. Transfer to resealable plastic freezer bags and freeze for up to 1 month.

COOKING AND SERVING DUMPLINGS

Dumplings are boiled, steamed, or fried, depending on the type. If you are boiling dumplings, such as gnocchi or *gnudi,* the best utensil to use for retrieving them from the pot and draining them is a wire skimmer, also known as a spider. The skimmer is ideal for three reasons: it enables you to retrieve the dumplings from the cooking water quickly and efficiently, thus avoiding overcooking; its wide webbing ensures the water will drain away freely; and it allows you to scoop up the dumplings the moment they float to the surface. Alternatively, you can use a large slotted spoon.

Tiered bamboo steamer baskets are ideal for cooking steamed dumplings, as they allow you to cook all of the dumplings at the same time. If you have only a single bamboo basket or a metal steamer insert, you will need to steam the dumplings in batches and keep the cooked batches warm in a 200°F (95°C) oven until all of the dumplings are cooked.

A large nonstick frying pan is usually the best type of pan to use for panfrying *gyoza* or other fried dumplings, because it ensures that the dumplings won't stick to the bottom and possibly tear, releasing the filling.

Not surprisingly, Western and Asian dumplings are served differently. Italian gnocchi, *gnudi,* and spoon gnocchi are typically dressed with a simple tomato sauce, flavored oil, or butter sauce and presented as a plated first or main course. Eastern European spaetzle are often served as an accompaniment to a main course of meat. Asian dumplings, unless cooked in broth, are usually served family style with a dipping sauce, either as an appetizer or as part of an assortment of dumplings. Because of these different serving conventions, the yields on the recipes in this chapter vary: the Italian recipe yields are for main-course portions, the two spaetzle recipes for side-dish portions, and the Asian recipes for appetizer portions, though a smaller group could enjoy the Asian dumplings as a main course.

DUMPLING SHAPES

1 **GNOCCHI** Italian potato dumplings, which are concave and dimpled or grooved.

2 **SHUMAI** Open-topped, pleated Chinese dumplings typically filled with a mixture of pork and shrimp and steamed.

3 **SPAETZLE** German dumplings made by scraping or dropping little bits of dough into simmering water.

4 **GNUDI** Meaning "naked gnocchi," these Italian spoon dumplings resemble the filling of ravioli without the pasta wrapper.

5 **GYOZA** Japanese half-moon–shaped, pleated dumplings that are usually panfried.

BASIC POTATO GNOCCHI

INGREDIENTS

2 lb (1 kg) Yukon gold or other
boiling potatoes, unpeeled

1¾ cups (9 oz/280 g) unbleached
all-purpose flour, or as needed

1 teaspoon fine sea salt

¼ teaspoon freshly ground pepper

MAKES ABOUT 2½ LB (1.25 KG)

1 RICE THE POTATOES	2 ADD FLOUR	3 FORM A DOUGH

In a saucepan, combine the potatoes with water to cover. Bring to a boil over high heat, then reduce the heat to medium and cook until the potatoes are tender, about 25 minutes. Drain and, when just cool enough to handle, peel. Pass them through a potato ricer onto a rimmed baking sheet. Spread out and let cool.

In a bowl, stir together the flour, salt, and pepper. Sprinkle 1½ cups (7½ oz/235 g) of the flour mixture evenly over the potatoes on the baking sheet. Using a bench scraper, scoop, lift, and fold the potatoes to mix them with the flour until a coarse dough forms. It should look raggedy.

Transfer the potato mixture to a lightly floured work surface and work in just enough of the remaining seasoned flour so that the dough is soft and smooth, but not dry. Shape the dough into a ball and flatten into a thick disk.

4–5 KNEAD THE DOUGH

6 ROLL INTO A CYLINDER

7 CUT INTO GNOCCHI

To knead the dough, using the heel of your hand, push it down and away from you, fold it in half back toward you, and then rotate it a quarter turn. Repeat until the dough is soft and pliable but no longer sticky, about 5 minutes. Divide the dough into quarters, and refrigerate three of the quarters.

Lightly flour the work surface, place a dough quarter on it, and shape it into a short, thick cylinder. Using the palms of both hands, roll the dough back and forth, gradually moving your palms to the ends of the cylinder as it elongates, until you have a "rope" about ½ inch (12 mm) in diameter.

Using the bench scraper or a knife, cut the rope crosswise into pieces ½–¾ inch (12 mm–2 cm) wide. Run the pieces lightly over the large holes of a box grater or a ridged butter paddle, or press the tines of a fork gently into each piece to create hollows (see page 172).

MAKING GNUDI

1 SCOOP UP SOME DOUGH	2 FORM THE DUMPLING	3 DROP IN WATER

Have ready two teaspoons and a large pot of simmering water. Use one teaspoon to scoop up a generous spoonful of the dough.

Use the second spoon to scoop under the dough, transferring it to the second spoon. Use the first spoon to scoop under the dough, transferring it back to the first spoon. Repeat several times, transferring the dough back and forth between the spoons until the dough forms a dumpling that holds its shape.

Once the dumpling has been shaped enough to hold together, drop the dumpling into the simmering water. Only cook as many at a time as you an easily retrieve without overcooking the others. Retrieve with a wire skimmer or slotted spoon.

MAKING OTHER DUMPLINGS

SPAETZLE

COOKING SPAETZLE

Place the dough in a colander held over simmering water. Use a flexible spatula to push the dough through the holes into the water. Cook until the spaeztle float to the surface, 3–4 minutes. Use a slotted spoon or wire skimmer to retrieve the spaetzle.

GYOZA

ASSEMBLING GYOZA

Place a teaspoonful of filling in the center of a wonton wrapper. Lightly brush the edges of the wrapper with water, and fold in half to form a half-moon. Make 4 or 5 pleats along the arc of the half-moon, pressing firmly to enclose the filling completely.

SHUMAI

ASSEMBLING SHUMAI

Place 1 heaping tablespoon of filling in the center of a wonton wrapper. Cup in your hand and, with the index finger and thumb of your other hand, pleat the top edge. Squeeze the dumpling gently in the center to indent slightly, and tap the bottom to flatten. Using the back of a teaspoon dipped in water, pack the filling gently and smooth the top.

POTATO GNOCCHI *with* ROASTED PEPPER SAUCE

Here, a simple combination of roasted red and yellow peppers, fruity olive oil, garlic, and basil provides a light sauce for these tender dumplings. To preserve the pretty colors of the peppers, do not use a food processor to chop them, as it will cause their colors to run together.

FOR THE SAUCE

½ cup *(4 fl oz/125 ml)* extra-virgin olive oil, plus more for baking sheet

1 large clove garlic, finely chopped or passed through a garlic press

2 yellow bell peppers

2 red bell peppers

6 fresh basil leaves, chopped

Fine sea salt and freshly ground pepper

Basic Potato Gnocchi *(page 176)*

Kosher salt for cooking gnocchi

¼ lb *(125 g)* aged Asiago cheese (optional)

To make the sauce, in a small bowl, combine the olive oil and garlic and let stand for about 1 hour to infuse the oil. Strain through a fine-mesh sieve and set the oil aside; discard the garlic.

Preheat the oven to 400°F (200°C). Oil a rimmed baking sheet with olive oil. Arrange the bell peppers on the baking sheet and roast, turning once halfway through cooking to color evenly, until they have collapsed and are blackened on all sides, 25–30 minutes.

When the peppers are cool enough to handle, peel off the skins, cut in half lengthwise, and remove and discard the stems, ribs, and seeds. Using a chef's knife or a *mezzaluna* (half-moon chopper), finely chop the peppers. Transfer to a bowl and add the infused olive oil and the basil. Season with sea salt and pepper and stir to mix well. Set aside.

You can begin making the gnocchi while the peppers are cooking. Make the dough as directed, then shape 1 dough portion into gnocchi as directed on page 177.

Select a large, wide, shallow serving platter, smear the bottom with a little of the sauce, and keep it warm in a 200°F (95°C) oven. In a large pot, bring 5 qt (5 l) water to a boil. Add 2 tablespoons kosher salt and the gnocchi and cook, stirring occasionally, until the gnocchi float to the top, about 3 minutes. Using a slotted spoon, lift out the cooked gnocchi, small batches at a time, drip-drying well over the pot, and transfer them to the serving dish, arranging them in a single layer. Cover loosely with aluminum foil and return the dish to the oven. Shape, cook, and drain the remaining gnocchi in the same way, and add them to the serving dish without layering them.

When all of the gnocchi have been cooked, spoon the pepper sauce over the gnocchi. If using the Asiago, use a vegetable peeler to shave the cheese over the top. Serve right away.

SERVES 6

SPAETZLE *with* BREAD CRUMBS

This simple, classic version of spaetzle is pure comfort food. The pea-sized dumplings are the perfect accompaniment to all sorts of meat dishes, from roasts to chops to saucy braises. An inexpensive spaetzle maker is customized for the task, but a standard colander works well, too.

1½ cups *(7½ oz/235 g)* unbleached all-purpose flour

⅛ teaspoon freshly grated nutmeg

Fine sea salt and freshly ground white or black pepper

3 extra-large eggs, beaten

2 tablespoons milk

Kosher salt for cooking spaetzle

4 tablespoons *(2 oz/60 g)* unsalted butter

¼ cup *(½ oz/15 g)* fresh bread crumbs, lightly toasted *(see page 233)*

To make the spaetzle, in a large bowl, combine the flour, nutmeg, a pinch of sea salt, and several grinds of pepper. In a separate bowl, whisk together the eggs and milk. Make a well in the center of the flour mixture and pour in the egg-milk mixture. Using your hands or a wooden spoon, gradually draw the flour mixture into the liquid and combine well. The dough should be smooth and thick. Let the dough rest for 10–15 minutes.

In a large pot, bring 3 qt (3 l) water to a rapid boil and add 1 tablespoon kosher salt. Reduce the heat slightly so the water is at a vigorous simmer.

If using a spaetzle maker, position it over the pot. Working in batches, add the dough to the hopper and slowly slide it back and forth to push the dough through the holes into the water.

If using a colander, hold it over the pot. Working in batches, add the dough to the colander and use a flexible spatula to push the dough through the holes into the water (see page 179).

Place a clean colander in the sink. Cook the spaetzle, stirring gently to prevent sticking, until they float to the surface, 3–4 minutes. Using a wire skimmer, transfer the spaetzle to the colander, rinse briefly under cold running water, drain again, and transfer to a large shallow bowl.

When all of the spaetzle are cooked, place a large frying pan over low heat and add the butter. When the butter has melted, add the crumbs and toss until lightly browned, about 1 minute. Add the spaetzle, toss to coat with the butter and crumbs, and sauté until lightly colored, about 2 minutes. Transfer to a warmed serving bowl and serve right away.

VEGETABLE DUMPLINGS *with* PONZU SAUCE

These delicate vegetable dumplings can be steamed, or fried like gyoza (page 186), and served with Soy-Ginger Sauce (page 232) or with tart Japanese *ponzu,* below. The steamed vegetable accompaniment makes this a beautiful plated meal. Alternatively, serve in broth as a soup course.

FOR THE PONZU SAUCE

¼ cup *(2 fl oz/60 ml)* fresh lime juice

¼ cup *(2 fl oz/60 ml)* fresh lemon juice

⅛ cup *(1 fl oz/30 ml)* fresh orange juice

⅛ cup *(1 fl oz/30 ml)* rice vinegar

½ cup *(4 fl oz/125 ml)* tamari or light soy sauce

⅛ cup *(1 fl oz/30 ml)* mirin

3 tablespoons dried bonito flakes

1-inch *(2.5-cm)* square piece of *kombu* (seaweed)

Pinch of cayenne pepper

FOR THE DUMPLINGS

2 tablespoons tamari or light soy sauce

½ teaspoon Asian sesame oil

3 tablespoons peanut or vegetable oil

1 large shallot, minced

1 teaspoon peeled and grated fresh ginger

1 pinch red pepper flakes, or to taste

1 small carrot, peeled and finely shredded

First, make the *ponzu* sauce. In a bowl, combine the lime juice, lemon juice, orange juice, vinegar, tamari, mirin, bonito, *kombu,* and cayenne and stir to mix well. Cover and let stand for at least 1 hour at room temperature or up to overnight in the refrigerator. Strain the sauce through a fine-mesh sieve placed over a bowl. Discard the solids. (The *ponzu* will keep, covered tightly, in the refrigerator for up to 4 days.)

To make the dumplings, in a large bowl, stir together the tamari and sesame oil. Set aside.

In a large frying pan, warm the peanut oil over medium heat. Add the shallot, ginger, and red pepper flakes and sauté until the shallot is translucent, about 4 minutes. Add the carrot and mushrooms and sauté until softened, 4–5 minutes. Stir in the spinach and toss to wilt lightly, about 1 minute. Remove from the heat.

Drain the noodles thoroughly and pat dry with paper towels. Spread on a cutting board and chop finely. You should have about 1 cup (6 oz/185 g).

Transfer the spinach mixture and the noodles to the bowl with the tamari–sesame oil mixture. Using your hands, toss to mix well. Taste and adjust the seasoning.

Work with 10 dumpling wrappers at a time, and keep the others covered with a damp kitchen towel. Lay the wrappers in a single layer on a work surface. Place a teaspoonful of filling in the center of each wrapper. Lightly brush the edge of the wrapper with water and fold in half to form a triangle, being sure to press out all the air before sealing to prevent the dumpling from inflating. Repeat to assemble the remaining dumplings.

Preheat the oven to 200°F (95°C). Place a large, wide, shallow serving platter in the oven to warm.

To steam the dumplings, select a bamboo or metal steamer insert. In a large pot, bring 2 inches (5 cm) of water to a simmer (make sure the water level will not reach the bottom of the steamer). Lightly oil the

3 oz *(90 g)* fresh oyster
mushrooms or shiitake
mushroom caps, minced

¼ lb *(125 g)* baby
spinach, stems removed,
finely chopped

1¼ oz *(37 g)* cellophane
(bean thread) noodles,
soaked in warm water
to cover until softened

About 40 square
wonton wrappers

Vegetable oil for greasing
steamer rack (optional)

8 tablespoons *(4 fl oz/125 ml)*
peanut oil for frying, or as
needed (optional)

1 bunch asparagus, trimmed

2 cups *(10 oz/315 g)* shelled
fresh or frozen baby peas

1 tablespoon snipped
fresh chives

steamer rack. Working in batches, arrange the dumplings on the rack
about 1 inch (2.5 cm) apart from one another. Place the steamer over
the simmering water and cover. Steam the dumplings until the filling
is firm and the wrapper is slightly translucent, 10–15 minutes. Remove the
steamer from the pot and, using a metal spatula, transfer the dumplings
to the platter in the oven. Steam the remaining dumplings in the same way.

To fry the dumplings, in a large nonstick frying pan over high heat,
warm 3 tablespoons of the peanut oil. When the oil is hot, add as many
dumplings as will fit comfortably in a single layer without crowding
and cook until browned on the first side, about 4 minutes. Using a metal
spatula, carefully flip the dumplings over and fry until browned on
the second side, about 2 minutes longer. Reduce the heat to low, add
4–5 tablespoons (2–3 fl oz/60–80 ml) water, cover tightly, and let
steam until the filling is cooked through and the water has evaporated,
about 5 minutes. Using the spatula, transfer the dumplings to the warmed
platter in the oven. Cook the remaining dumplings the same way.

While the last batch of dumplings is cooking, in a large saucepan
fitted with a steamer insert, bring 1 inch (2.5 cm) water to a boil over
medium-high heat. Snap the tough ends off the asparagus spears and use
a vegetable peeler to peel off the thick skin to within 2 inches (5 cm) of
the tips. Arrange the fresh peas and the asparagus on the steamer rack,
cover, and cook until tender, about 10 minutes. If using frozen peas, add
during the last 3 minutes of cooking time. Remove from the heat and
remove the steamer insert with the vegetables. Drain the pan, transfer the
vegetables from the steamer back to the pan, and cover to keep warm.

Remove the dumplings from the oven and serve right away, accompanied
by the steamed vegetables and garnished with the chives. Pass the *ponzu*
sauce at the table or serve it in individual dipping bowls.

Pork and Cabbage Gyoza

The origins of *gyoza* are Chinese, but the pot stickers were adopted in Japan, where they are even more popular. This recipe borrows from both traditions. *Gyoza* wrappers are sold at Asian markets and in the refrigerated section of many supermarkets. Do not use lean pork or the filling will be dry.

FOR THE FILLING

3 cups *(8 oz/250 g)* minced napa cabbage

Fine sea salt and freshly ground pepper

⅓ lb *(5 oz/155 g)* ground pork *(see Note)*

1 tablespoon peeled and minced fresh ginger

1 small carrot, peeled and finely shredded

9 green onions, including 1 inch *(2.5 cm)* of green tops, minced

3 tablespoons minced fresh cilantro

2 large cloves garlic, minced

1 tablespoon tamari or soy sauce

¼ teaspoon Asian sesame oil

2 teaspoons sesame seeds, lightly toasted

2 tablespoons lightly beaten egg

40 *gyoza* wrappers *(see Note)*

8 tablespoons *(4 fl oz/125 ml)* peanut oil for frying, or as needed

Soy-Ginger Sauce *(page 232)* for serving

To make the filling, place the cabbage in a colander in the sink and toss with ½ teaspoon sea salt. Top with a flat plate, and then with a heavy can or other weight and let drain for 30 minutes. Squeeze out as much water from the cabbage as possible.

In a large bowl, combine the cabbage, pork, ginger, carrot, green onions, cilantro, garlic, tamari, sesame oil, sesame seeds, egg, ¼ teaspoon sea salt, and a few grinds of pepper. Using your hands, mix to distribute the ingredients evenly.

Work with 10 *gyoza* wrappers at a time, and keep the others covered with a damp kitchen towel. Lay the wrappers in a single layer on a work surface. Place a teaspoonful of filling in the center of each wrapper. Lightly brush the edge of the wrapper with water, and fold the wrapper in half to form a half-moon. Then, holding the half-moon in one hand, use the thumb and index finger of your other hand to make 4 or 5 pleats along the arc of the half-moon, pressing firmly to enclose the filling completely (see page 179). Repeat to assemble the remaining *gyoza*.

Preheat the oven to 200°F (95°C). In a large nonstick frying pan over high heat, warm 3 tablespoons of the peanut oil. When the oil is hot, add as many dumplings as will fit comfortably in a single layer without crowding and sear until browned on the first side, about 4 minutes. Using a metal spatula, carefully flip the dumplings over and fry until browned on the second side, about 2 minutes longer. Reduce the heat to low, add 4–5 tablespoons (2–3 fl oz/60–80 ml) water, cover tightly, and let steam until the filling is cooked through and the water has evaporated, about 5 minutes. Using the spatula, transfer the dumplings to a heatproof platter and keep warm in the oven. Cook the remaining dumplings the same way.

Serve the *gyoza* hot, and pass the Soy-Ginger Sauce at the table or serve it in individual dipping bowls.

POTATO GNOCCHI *with* BEEF-CINNAMON SAUCE

Potato gnocchi are a specialty of the city of Verona, in the Veneto, where a festival is held at Carnival time each year to celebrate the dumpling. Here, they are paired with an eastern Mediterranean–influenced *ragù* spiced with cinnamon, coriander, and cloves.

FOR THE SAUCE

1 can *(28 oz/875 g)* plum tomatoes

2 tablespoons unsalted butter

1 tablespoon extra-virgin olive oil

2 oz *(60 g)* pancetta, finely diced

1 large clove garlic, minced

1 small yellow onion, chopped

1 small carrot, peeled and chopped

1 small celery stalk, including leaves, chopped

1 bay leaf

1 cinnamon stick, 3 inches *(7.5 cm)* long

Scant ½ teaspoon ground coriander

¼ teaspoon ground cloves

1½ lb *(750 g)* ground beef

½ cup *(4 fl oz/125 ml)* dry red wine

2 tablespoons tomato paste

Fine sea salt and freshly ground white or black pepper

Basic Potato Gnocchi *(page 176)*

Kosher salt for cooking gnocchi

To make the sauce, drain the tomatoes, reserving their juice. Strain the captured juice to hold back the seeds. Using your fingers, push out the excess seeds from the tomatoes, then chop and set aside with the juice. In a large saucepan over medium-low heat, melt the butter with the olive oil. Add the pancetta and sauté until golden, 7–9 minutes. Add the garlic, onion, carrot, celery, bay leaf, cinnamon stick, coriander, and cloves; reduce the heat to low and cook, stirring occasionally, until the vegetables have softened, 12–15 minutes. Add the beef and cook, breaking up any clumps with a wooden spoon and stirring as needed, until lightly colored, 5–7 minutes. Add the wine and cook until most of the alcohol has evaporated, about 3 minutes. Stir in the tomato paste and cook, stirring occasionally, for 2–3 minutes. Add the tomatoes and their juice, ¾ teaspoon sea salt, and several grinds of pepper; cover partially and simmer gently, stirring occasionally, until the sauce thickens and is aromatic, about 1½ hours. If the pan begins to dry out, add a few tablespoons of water to moisten. Remove from the heat and remove and discard the bay leaf and cinnamon stick. Cover and set aside.

When the sauce is almost done, make the gnocchi dough as directed, then shape 1 dough portion into gnocchi as directed on page 177.

Select a large, wide, shallow serving platter, smear the bottom with a little of the sauce, and keep it warm in a 200°F (95°C) oven. In a large pot, bring 5 qt (5 l) water to a boil. Add 2 tablespoons kosher salt and the gnocchi and cook, stirring occasionally, until the gnocchi float to the top, about 3 minutes. Using a slotted spoon, lift out the cooked gnocchi, small batches at a time, drip-drying well over the pot, and transfer them to the serving dish, arranging them in a single layer. Cover loosely with aluminum foil and return the dish to the oven. Shape, cook, and drain the remaining gnocchi in the same way, and add them to the serving dish without layering them.

Just before the final batch of gnocchi is ready, reheat the sauce. Spoon the sauce over the gnocchi. Serve right away.

CHICKEN DUMPLINGS *with* SOY-GINGER SAUCE

Here is a Chinese-inspired dumpling that uses dark chicken meat to ensure the filling is moist and flavorful. See the Note on page 194 for a tip on how to cook all the dumplings at once. For a spicier dipping sauce, you can add thin slices of fresh chile to the Soy-Ginger Sauce to taste.

FOR THE FILLING

1 lb *(500 g)* ground dark chicken meat

2 tablespoons minced fresh cilantro

3 tablespoons minced green onion

1 tablespoon dry sherry

1 teaspoon Asian sesame oil

1 teaspoon sugar

Fine sea salt and freshly ground pepper

30 round dumpling wrappers

Napa cabbage leaves for lining steamer

Soy-Ginger Sauce *(page 232)* for serving

To make the filling, in a bowl, combine the chicken, cilantro, green onion, sherry, sesame oil, sugar, ¾ teaspoon sea salt, and ¼ teaspoon pepper and stir until the mixture has a smooth, even consistency.

Work with 1 dumpling wrapper at a time, and keep the others covered with a damp kitchen towel. Place a wrapper in the palm of one hand and place 1 heaping tablespoon of filling in the center of the wrapper. Lightly brush the edge of the wrapper with water, and fold in half over the filling to form a half-moon. Still holding the half-moon, use the thumb and index finger of your other hand to make 4 or 5 pleats along the round edge of the half-moon, pinching well to seal (see page 179). Repeat with the remaining filling and wrappers to make 24 dumplings. (The extra dumpling wrappers allow you to lose a few while practicing.)

Pour water to a depth of 2 inches (5 cm) into a wok or large, wide saucepan and bring to a boil over high heat. Line a bamboo steamer basket or a plate with a single layer of cabbage leaves, and top with half of the dumplings, spacing them about ½ inch (12 mm) apart. Place the basket in the wok or on top of the pan, or place the plate on a steamer rack in the wok or pan. Make sure the steaming water does not touch the basket or plate. Cover tightly and steam until the wrappers are translucent and the filling can be seen through the wrapper, about 6 minutes. Transfer the dumplings to a large, wide, shallow serving platter and keep warm in a 200°F (95°C) oven while you steam the remaining dumplings.

When all the dumplings are cooked, serve right away with the Soy-Ginger Sauce.

BUTTERNUT SQUASH GNUDI *with* SAGE BUTTER

The Italian name for these light, fluffy dumplings translates to "nude" in English because they resemble the filling of ravioli without the pasta wrapper. Enjoy this dish as is, or serve with roast chicken and an Italian red wine for a warming meal when the weather turns cold.

Olive oil for brushing

1 butternut squash, about 3 lb *(1.5 kg)*

2 large eggs, lightly beaten

¼ teaspoon freshly grated nutmeg

Fine sea salt and freshly ground white pepper

2 cups *(10 oz/315 g)* unbleached all-purpose flour, sifted

½ cup *(4 oz/125 g)* unsalted butter, clarified *(see page 233)*

10 fresh sage leaves

Kosher salt for cooking *gnudi*

⅓ cup *(1½ oz/45 g)* freshly grated Parmigiano-Reggiano cheese

Preheat the oven to 450°F (230°C). Line a rimmed baking sheet with parchment paper and brush the surface lightly with olive oil. Cut the squash in half lengthwise and place the halves, cut side down, on the prepared baking sheet. Using a sharp paring knife, poke the skin of each half in a few places to create steam holes. Bake until the halves have begun to collapse and are thoroughly tender when pierced with the knife, 40–50 minutes. Remove from the oven and, when cool enough to handle, scoop out and discard the seeds and fibers. Using a large spoon, scoop out the flesh and pass it through a ricer or food mill into a bowl, or place the flesh in a bowl and mash with a potato masher until smooth. (The squash purée can be covered and refrigerated for up to 3 days before continuing.)

Add the eggs, nutmeg, 1 teaspoon sea salt, and several grinds of pepper to the squash and mix well. Slowly re-sift the flour into the squash mixture while stirring with a wooden spoon, and continue to stir until well mixed. Cover and refrigerate for at least 1 hour or up to overnight. The mixture will be very soft but cohesive enough to form *gnudi*.

In a large pot, bring 5 qt (5 l) water to a rapid boil.

Add the clarified butter to a frying pan large enough to hold the cooked *gnudi* later and place over medium-low heat. Add the sage and warm until aromatic and the butter is infused with the flavor of the sage, about 4 minutes. Remove from the heat and cover to keep warm.

Add 1 tablespoon kosher salt to the boiling water. Follow the directions on page 178 to form the *gnudi*. Cook as many *gnudi* as you can right away without breaking the boil, and adjust the heat as needed to prevent the *gnudi* from knocking against one another and breaking. When the *gnudi* rise to the surface, after about 1 minute, use a slotted spoon or wire skimmer to transfer them to the frying pan with the sage butter. Repeat until all of the *gnudi* are cooked. Turn the *gnudi* in the butter to coat evenly, then transfer them to a warmed platter or individual plates. Serve right away, passing the cheese at the table.

SPAETZLE *with* LAMB RAGÙ

The recipe for this winy Apulian *ragù* is inspired by one from Italian food expert Ann Amendolara Nurse. Originally used as a sauce for pasta, its pleasantly acidic edge marries deliciously with tender spaetzle in this hearty dish. Use the freshest lamb shank you can find, which will be pink and fat.

FOR THE RAGÙ

2 cans *(28 oz/875 g each)* plum tomatoes

½ cup *(4 fl oz/125 ml)* extra-virgin olive oil

4 meaty lamb shanks *(1–1¼ lb/500–625 g) (see Note)*

4 cloves garlic, bruised *(see page 233)*

1 large yellow onion, chopped

¾ cup *(6 fl oz/180 ml)* dry red wine

¾ cup *(6 oz/185 g)* tomato paste

Fine sea salt

Pinch of red pepper flakes

5 large fresh basil leaves

FOR THE SPAETZLE

1½ cups *(7½ oz/235 g)* unbleached all-purpose flour

⅛ teaspoon freshly grated nutmeg

Fine sea salt and freshly ground white or black pepper

3 extra-large eggs, beaten

2 tablespoons milk

Kosher salt for cooking spaetzle

2 tablespoons unsalted butter

To make the *ragù,* pass the tomatoes and their juice through a food mill or fine-mesh sieve directly into a pot large enough to accommodate the shanks later. Bring to a boil over medium-high heat, then reduce the heat to low to maintain a gentle simmer.

In a frying pan large enough to accommodate the lamb shanks comfortably, warm the olive oil over medium-high heat. When the oil is hot, add the shanks and brown on all sides, turning as needed to color them evenly, about 15 minutes. Transfer the shanks to the pot with the tomatoes. Drain off all but ⅓ cup (3 fl oz/80 ml) oil from the pan. Add the garlic to the remaining oil in the pan and sauté over medium-low heat until golden, 1–2 minutes. Using a slotted spoon, transfer the garlic to the pot with the lamb and tomatoes. Add the onion to the oil and sauté over medium-low heat until softened and golden, 10–15 minutes. Raise the heat to medium, pour in the wine, and simmer until most of the alcohol has evaporated, about 3 minutes. Add the tomato paste to the pan and stir, using a wooden spoon to scrape up any browned bits stuck to the bottom of the pan. Sauté for 5 minutes to allow the flavors to blend.

Add the onion mixture, 1 teaspoon sea salt, and the red pepper flakes to the pot of simmering tomatoes and lamb and stir well. Cover partially and simmer, stirring occasionally, until the meat is tender but not yet falling off the bones, no longer than 1½ hours. Keep an eye on the heat to be sure the sauce bubbles gently and steadily as it simmers; it should not bubble vigorously. Stir in the basil. Taste and adjust the seasoning. Remove from the heat and cover to keep warm.

While the *ragù* is cooking, make the spaetzle dough. In a large bowl, combine the flour, nutmeg, and a pinch each of sea salt and pepper. In a separate bowl, whisk together the eggs and milk. Make a well in the center of the flour mixture and pour in the egg-milk mixture. Using your hands or a wooden spoon, gradually draw the flour mixture into the liquid and combine well. The dough should be smooth and thick. Let the dough rest for 10–15 minutes.

The light, fluffy dumplings known as *spätzle* in Germany, Austria, and the German-speaking parts of Switzerland, are also popular in Hungary where they are called *galuska, nokedli,* or *csipetke.*

In a large pot, bring 3 qt (3 l) water to a rapid boil and add 1 tablespoon kosher salt. Reduce the heat slightly so the water is at a vigorous simmer.

If using a spaetzle maker, position it over the pot. Working in batches, add the dough to the hopper and slowly slide it back and forth to push the dough through the holes into the water.

If using a colander, hold it over the pot. Working in batches, add the dough to the colander and use a flexible spatula to push the dough through the holes into the water (see page 179).

Place a clean colander in the sink. Cook the spaetzle, stirring gently to prevent sticking, until they float to the surface, 3–4 minutes. Using a wire skimmer, transfer the spaetzle to the colander, rinse briefly under cold running water, drain again, and transfer to a large shallow bowl.

When all of the spaetzle are cooked, reheat the *ragù* gently.

Place a large frying pan over medium-low heat and add the butter. When the butter has melted, add the spaetzle, toss to coat with the butter, and sauté until lightly colored, about 2 minutes. Transfer the spaetzle to a warmed serving bowl, and transfer the *ragù,* with the lamb still clinging to the shank bones, to a second warmed serving bowl. (Alternatively, remove the shanks from the sauce, shred the meat, and return the shredded meat to the sauce; discard the shank bones.) Serve right away.

SERVES 4–6

SHRIMP AND PORK SHUMAI

Shumai are traditional fare on the Chinese *dim sum* table. In this version, the preparation is simplified with purchased dumpling wrappers (sometimes labeled *shumai* wrappers). If you have two bamboo steamer baskets (or a two-tiered metal steamer), you can steam all of the dumplings at once.

FOR THE FILLING

½ lb *(250 g)* boneless pork loin, ground

¼ cup *(1½ oz/45 g)* minced raw shrimp

1½ oz *(45 g)* pork fatback, minced

2 oz *(60 g)* fresh shiitake or oyster mushrooms, brushed clean and tough stems removed, minced

2 tablespoons minced bamboo shoot

1 tablespoon peeled and finely grated fresh ginger

1½ tablespoons cornstarch

1 tablespoon dry sherry

2 teaspoons Asian sesame oil

1 teaspoon sugar

Fine sea salt and freshly ground pepper

30 round dumpling wrappers *(see Note)*

Napa cabbage leaves for lining steamer

Soy-Ginger Sauce *(page 232)* for serving

To make the filling, in a bowl, combine the pork, shrimp, fatback, mushrooms, bamboo shoot, and ginger and toss briefly to combine. Add the cornstarch, sherry, sesame oil, sugar, ¾ teaspoon salt, and ¼ teaspoon pepper and stir until the mixture has a smooth, even consistency.

Working with 1 dumpling wrapper at a time, and keeping the others covered with a damp kitchen towel, follow the instructions on page 179 to assemble the *shumai*. Repeat with the remaining filling and wrappers to make 24 dumplings. (The extra dumpling wrappers allow you to lose a few while practicing.)

Pour water to a depth of 2 inches (5 cm) into a wok or a large, wide saucepan and bring to a boil over high heat. Line a bamboo steamer basket or a plate with a single layer of cabbage leaves, and top with half of the dumplings, spacing them about ½ inch (12 mm) apart. Place the basket in the wok or on top of the pan, or place the plate on a steamer rack in the wok or pan. Make sure the steaming water does not touch the basket or plate. Cover tightly and steam until the wrapper is translucent and the visible filling is opaque, about 6 minutes. Transfer the dumplings to a large, wide, shallow serving platter and keep warm in a 200°F (95°C) oven while you steam the remaining dumplings.

Serve the dumplings right away. Pass the Soy-Ginger Sauce at the table or serve it in individual dipping bowls.

RICOTTA SPOON GNOCCHI *with* TOMATO SAUCE

These gnocchi are easy to make, as long as care is taken to drain the ricotta well—much longer than for other fillings. The drier the ricotta, the less flour needed to hold the dough together, and the lighter the dumpling. The acidity of the tomato sauce is a nice contrast to the creamy gnocchi.

FOR THE GNOCCHI

2 lb *(1 kg)* whole-milk ricotta cheese

¼ cup *(1 oz/30 g)* freshly grated Parmigiano-Reggiano or grana padano cheese

2 tablespoons chopped fresh basil

1 tablespoon chopped fresh flat-leaf parsley

¾ cup *(4 oz/125 g)* unbleached all-purpose flour, or as needed

Fine sea salt

⅛ teaspoon freshly grated nutmeg

Simple Tomato Sauce *(page 232)*

Kosher salt for cooking gnocchi

6 large fresh basil leaves, torn into pieces, plus basil leaves for garnish

3 tablespoons unsalted butter, at room temperature, or extra-virgin olive oil

Freshly grated Parmigiano-Reggiano cheese for serving

To make the gnocchi, place the ricotta in a fine-mesh sieve set over a bowl. Cover and refrigerate for at least 1 day and up to 2 days to drain off as much excess moisture as possible. The drained cheese should have a firm consistency.

To finish the gnocchi dough, transfer the ricotta to a bowl and discard the liquid. Add the grated cheese, basil, parsley, flour, 1 teaspoon sea salt, and nutmeg. Using a wooden spoon, stir until well blended.

Place a large, wide, shallow serving platter in a 200°F (95°C) oven to warm. In a large pot, bring 5 qt (5 l) water to a boil. While the water heats, make the tomato sauce as directed and set aside.

When the water is boiling, add 2 tablespoons kosher salt and reduce to a simmer. Using a small spoon, scoop up enough of the dough to form a dumpling about the size of a walnut, then use a second spoon to nudge the dumpling into the simmering water. When it floats to the surface, after 30–45 seconds, retrieve it with a wire skimmer or slotted spoon. If the dumpling holds together nicely, proceed to make the gnocchi. If the dumpling is too soft, add flour as needed to the dough to make a dumpling firm enough to hold its shape. Be careful not to add more flour than is necessary, or the dumplings will be heavy. Cook the gnocchi, dropping in only as many at a time as you can easily retrieve without overcooking the others; transfer the gnocchi to the platter as they are finished, arranging them in a single layer, and returning the dish to the oven between batches.

While the gnocchi are cooking, gently reheat the tomato sauce; remove from the heat. Add the torn basil and the butter to the sauce and stir to mix. Spoon the sauce over the gnocchi and garnish with the additional basil leaves. Serve right away. Pass the cheese at the table.

BREAD GNOCCHI *in* BRODO

These bread gnocchi, served in a rich broth, come from the northern Italian regions. They are reminiscent of dumplings served in Austria and throughout eastern Europe. Be sure to use a sturdy artisanal bread that is a couple of days old to achieve the best texture.

1 cup *(8 fl oz/250 ml)* milk

4 large eggs

1 large egg white

Fine sea salt and freshly ground white or black pepper

½ lb *(250 g)* two-day-old artisanal bread, or as needed, crusts removed and finely torn

3 tablespoons unsalted butter

1 large yellow onion, finely minced

¼ lb *(125 g)* thinly sliced prosciutto, chopped

2 tablespoons olive oil–packed sun-dried tomatoes, minced

¼ cup *(1½ oz/45 g)* unbleached all-purpose flour, or as needed

3 tablespoons chopped fresh flat-leaf parsley

2 teaspoons minced fresh thyme, or 1 teaspoon crumbled dried thyme

2 qt *(2 l)* low-sodium chicken or beef broth

Freshly grated Parmigiano-Reggiano cheese for serving

In a large bowl, whisk together the milk, eggs, egg white, and ½ teaspoon sea salt until well blended. Add the bread to the bowl and let stand until the bread is thoroughly moistened, about 5 minutes. If there is liquid remaining in the bowl, add additional bread as needed until all of the liquid has been absorbed. Use your hands as needed to work together the bread and liquid until it forms a cohesive mixture.

While the bread is soaking, in a frying pan over medium-low heat, melt the butter. Add the onion and sauté, stirring occasionally, until thoroughly softened, about 6 minutes. Add the prosciutto and tomatoes and continue to sauté for 2 minutes to allow the flavors to blend. Remove from the heat.

Add the onion mixture, flour, parsley, thyme, and a few grinds of pepper to the bread mixture and mix well with your hands. The mixture should be moist but cohesive.

Pour the broth into a large saucepan, place over medium-high heat, and bring to a boil. Cover partially to prevent excessive evaporation.

Meanwhile, using your palms, form a scoop of the bread mixture into a round gnocchi about 1 inch (2.5 cm) in diameter. When the broth is boiling, drop in the gnocchi. If it does not hold its shape, add a little more flour to the mixture, mixing it in well, and then test again. If it holds its shape, form the remaining mixture into 2-inch (5-cm) round gnocchi. To cook, add the gnocchi to the simmering broth all at once and cook until they float to the surface, 3–4 minutes.

Remove from the heat and ladle the gnocchi and broth into warmed shallow bowls. Serve right away. Pass the cheese at the table.

POTATO GNOCCHI *with* MIXED HERB PESTO

This twist on basic basil pesto brings together a trio of harmonious herbs. To make the sauce in advance, prepare as directed, omitting the cheese, salt, and butter. Cover tightly and refrigerate for up to 5 days or freeze for up to 3 months. Just before using, whisk in the cheese, salt, and butter.

FOR THE MIXED HERB PESTO

Kosher salt for blanching basil

2 cups *(2 oz/60 g)* firmly packed fresh basil leaves

¼ cup *(¼ oz/7 g)* firmly packed fresh parsley leaves

1 teaspoon chopped fresh thyme

3 cloves garlic, coarsely chopped

⅓ cup *(2 oz/60 g)* pine nuts, lightly toasted

½ cup *(4 fl oz/125 ml)* extra-virgin olive oil

Fine sea salt and freshly ground pepper

½ cup *(2 oz/60 g)* freshly grated Parmigiano-Reggiano cheese

2 tablespoons unsalted butter, at room temperature

Basic Potato Gnocchi *(page 176)*

Kosher salt for cooking gnocchi

Freshly grated Parmigiano-Reggiano cheese for serving

To make the pesto, have ready a bowl filled with ice water. In a saucepan, bring 4 cups (32 fl oz/1 l) water to a boil and add 2 teaspoons kosher salt and the basil leaves. Using a wire skimmer or other wide, flat strainer, stir the basil and then press on it to keep it submerged for 30 seconds. Drain immediately and transfer to the ice water to halt the cooking. Squeeze the leaves to remove excess water, then chop coarsely.

In a food processor, combine the basil, parsley, thyme, garlic, pine nuts, olive oil, ½ teaspoon sea salt, and a few grinds of pepper. Process until smooth, stopping the machine once or twice to scrape down the sides of the bowl. Add the cheese and the butter and process for about 15 seconds. Scrape down the sides again, then process for a few seconds longer. Be careful not to overprocess; the consistency of the pesto should be thick and fluid and have a slightly grainy texture. Transfer to a bowl, taste and adjust the seasoning, and set aside.

Make the gnocchi dough as directed, then shape 1 dough portion into gnocchi as directed on page 177.

Preheat the oven to 200°F (95°C) and place a large, wide, shallow serving platter in it to warm. In a large pot, bring 5 qt (5 l) water to a boil. Add 2 tablespoons kosher salt and the gnocchi and cook, stirring occasionally, until the gnocchi float to the top, about 3 minutes. Using a slotted spoon, lift out the cooked gnocchi, small batches at a time, drip-drying well over the pot, and transfer them to the serving dish, arranging them in a single layer. Cover loosely with aluminum foil and return the dish to the oven. Shape, cook, and drain the remaining gnocchi in the same way, and add them to the serving dish without layering them.

Stir about 1 tablespoon of the gnocchi cooking water into the pesto to make a saucy consistency. Spoon the sauce over the gnocchi and sprinkle with a little grated cheese. Serve right away, and pass the additional cheese at the table.

SPINACH-RICOTTA GNUDI *with* FRESH TOMATO SAUCE

These *gnudi* showcase the classic Italian combination of spinach and ricotta. They are not the simplest dumplings to make, and it takes practice to achieve the proper texture for the mixture, which needs to be soft, yet firm and compact. The results, however, are well worth the effort.

FOR THE GNUDI

¾ cup *(6 oz/185 g)* whole-milk ricotta cheese

1 lb *(500 g)* spinach

1 large egg, beaten

⅔ cup *(2½ oz/75 g)* freshly grated Parmigiano-Reggiano or grana padano cheese

¾–1 cup *(4–5 oz/125–155 g)* unbleached all-purpose flour, or as needed

¼ teaspoon freshly grated nutmeg

Fine sea salt and freshly ground pepper

FOR THE SAUCE

2½ lb *(1.25 kg)* fresh plum tomatoes, peeled and seeded *(see page 233)*

⅓ cup *(3 fl oz/80 ml)* extra-virgin olive oil

6 cloves garlic, bruised *(see page 233)*

Fine sea salt and freshly ground white or black pepper

Kosher salt for cooking *gnudi*

Freshly grated Parmigiano-Reggiano for serving

To make the *gnudi,* place the ricotta in a fine-mesh sieve set over a bowl. Cover and refrigerate for at least 1 day and up to 2 days to drain off as much excess moisture as possible. The drained cheese should have a firm consistency. This is an important step because if the ricotta is too wet, the *gnudi* will disintegrate during cooking or will absorb too much flour and be heavy.

Trim off the stems from the spinach. Rinse the leaves thoroughly, and then place them in a large, deep frying pan or other pot with a tight-fitting lid with only the water clinging to them. Cover, place over medium-low heat, and cook, stirring several times, until tender, 5–10 minutes. The timing will depend on the freshness and tenderness of the spinach. Remove from the heat and let cool. Squeeze out the excess water; this step is very important, as the drier the spinach the less flour the *gnudi* will absorb and the lighter the dumplings will be. Chop the leaves and set aside.

Preheat the oven to 200°F (95°C) and place a large, wide, shallow serving platter in it to warm. In a large pot, bring 5 qt (5 l) water to a rapid boil.

While the water is heating, make the sauce. Coarsely chop the tomatoes, place in a colander in the sink, and let drain for 5 minutes. In a saucepan over medium heat, warm the olive oil. Add the garlic and sauté, pressing with the back of a wooden spoon to release its juices, until it takes on a rich golden color but has not yet turned brown, 1–2 minutes. Remove and discard the garlic and immediately add the tomatoes, ½ teaspoon sea salt, and season to taste with pepper. Using a fork or potato masher, press down on the tomatoes to break them up until they are in fairly fine pieces. Raise the heat to high and bring the tomatoes to a simmer. Reduce the heat to medium-low and continue to simmer, stirring occasionally, until the tomatoes form a thick sauce, about 20 minutes. Remove from the heat and set aside.

SPOON GNOCCHI VARIATION

Instead of forming this mixture into neatly shaped *gnudi,* you can make the more irregular-shaped spoon gnocchi. Using a teaspoon, take enough of the filling to make a dumpling approximately the size of a walnut. Working over simmering water, use another teaspoon to nudge the dumpling into the water. Cook as directed for *gnudi.*

To finish the *gnudi* dough, transfer the ricotta to a bowl and discard the liquid. Add the spinach, egg, grated cheese, flour, nutmeg, 1 teaspoon sea salt, and a few grinds of pepper. Stir until well blended.

When the water is boiling, add 1 tablespoon kosher salt to the boiling water. Follow the directions on page 178 to form the *gnudi.* Cook as many *gnudi* as you can right away without breaking the boil, and adjust the heat as needed to prevent the *gnudi* from knocking against one another and breaking. When the *gnudi* rise to the surface, after about 1 minute, use a slotted spoon or wire skimmer to transfer them to the platter in the oven. Repeat until all of the *gnudi* are cooked.

Reheat the sauce over medium-low heat. When all of the *gnudi* are cooked and arranged on the platter, drizzle with the sauce and serve right away. Pass the cheese at the table.

ASIAN NOODLES

ABOUT ASIAN NOODLES

Asian noodles form a diverse family: wiry rice sticks, translucent "glass" noodles; coiled green tea noodles; wide, flat, opaque rice noodles; pale yellow, rodlike egg noodles; thick, white udon; and thin, pale brown soba, to name only a few. Asian ingredients, including noodles, are widely available today, making it easier than ever to cook Asian food at home. The recipes in this chapter reflect the rich traditions of the Asian kitchen.

TYPES OF ASIAN NOODLES

Noodles are as ubiquitous and loved in Asian cuisine as pasta is in Italian cuisine. From China to Vietnam, Japan to Thailand, noodles are fashioned primarily from flour or starch made from wheat, rice, buckwheat, or legumes, served both hot and cold, and turn up in soups, stir-fries, braises, and salads. Many of the different types are sold both fresh and dried, and either can be used in most recipes. Because the sheer variety of Asian noodles can make describing them difficult, and the same noodle can have more than one name, they are divided here by the primary ingredient used to make them.

Wheat noodles, available both dried and fresh, come flat and round and can be as thin as thread or as thick as window-shade cord, with most of them somewhere in between. Some contain egg; others are flavored with shrimp or crab. Chinese noodles, both with egg and without, and Japanese udon and ramen are among the best known. Chinese wheat noodles are particularly versatile, used in soups, stir-fries, braised in clay pots, and panfried. Ramen and udon are primarily served in broth, but the latter also occasionally appears sukiyaki style, with meat and vegetables, or cold, with a dipping sauce.

Buckwheat flour, mixed with a smaller proportion of wheat flour, is used to make pale brown, square-cut, thin Japanese soba, sold both fresh and dried. Green soba, which includes powdered green tea in the dough, has a pleasantly bitter flavor. Soba is traditionally served cold with a dipping sauce or hot in broth. It can also be stir-fried, as it is in Stir-Fried Soba Noodles with Beef and Cabbage (page 220).

Noodles made from rice, which are routinely used by both Chinese and Southeast Asian cooks, are sold in Asian markets and many supermarkets. They come in a variety of sizes, from thin, wiry dried rice vermicelli to fresh or dried flat noodles ¼ inch (6 mm) or ½ inch (12 mm) wide. You can also purchase wide, fresh rice-noodle sheets that can be cut into noodles of any width, as well as long, round fresh rice noodles similar to spaghetti.

Cellophane noodles, also known as glass noodles, are made from a variety of plant starches, but they are most typically based on mung bean starch, which accounts for yet another common name, bean thread noodles. They are thin and brittle when dried, and turn translucent when rehydrated. Cellophane noodles, which readily absorb the flavors of the dish in which they are used, are popular additions to braised dishes, such as Cellophane Noodles with Spinach and Carrots (page 227), or to quick stir-fries, such as Cellophane Noodles with Shrimp and Garlic (page 219).

WORKING WITH FRESH NOODLES

If possible, use fresh rice noodles the day they are purchased and keep them at room temperature, so they are soft and supple enough to combine with other ingredients. Use your fingers to gently loosen and separate them just before using. If they have been refrigerated or do not separate easily, immerse them in a bowl of warm water for about 1 minute, loosen them with your fingers, and then drain. Because fresh rice noodles are made from a batter and thus already cooked, they require little cooking time, and are often added to dishes toward the end of cooking just to warm through.

Fresh wheat and buckwheat noodles are often liberally dusted with cornstarch before packaging to prevent them from sticking together. Just before cooking them in rapidly boiling salted water, shake them gently to separate them and remove some of the cornstarch. Cooking times are included in the recipes, but you should also check the packages for times and begin checking for doneness about a minute in advance of the suggested times.

WORKING WITH DRIED NOODLES

Similar to Italian pasta, dried Asian noodles take significantly longer to cook than fresh noodles. Cook dried wheat and buckwheat noodles in plenty of rapidly boiling salted water. As with their fresh noodle counterparts, take note of the cooking times in both the recipes and on the packages and begin checking in advance of the suggested times. Some dried rice noodles are also cooked in boiling salted water. Other dried rice noodles, especially rice vermicelli, and cellophane noodles need only be rehydrated in hot water until fully softened, usually about 20 minutes. They are then drained, added to a dish, and cooked just until they are heated through and have absorbed the flavors and usually some of the liquid of the dish.

Both rice vermicelli and cellophane noodles can also be deep-fried—they puff up within seconds of being immersed in hot oil—and used as a garnish. If you are using them this way, add them to the oil directly from the package.

SEASONING AND SERVING

The vast Asian pantry provides a wealth of potent flavors, such as soy sauce, fish sauce, garlic, onions, shallots, and ginger, and Asian cooks are masters of blending them harmoniously in noodle dishes. For example, in Rice Noodles with Shrimp and Cashews (page 215), a robust mix of Thai curry paste, garlic, chiles, and cilantro seasons the shrimp and noodles without overpowering either main ingredient. The same is true in Sweet and Sour Noodles (page 213), where a lively fusion of fish sauce, shallots, ginger, chile, tamarind, lime, basil, and mint complements, rather than buries, the noodles and seafood. Some noodles are tossed with a piquant sauce just before serving, such as in Rice Noodle Salad with Grilled Steak (page 222), and then additional sauce is passed at the table for dipping.

Authentic recipes for Asian noodles can sometimes have long, daunting ingredient lists. These recipes have pared down the ingredients for ease, but if you cannot get ahold of something, you can still successfully make most dishes by using ingredients you have on hand and adjusting the seasoning with the Asian condiments already in your pantry. Spiciness is a common feature of Asian cuisine, especially in the cooking of the Sichuan province of China. The recipes in this chapter use a moderate amount of spice in the form of fresh chiles, dried red pepper flakes, and Asian chile oil, but if you prefer spicier dishes, you can increase the amount of these ingredients to suit your taste.

The recipe yields in this chapter are for main-course portions, even though many of the dishes call for a smaller amount of noodles than is used in other recipes in this book. This is because the noodles are generally tossed with many more ingredients, which bulks up the overall serving size. You can always adjust the amount of noodles used to achieve the desired noodle-to-ingredient-and-sauce-ratio.

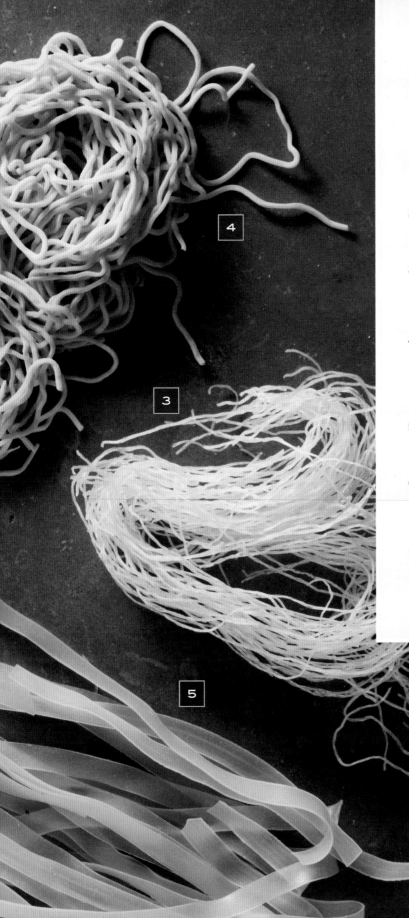

ASIAN NOODLE SHAPES

1 **DRIED SOBA NOODLES** These square-cut Japanese buckwheat noodles are made with varying amounts of buckwheat flour, accounting for a range of light to dark colors.

2 **FRESH RICE NOODLES** Fresh rice noodles are sold both pre-cut and in sheets, and are often served in broth.

3 **CELLOPHANE NOODLES** Also called bean thread, mung bean, or glass noodles, cellophane noodles are made from mung beans and turn clear when cooked.

4 **FRESH SOBA NOODLES** These fresh buckwheat noodles are harder to find than their dried counterpart, but they are easy to make at home and have a pleasant earthy flavor and chewy texture.

5 **DRIED RICE NOODLES** Dried rice noodles, often added to stir-fried noodle dishes, are most commonly found ½ inch (12 mm) wide.

6 **CHINESE EGG NOODLES** Available both fresh and dried, these versatile noodles are used in a variety of cooking methods from stir-frying to deep-frying.

7 **UDON NOODLES** These wide Japanese wheat noodles, available both dried and fresh, are most often served in hearty soups.

MAKING FRESH SOBA NOODLES

INGREDIENTS

1¼ cups (6 oz/185 g) Japanese
buckwheat flour

¾ cup (4 oz/125 g) unbleached
all-purpose flour, plus more
for dusting

2 teaspoons kosher salt dissolved
in ½ cup (4 fl oz/125 ml) water

MAKES ABOUT 1 LB (500 G)

1 MAKE THE DOUGH

Fit a food processor with the metal blade
and add both of the flours to the work
bowl. Turn on the machine and pour
the salt-water mixture through the feed
tube. Process just until the mixture forms
a ball of dough on top of the blade, about
30 seconds, adding 1–2 tablespoons
more water, if needed.

2 KNEAD THE DOUGH

Transfer the dough to a lightly floured
work surface. Use the heel of one hand
to push the dough away from you, then
rotate it a quarter turn. Repeat, dusting
with flour, until the dough feels damp
but not sticky, 1–2 minutes. Shape into
a ball, cover with an overturned bowl,
and let rest for 30 minutes.

3 ROLL OUT THE DOUGH

Divide the dough into 4 pieces. Slip 3 of
the pieces back under the bowl. Set the
rollers of a pasta machine at the widest
setting and dust with flour. Crank the
dough piece through the machine. Fold
into thirds and repeat. Repeat, moving
the dial 1 notch narrower after each
pass. Stop at the second-to-last setting.

4 CUT INTO SECTIONS

5 CUT INTO NOODLES

6 LET THE NOODLES DRY

Cut the pasta sheet into sections about 10 inches (25 cm) long. Lay the sections flat on a floured baking sheet, layering them as needed and separating the layers with floured kitchen towels. Repeat step 3 to roll out the remaining dough pieces. Let the sections dry for 10–20 minutes before cutting.

Secure the taglierini attachment (see page 13) onto the pasta machine and attach the crank. One at a time, insert a section of dough into the taglierini cutting blades and turn the crank to pass it through, creating strands about $\frac{1}{16}$ inch (2 mm) wide.

Spread the soba noodles out onto a lightly floured rimmed baking sheet and let dry for 10–20 minutes. Cook right away or coil into nests and let dry for up to 3 hours.

SOBA NOODLES *with* BELL PEPPER AND MANGO

Here is an improvisational dish for those who like the melding of sweet and savory. Earthy buckwheat noodles and salty peanuts meet the bright, sweet notes of mango, bell pepper, lemon zest, basil, and mint. A savory dressing with a hint of honey pulls the diverse flavors together.

FOR THE DRESSING

¾ cup *(6 fl oz/180 ml)* rice vinegar

¼ cup *(2 fl oz/60 ml)* peanut oil

1 tablespoon honey

1 tablespoon prepared hot Chinese mustard

FOR THE SALAD

Kosher salt for blanching cabbage and cooking noodles

1 head napa cabbage, about 2 lb *(1 kg)*, cored and shredded

6 green onions, including 2 inches *(5 cm)* of green tops, thinly sliced on the diagonal

1 jalapeño chile, seeded and minced

1 lb *(500 g)* fresh *(page 208)* or ¾ lb *(375 g)* dried soba noodles

1 firm yet ripe mango

Grated zest of 1 lemon

3 tablespoons fresh lemon juice

1 large red bell pepper, seeded and thinly sliced

½ cup *(½ oz/15 g)* fresh Thai or sweet basil leaves, chopped

½ cup *(½ oz/15 g)* fresh mint leaves, chopped

⅓ cup *(2 oz/60 g)* salted roasted peanuts, chopped

In a large pot, bring 4 qt (4 l) water to a rapid boil.

While the water is heating, make the dressing. In a small saucepan over medium heat, stir together the vinegar, peanut oil, honey, and mustard and bring to a boil. Adjust the heat so the mixture simmers and cook, stirring, for 3 minutes. Remove from the heat and cover to keep warm.

To make the salad, have ready a bowl of ice water. Add 1 tablespoon kosher salt and the cabbage to the boiling water and cook for 10 seconds; use a wire skimmer to transfer the cabbage immediately to the ice water to halt the cooking. Drain the cabbage thoroughly.

In a large serving bowl, combine the cabbage, green onions, and chile. Pour the hot dressing over the top and stir to mix and wilt the cabbage. Let stand while the noodles are cooking.

Return the water to a boil and add the noodles, stir well, and cook, stirring occasionally, until just tender, 2–3 minutes for fresh noodles or 5–7 minutes for dried noodles.

Meanwhile, to prepare the mango, stand it on its blossom end on a cutting board. Using a sharp chef's knife, slice downward to cut away one side of the flesh from the large, flat pit, pressing the flat side of the knife as close to the pit as possible. Repeat on the second side. Using the tip of the knife, cut the flesh side of each half lengthwise into 3 or 4 sections, up to but without piercing the skin. Turn the skin inside out and cut out the sections. Cut each section lengthwise into thin slices.

Drain the noodles, rinse under cold running water, and drain again. Add the lemon zest and juice, bell pepper, basil, and mint to the cabbage mixture and toss to mix well. Add the noodles and toss again to mix well. Top with the mango slices and peanuts and serve at room temperature.

SWEET AND SOUR NOODLES

The stir-fry sauce used here—a combination of spicy ginger and chile, sweet tomato and tamarind, tart lime, and salty fish sauce—goes equally well with shrimp (as in this dish), chicken, or pork. Substitute fresh or dried flat rice noodles for a Vietnamese-inspired version.

2 tablespoons peanut oil

2 shallots, minced

4 cloves garlic, minced

3 or 4 Thai chiles, seeded and minced

1 tablespoon peeled and grated fresh ginger

6 green onions, including 3 inches *(7.5 cm)* of green tops, thinly sliced

1¼ lb *(625 g)* shrimp, peeled and deveined

2 firm tomatoes, peeled, seeded, and chopped

2 tablespoons tamarind paste, mixed with 2 tablespoons low-sodium chicken broth

2 tablespoons fish sauce

Grated zest and juice of 1 lime, plus more juice if needed

4 teaspoons sugar, plus more if needed

½ cup *(4 fl oz/125 ml)* low-sodium chicken broth

Kosher salt for cooking noodles

½ lb *(250 g)* fresh or 1 lb *(500 g)* dried Chinese egg noodles

1 cup *(1 oz/30 g)* fresh Thai or sweet basil leaves, chopped

¼ cup *(¼ oz/7 g)* fresh mint leaves, chopped

1 tablespoon Asian sesame oil

In a wok or large, nonstick frying pan over high heat, warm the peanut oil. When the oil is hot, add the shallots, garlic, chiles, and ginger and stir-fry until they begin to color, 1–2 minutes. Add the green onions and stir-fry for 1 minute. Add the shrimp and stir-fry until they turn pink and are nearly opaque, 1–2 minutes. Add the tomatoes and stir to combine. Add the diluted tamarind paste, fish sauce, lime zest and juice, and sugar and mix well. Pour in the broth, stir well, and cook for 2 minutes to allow the flavors to blend. Remove from the heat and cover to keep warm.

In a large pot, bring 4 qt (4 l) water to a rapid boil. Add 1 tablespoon kosher salt and the noodles, stir well, and cook, stirring occasionally, until just tender, 2–3 minutes for fresh noodles or 5–7 minutes for dried noodles. Drain the noodles.

Place the pan with the shrimp mixture over medium heat, add the noodles, and toss and stir until the noodles are nicely coated with the sauce and the mixture is piping hot. Taste and adjust the balance of sweet and sour with more sugar or lime juice. Add the basil and mint, toss to mix, and transfer to a warmed large, shallow platter. Drizzle with the sesame oil and serve right away.

RICE NOODLES *with* CURRIED CHICKEN

This delicately scented curried noodle dish captures the appeal of fusion cooking. A simple preparation for chicken is dressed in a rich coconut milk–based curry and topped with ample fresh herbs. Take care not to overcook the chicken breast to ensure moist, tender results.

Kosher salt for cooking noodles

½ lb *(250 g)* dried flat rice noodles, about ½ inch *(12 mm)* wide

1 lb *(500 g)* skinless, boneless chicken breasts, thinly sliced against the grain

1 tablespoon curry powder

¼ teaspoon cayenne pepper

Pinch of red pepper flakes

¼ cup *(2 fl oz/60 ml)* safflower or grapeseed oil

2 cups *(16 fl oz/500 ml)* coconut milk

Fine sea salt

½ cup *(2½ oz/75 g)* salted roasted peanuts, roughly chopped

½ cup *(½ oz/15 g)* fresh cilantro leaves, chopped

¼ cup *(¼ oz/7 g)* fresh Thai or sweet basil leaves, chopped

In a wide saucepan, bring 4 cups (32 fl oz/1 l) water to a boil. Add 1 tablespoon kosher salt and the noodles, stir well, and cook, stirring occasionally, until just tender, 3–5 minutes. Drain well and transfer to a warmed shallow serving bowl.

While the noodles are cooking, pat the chicken slices thoroughly dry with paper towels. In a small bowl, stir together the curry powder, cayenne, and red pepper flakes. Sprinkle the spice mixture on the chicken, distributing it evenly.

In a large frying pan over medium-high heat, warm the oil. Add the chicken and sauté until half-cooked, about 2 minutes. Add the coconut milk and ½ teaspoon sea salt, reduce the heat to medium, and simmer until the coconut milk is hot and the chicken is just cooked through, about 2 minutes longer. Immediately remove from the heat.

Spoon the chicken and its sauce over the noodles; the noodles will absorb the excess liquid. Scatter the peanuts, cilantro, and basil on top. Serve right away.

RICE NOODLES *with* SHRIMP AND CASHEWS

Whether in authentic Asian dishes or Asian-inspired dishes, the lightness and tender texture of rice noodles make them an inviting canvas for a wide range of ingredients. In this recipe, they are in perfect harmony with shrimp, cashews, and tender baby spinach leaves.

1½ lb *(750 g)* large shrimp, peeled and deveined

1½ tablespoons Thai green curry paste

¾ cup *(4 oz/125 g)* raw cashews

Kosher salt for cooking noodles

½ lb *(250 g)* dried flat rice noodles, about ¼ inch *(6 mm)* wide

1 tablespoon cornstarch

2 cups *(16 fl oz/500 ml)* low-sodium chicken broth

2 tablespoons safflower or grape seed oil

2 large cloves garlic, chopped

1 or 2 small dried chiles, crushed and some seeds removed

¾ lb *(375 g)* baby spinach

¼ cup *(⅓ oz/10 g)* chopped fresh cilantro

In a bowl, combine the shrimp and curry paste and stir to coat the shrimp evenly. Cover and refrigerate for at least 1 hour or up to 3 hours.

In a small, dry frying pan over medium-low heat, toast the cashews, tossing often to color evenly, until lightly browned, about 5 minutes. Pour onto a plate to cool, and set aside.

In a large pot, bring 4 qt (4 l) water to a rapid boil. Add 1 tablespoon kosher salt and the noodles, stir well, and cook, stirring occasionally, until just tender, 3–5 minutes. Drain in a colander, place under cold running water to cool, and drain again thoroughly.

While the noodles are cooking, whisk the cornstarch into the broth and set aside. In a large nonstick frying pan over medium-high heat, warm the oil. Add the garlic and the chiles to taste and sauté quickly until lightly toasted, about 1 minute, being careful not to burn the garlic. Add the spinach and sauté briefly to wilt, about 1 minute. Quickly stir the broth if the cornstarch has settled, add to the pan, and bring to a simmer, stirring occasionally. Add the shrimp and simmer just until opaque throughout, no more than 3 minutes.

Transfer the noodles to the pan holding the shrimp mixture, raise the heat to high, and toss together to warm the noodles and distribute all the ingredients evenly. Transfer to a warmed large, shallow serving platter and top with the cashews and cilantro. Serve right away.

BEEF AND NOODLE SOUP

Pho bo is one of Vietnam's most famous soups. It's composed of a hearty bowl of broth, rice noodles, and thinly sliced beef, and is typically served with a variety of garnishes for diners to add to taste. Though not traditional, this recipe adds fresh tomatoes for additional freshness and color.

FOR THE BROTH

5 lb *(2.5 kg)* short ribs
or meaty beef shanks

3 yellow onions, quartered

1 small carrot, peeled
and quartered

1 cinnamon stick, about
3 inches *(7.5 cm)* long

3-inch *(7.5-cm)* piece fresh
ginger, peeled and quartered
lengthwise

Fine sea salt

1 lb *(500 g)* fresh or ½ lb
(250 g) dried flat rice noodles,
about ½ inch *(12 mm)* wide

1 tablespoon Asian sesame oil

Kosher salt for cooking
noodles

1 lb *(500 g)* boneless beef
chuck, partially frozen

1 cup *(1 oz/30 g)* mung
bean sprouts

4 tomatoes, halved from stem
end to bottom and thinly
sliced lengthwise

4 small white onions, quartered
through the stem end and thinly
sliced lengthwise

Leaves from 1 small
bunch fresh cilantro

2 or 3 fresh hot chiles, seeded
and thinly sliced

Fish sauce for serving

2 limes, cut into wedges

To make the broth, in a stockpot over medium-high heat, combine the short ribs, yellow onions, carrot, cinnamon, ginger, and 2½ qt *(2.5 l)* water. Bring just to a boil, skimming any foam that forms on the surface. Immediately reduce the heat to medium-low and cover partially; the liquid should be at a gentle but steady simmer. Cook, continuing to skim as necessary and adding water as needed to keep the ingredients covered, until the meat is fork-tender and falling off the bone, about 3 hours. Remove from the heat. Remove and reserve the short ribs for another use. Strain the broth through a fine-mesh sieve into a wide saucepan. Using a large spoon, skim off the fat from the surface. Season to taste with sea salt.

If using fresh rice noodles, have them at room temperature, and gently loosen to separate the noodles. If they have been refrigerated, place them in a bowl, cover with warm water, and let soak for 1 minute, then gently separate them and drain in a colander. Toss the noodles with the sesame oil. If using dried noodles, in a large pot, bring 5 qt *(5 l)* water to a rapid boil. Add 2 tablespoons kosher salt and the dried noodles, stir well, and cook, stirring occasionally, until just tender, 3–5 minutes. Drain well and toss with the sesame oil.

To serve, have ready large soup bowls. Using a sharp knife, cut the beef against the grain into paper-thin strips about 2 inches (5 cm) long and ½ inch (12 mm) wide. Divide the noodles evenly among the bowls, then top with the bean sprouts, again dividing evenly. Bring the broth to a boil over high heat. Place one portion of the beef, tomato, and white onion in a wire skimmer and slowly immerse the skimmer in the boiling broth. Cook only until the beef turns from bright pink to pale pink, about 1 minute, then transfer the beef, tomato, and onion to a bowl, placing them on top of the bean sprouts. Top the remaining bowls the same way, then ladle the boiling broth over the top of all of the bowls, dividing it evenly. Top with the cilantro and chiles, and add a dash of fish sauce to each bowl. Serve right away. Pass the lime wedges and additional fish sauce at the table.

CELLOPHANE NOODLES *with* SHRIMP AND GARLIC

Heads of pickled garlic, available at Southeast Asian markets, need no peeling and add a pleasantly sweet-sour flavor to offset the sweetness of the shrimp. If you cannot find pickled garlic, substitute 4 cloves chopped garlic and increase the fish sauce or lime juice by 1–2 tablespoons.

12 oz *(750 g)* cellophane (bean thread) noodles

1 lb *(500 g)* small shrimp, peeled and deveined

¼ cup *(2 fl oz/60 ml)* peanut or canola oil

3 shallots, thinly sliced

1 head pickled garlic, chopped *(see Note)*

2–4 Thai chiles, seeded and sliced

½ lb *(250 g)* ground pork

1½ cups *(10 oz/275 g)* grape tomatoes, halved lengthwise

¼ cup *(2 fl oz/60 ml)* fish sauce or soy sauce, or as needed

2 tablespoons fresh lime juice, or as needed

¼ cup *(¼ oz/7 g)* fresh Thai or sweet basil leaves

¼ cup *(¼ oz/7 g)* fresh cilantro leaves

Place the noodles in a large bowl, add hot water to cover generously, and let stand until softened, about 20 minutes. Drain the noodles and set aside.

Fill a saucepan three-fourths full of water and bring to a boil over high heat. Add the shrimp and boil just until they turn pink and curl, 1–2 minutes. Drain in a colander and place under cold running water until cool. Set aside.

In a wok or large nonstick frying pan over high heat, warm the oil. Add the shallots and stir-fry for about 30 seconds to soften slightly. Add the pickled garlic and the chiles to taste and continue to stir-fry until the shallots begin to color, about 2 minutes. Add the pork and cook, stirring to break up any clumps, until it has lost its pink color, 1–2 minutes.

Add the tomatoes and stir-fry for 1 minute. Push the contents of the pan to one side, add the fish sauce to the other side, let it bubble up for a second, and then add the noodles. Quickly stir and toss to combine the noodles, fish sauce, and pork mixture. Add the shrimp, toss to combine, and sprinkle with the lime juice.

Remove from the heat. Taste and adjust the seasoning with more fish sauce and/or lime juice. The dish should have a nice balance of salty, sour, and hot. Add the basil and cilantro and toss to mix well. Transfer to a platter or individual bowls and serve hot or at room temperature.

STIR-FRIED SOBA NOODLES *with* BEEF AND CABBAGE

The nutty flavor and delicately grainy texture of soba noodles pair particularly well with cabbage, and the pure white ribs and bright green curly-edged leaves of napa cabbage make any dish prettier. Napa cabbage is crisp and mild-flavored, contributing subtly to this full-flavored dish.

1 lb *(500 g)* boneless beef sirloin or tenderloin, partially frozen

¼ cup *(2 fl oz/60 ml)* Asian sesame oil

¼ cup *(2 fl oz/60 ml)* soy sauce

¼ cup *(2 fl oz/60 ml)* plus 1 tablespoon peanut oil

2 tablespoons peeled and grated fresh ginger

2 large cloves garlic, chopped

4 green onions, including 3 inches *(7.5 cm)* of green tops, thinly sliced on the diagonal

1 head napa cabbage, about 2 lb *(1 kg)*, cored and shredded

2 cups *(16 fl oz/500 ml)* low-sodium chicken or beef broth

2 tablespoons cornstarch

½ lb *(250 g)* snow peas, trimmed and halved on the diagonal

Kosher salt for cooking noodles

1 lb *(500 g)* fresh *(page 208)* or ¾ lb *(375 g)* dried soba noodles

¼ cup *(1 oz/30 g)* sesame seeds, lightly toasted

Using a sharp knife, cut the beef against the grain into thin slices, then cut the slices into matchsticks. In a bowl, whisk together the sesame oil, soy sauce, the ¼ cup (2 fl oz/60 ml) peanut oil, and the ginger. Add the beef and stir to coat evenly. Cover and refrigerate, stirring occasionally, for at least 1 hour or up to 3 hours.

In a large pot, bring 5 qt (5 l) water to a rapid boil.

While the water is heating, in a wok or large nonstick frying pan over medium-high heat, warm the 1 tablespoon peanut oil. Add the garlic and green onions and stir-fry until lightly colored, about 1 minute. Raise the heat to high, add the beef and its marinade, and stir-fry until lightly browned, about 8 minutes. Add the cabbage and 1½ cups (12 fl oz/375 ml) of the broth and toss to combine. Cover, reduce the heat to medium-high, and cook until the cabbage wilts, about 4 minutes.

In a small bowl, whisk the cornstarch into the remaining ½ cup (4 fl oz/125 ml) broth. Uncover the wok, add the cornstarch mixture to the pan, and stir and toss to incorporate. Add the snow peas, stir and toss to combine, cover, and cook until just tender, about 2 minutes. Take care not to overcook; the snow peas and cabbage should remain crisp.

Add 2 tablespoons kosher salt and the noodles to the boiling water, stir well, and cook, stirring occasionally, until just tender, 2–3 minutes for fresh noodles or 5–7 minutes for dried noodles. Drain the noodles.

Off the heat, add the noodles to the wok and stir and toss until well combined. Transfer to a warmed large, shallow platter and garnish with the sesame seeds. Serve right away.

Chinese Egg Noodles *with* Pork and Bok Choy

Sweet and tender, baby bok choy is often paired with spicy stir-fried pork in Sichuan cooking, which is known for its fiery character. This dish has a kick to it, but you can adjust the intensity of the heat by increasing or decreasing the amount of red pepper flakes in the marinade.

FOR THE MARINADE

2 large cloves garlic, chopped

3 tablespoons peeled and minced fresh ginger

3 tablespoons soy sauce

3 tablespoons Asian sesame oil

2 tablespoons rice vinegar or dry sherry

1 tablespoon honey

1 teaspoon red pepper flakes

1 lb *(500 g)* boneless pork loin, partially frozen

Kosher salt for cooking noodles

1 lb *(500 g)* fresh or ¾ lb *(375 g)* dried Chinese egg noodles

3 tablespoons peanut oil

1 lb *(500 g)* baby bok choy, quartered lengthwise

½ lb *(500 g)* fresh oyster mushrooms, brushed clean, tough stems removed, and thinly sliced

6 green onions, including 3 inches *(7.5 cm)* of green tops, thinly sliced on the diagonal

2 tablespoons cornstarch

¾ cup *(6 fl oz/180 ml)* low-sodium chicken broth

1 tablespoon Asian sesame oil

¼ cup *(1 oz/30 g)* sesame seeds, lightly toasted

To make the marinade, in a large bowl, whisk together the garlic, ginger, soy sauce, sesame oil, vinegar, honey, and red pepper flakes until well blended. Set aside.

Using a sharp knife, cut the pork against the grain into thin slices, then cut the slices into matchsticks. Add the pork to the marinade and stir to coat evenly. Cover and marinate, stirring occasionally, for at least 1 hour at room temperature or up to 4 hours in the refrigerator.

In a large pot, bring 4 qt (4 l) water to a rapid boil. Add 1 tablespoon kosher salt and the noodles, stir well, and cook, stirring occasionally, until just tender, 2–3 minutes for fresh noodles and 5–7 minutes for dried noodles. Drain the noodles.

While the noodles are cooking, in a wok or large nonstick frying pan over high heat, warm the peanut oil. When the oil is hot, add the pork and its marinade and stir-fry until nicely colored, 3–4 minutes. Add the bok choy, mushrooms, and green onions and stir and toss to distribute the ingredients evenly. Cover, reduce the heat to medium, and cook until the bok choy is bright green, about 3 minutes.

In a small bowl, whisk the cornstarch into the broth. Uncover the wok, raise the heat to high, and add the cornstarch mixture to the pan. Stir-fry until the liquid thickens slightly, 1–2 minutes. Add the noodles and stir and toss until well combined. Remove from the heat, add the sesame oil, and toss to mix well. Transfer to a warmed large, shallow serving platter and scatter the sesame seeds over the top. Serve right away.

RICE NOODLE SALAD *with* GRILLED STEAK

In this rendition of the perennially popular Vietnamese grilled steak salad, flank steak is marinated in a slurry of red curry paste, sesame oil, and garlic, and then grilled, thinly sliced, and placed on a bed of delicate butter lettuce, rice noodles, and herbs. A refreshing coconut dressing is drizzled on top.

1 tablespoon soy sauce

2 tablespoons red curry paste

2 large cloves garlic, minced

2 tablespoons Asian sesame oil

2 tablespoons grape seed oil

1¼ lb *(625 g)* flank steak

Kosher salt

½ lb *(250 g)* dried flat rice noodles, about ½ inch *(12 mm)* wide

FOR THE DRESSING

½ cup *(4 fl oz/125 ml)* coconut water

2 tablespoons rice vinegar

2 tablespoons sugar

2 tablespoons fish sauce

1 teaspoon fresh lime juice

½ red chile, seeded and sliced

FOR THE SALAD

1 head butter lettuce

½ English cucumber, thinly sliced

¼ cup *(¼ oz/7 g)* fresh cilantro leaves

¼ cup *(¼ oz/7 g)* fresh Thai basil leaves

½ red chile, seeded and minced

2 tablespoons sesame seeds, lightly toasted

In a small bowl, stir together the soy sauce, curry paste, garlic, sesame oil, and grape seed oil. Place the steak in a shallow glass or ceramic dish, and rub on both sides with the curry mixture. Cover and refrigerate for at least 1 hour or up to 3 days.

Prepare a hot fire in a charcoal or gas grill or preheat the broiler.

Meanwhile, in a large pot, bring 4 qt (4 l) water to a rapid boil. Add 1 tablespoon kosher salt and the noodles, stir well, and cook, stirring occasionally, until just tender, 3–5 minutes. Drain the noodles, rinse under cold running water, and drain again thoroughly. Set aside.

Remove the steak from the marinade and pat dry with paper towels. Place on the grill rack directly over the fire, or place on a broiler pan and slip in the broiler. Cook until well seared and dark brown on the first side, about 5 minutes. Turn the steak and cook on the second side until well seared, dark brown, and done to your liking, 2–5 minutes total for medium-rare, depending on the thickness of the steak. Transfer to a cutting board and let rest for 5–10 minutes. Using a sharp chef's knife, thinly slice the steak against the grain on the diagonal.

While the meat is cooking, make the dressing. In a small saucepan, combine the coconut water, vinegar, and sugar and bring to a boil, stirring to dissolve the sugar. Remove from the heat and let cool. Whisk in the fish sauce, lime juice, and sliced chile. Set aside.

In a large bowl, toss the noodles with half of the dressing. Separate the head of lettuce into leaves. To assemble the salad, on a platter or individual plates, arrange the lettuce leaves, cucumber, and half of the cilantro and basil. Top with the noodles and beef slices. Serve the remaining dressing on the side or pour it over the meat. Scatter the remaining cilantro and basil leaves, the minced chile, and the sesame seeds on top. Serve at room temperature.

RICE NOODLES *with* FRESH CRAB

This Thai-flavored salad depends on the availability of very fresh lump crabmeat. Always use pre-cooked, high-quality crabmeat, which is moist and ivory colored. Or, try using mussels in place of the crab: simply steam open 1 lb (2 kg) small mussels, and then shell them and toss in with the noodles.

Kosher salt for
cooking noodles

½ lb *(250 g)* dried flat
rice noodles, about ¼ inch
(6 mm) wide

¼ cup *(2 fl oz/60 ml)*
coconut milk

2–3 tablespoons fish sauce

2 tablespoons fresh
lime juice

Grated zest of 1 lime

2–4 Thai chiles, sliced
(optional)

1 cup *(1 oz/30 g)*
mung bean sprouts

½ English cucumber,
cut into paper-thin slices

½ lb *(250 g)* fresh lump
crabmeat, picked over for
shell fragments and cartilage
and flaked

½ cup *(½ oz/15 g)*
fresh cilantro leaves

In a large pot, bring 4 qt (4 l) water to a rapid boil. Add 1 tablespoon kosher salt and the noodles, stir well, and cook, stirring occasionally, until just tender, 3–5 minutes. Drain in a colander, place under cold running water to cool, and drain again thoroughly.

In a bowl, stir together the coconut milk, fish sauce to taste, lime juice, lime zest, and chiles to taste, if using. Add the bean sprouts, cucumber, and crabmeat and toss gently to combine.

Transfer the noodles to a large, shallow serving bowl. Arrange the crab mixture over the noodles. Scatter the cilantro on top. Serve at room temperature, or cover and refrigerate for up to 3 hours and serve chilled.

CHINESE EGG NOODLES *with* PEANUT SAUCE

Plain old peanut butter takes on richness and nuance when called on for a classic Asian peanut sauce. You can adjust the quantities of soy, honey, and vinegar in the sauce to suit your tastes. The sauce can be made well in advance; it keeps for up to a month in the refrigerator.

FOR THE SAUCE

1 cup *(10 oz/315 g)* smooth peanut butter

½ cup *(4 fl oz/125 ml)* soy sauce

½ cup *(6 oz/185 g)* honey

¼ cup *(2 fl oz/60 ml)* rice vinegar

1 tablespoon Asian sesame oil

Chile oil or chile paste

Kosher salt for cooking noodles

1 lb *(500 g)* fresh or ¾ lb *(375 g)* dried Chinese egg noodles

1 English cucumber, peeled, halved lengthwise, and cut into matchsticks

2 tablespoons untoasted sesame seeds

To make the sauce, in a food processor, combine the peanut butter, soy sauce, honey, vinegar, and sesame oil and process until smooth. Add the chile oil to taste and process until combined. Taste and adjust with soy sauce, honey, and vinegar as needed.

In a large pot, bring 5 qt (5 l) water to a rapid boil. Add 2 tablespoons kosher salt and the noodles, stir well, and cook, stirring occasionally, until just tender, 2–3 minutes for fresh noodles and 5–7 minutes for dried noodles. Drain, reserving a few tablespoons of the cooking water.

In a large bowl, combine the noodles and half of the sauce and toss to coat the strands evenly; add some of the reserved cooking water to loosen the sauce, if necessary. Transfer to a large, shallow serving platter and top with the remaining sauce and the cucumber. Sprinkle with the sesame seeds and serve at room temperature.

Cellophane Noodles *with* Spinach and Carrots

Here is a quick and fresh recipe for sauce-friendly cellophane noodles tossed with the perfect balance of savory ingredients. Serve this dish as a vegetarian main course for four or as a side dish for six. A toasted sesame seed topping is added before serving for a nutty crunch.

½ lb *(250 g)* cellophane (bean thread) noodles

4 tablespoons *(2 fl oz/60 ml)* sesame oil

3 tablespoons peanut oil

2 cloves garlic, minced

4 green onions, including 2 inches *(5 cm)* of tender green tops, thinly sliced on the diagonal

4 large carrots, peeled and cut into matchsticks

1 cup *(8 fl oz/250 ml)* low-sodium vegetable broth

3 tablespoons dark soy sauce

¾ lb *(375 g)* baby spinach

2 cups *(2 oz/60 g)* mung bean sprouts

5 oz *(150 g)* fresh shiitake mushrooms, brushed clean, tough stems removed, caps thinly sliced

½ teaspoon red pepper flakes

¼ cup *(1 oz/30 g)* sesame seeds

¼ cup *(⅓ oz/7 g)* chopped fresh cilantro

Place the noodles in a large bowl, add hot water to cover generously, and let stand until softened and translucent, about 20 minutes. Drain thoroughly, toss with 2 tablespoons of the sesame oil, and set aside.

In a wok or large nonstick frying pan over medium heat, warm the peanut oil. When the oil is hot, add the garlic and green onions and stir-fry until the garlic is golden, about 2 minutes. Add the carrots and stir to coat with the oil. Add the broth and 2 tablespoons of the soy sauce. Bring to a boil and cook until the carrots are half-cooked, 3–4 minutes. Add the spinach, bean sprouts, mushrooms, and red pepper flakes and toss until the mushrooms are tender, about 5 minutes. Add the noodles and stir and toss until well mixed and the noodles are heated through. Remove from the heat and cover to keep warm.

In a small, dry frying pan over medium heat, toast the sesame seeds, stirring constantly, until lightly browned, 2–3 minutes. Add the remaining 2 tablespoons sesame oil and 1 tablespoon soy sauce to the pan and stir to coat the seeds. Remove from the heat.

Transfer the noodle mixture to a warmed large, shallow serving platter or individual shallow serving plates. Garnish with the sesame seed mixture and the cilantro and serve right away.

UDON NOODLE SOUP *with* PORK

This soup is inspired by the soothing noodle soups that are so popular in Japanese cuisine, filled with thick, chewy udon noodles and meaty shiitake mushrooms. Its success depends largely on the quality of the broth; make your own or seek out the highest-quality, low-sodium broth you can find.

½ lb *(250 g)* fresh or ¾ lb *(375 g)* dried udon noodles

1 lb *(500 g)* pork tenderloin, partially frozen

2 qt *(2 l)* low-sodium beef or chicken broth

1 carrot, peeled and cut into julienne

4 fresh shiitake mushrooms, brushed clean, stems removed, and caps thinly sliced

1½ oz *(45 g)* enoki mushrooms, trimmed and rinsed

1 tablespoon peeled and grated fresh ginger

1 or 2 fresh red chiles

¼ cup *(2 fl oz/60 ml)* mirin

1 tablespoon soy sauce

1 teaspoon sugar, or to taste

1 bunch watercress, stems removed

1 bunch green onions, including 2 inches *(5 cm)* of green tops, thinly sliced

¼ cup *(1 oz/30 g)* sesame seeds, lightly toasted

In a large pot, bring 4 qt (4 l) water to a rapid boil. If using fresh udon, add the noodles and cover the pot. When the water returns to a boil, uncover and cook for about 10 seconds. Drain in a colander, rinse under cold running water, and set aside. If using dried udon, add to the boiling water, stir well, and cook, stirring occasionally, until just tender, about 5 minutes. Drain in a colander, rinse under cold running water, and drain again thoroughly. Set aside.

Using a sharp knife, cut the pork against the grain into thin slices, then cut the slices into matchsticks. In a large saucepan over high heat, combine the broth, carrot, shiitake and enoki mushrooms, ginger, chile(s) to taste, mirin, soy sauce, and sugar and bring to a boil. Reduce the heat to medium and simmer for 2 minutes. Add the pork, raise the heat to high, and cook for 1 minute. Stir in the cooked noodles, watercress, and green onions and simmer until the watercress and green onions have wilted and the noodles are just heated through, about 1 minute.

Remove from the heat, and remove and discard the chile(s). Taste and adjust the seasoning, then ladle into warmed individual bowls. Sprinkle with the sesame seeds, dividing evenly, and serve right away.

CHINESE EGG NOODLES *with* CHICKEN AND PEA SHOOTS

Pea shoots, also known as pea tendrils, are the delicate curling tips of the snow pea vine. Look for them in Asian markets, in well-stocked produce stores, or at farmers' markets. They are very fragile and wilt quickly with heat, so toss them in with the noodles at the end of cooking.

FOR THE MARINADE

1 teaspoon Thai green curry paste

2 large cloves garlic, minced

1 teaspoon peeled and grated fresh ginger

2 red Thai chiles, seeded and finely chopped

1 tablespoon soy sauce

1 teaspoon Asian sesame oil

Juice of 1 lime

1 teaspoon sugar

1 lb *(500 g)* skinless, boneless chicken breasts, partially frozen

Kosher salt for cooking noodles

¾ lb *(375 g)* fresh or ½ lb *(250 g)* dried Chinese egg noodles

3 tablespoons peanut oil

3 oz *(90 g)* fresh shiitake or oyster mushrooms, brushed clean, tough stems removed, and caps thinly sliced

1½ cups *(12 fl oz/375 ml)* low-sodium chicken broth

1 lb *(500 g)* pea shoots, tough stem portions and leaves removed *(about 5 cups/5 oz/155 g after trimming)*

To make the marinade, in a small bowl, whisk together the curry paste, garlic, ginger, chiles, soy sauce, sesame oil, lime juice, and sugar until well blended.

Using a sharp knife, cut the chicken against the grain into thin strips about 3 inches (7.5 cm) long and ½ inch (12 mm) wide. Place in a bowl, add half of the marinade, and work the marinade into the chicken with your hands. Set the remaining marinade aside.

In a large pot, bring 4 qt (4 l) water to a rapid boil. Add 1 tablespoon kosher salt and the noodles, stir well, and cook, stirring occasionally, until just tender, 2–3 minutes for fresh noodles and 5–7 minutes for dried noodles. Drain the noodles thoroughly.

Meanwhile, in a wok or large nonstick frying pan over high heat, warm the peanut oil. When the oil is hot, add the chicken and mushrooms and stir-fry until the chicken is half-cooked, about 2 minutes. Add the broth and the reserved marinade, stir to coat the chicken evenly, and cook, stirring, just until the chicken is opaque throughout and the mushrooms are tender, about 5 minutes longer. Add the drained noodles and the pea shoots and stir and toss until the noodles are evenly coated with the sauce and the pea shoots are just wilted, about 1 minute.

Transfer to a warmed large, shallow serving platter and serve right away.

SERVES 4

RICE NOODLES *with* CHICKEN AND PAPAYA

In this simple pasta dish, cinnamon and cardamom mix with coconut milk, papaya, and rice noodles in a fusion of Middle Eastern and Southeast Asian flavors. Seek out the yellow, pear-shaped Hawaiian papaya, which is sweeter than the larger green papaya.

Kosher salt for
cooking noodles

½ lb *(250 g)* dried flat
rice noodles, about ½ inch
(12 mm) wide

6 tablespoons *(3 fl oz/90 ml)*
safflower or grapeseed oil

1 lb *(500 g)* skinless, boneless
chicken breasts, thinly sliced
against the grain

Fine sea salt

1 teaspoon ground
fennel powder

1 teaspoon ground cardamom

¼ teaspoon cayenne pepper

Pinch of red pepper flakes

2 tablespoons peeled and
minced fresh ginger

1 large shallot, finely sliced

1¾ cups *(14 fl oz/430 ml)*
coconut milk

1 cinnamon stick,
3 inches *(7.5 cm)* long

1 small papaya, peeled,
seeded, and diced

½ cup *(½ oz/15 g)* fresh
cilantro leaves, chopped

In a wide saucepan, bring 4 cups (32 fl oz/1 l) water to a boil. Add 1 tablespoon kosher salt and the noodles, remove the pan from the heat, and let the noodles stand in the water until softened, about 5 minutes. Drain and transfer to a warmed large, shallow serving bowl; toss with 2 tablespoons of the oil.

While the noodles are soaking, pat the chicken slices thoroughly dry. In a small bowl, combine ½ teaspoon sea salt, the fennel, cardamom, cayenne, and red pepper flakes. Work the spice mixture into the chicken slices, distributing it evenly.

In a large frying pan over medium-high heat, warm the remaining 4 tablespoons (2 fl oz/60 ml) oil. Add the ginger and shallot and sauté until nearly tender, 1 minute. Add the chicken and sauté until half-cooked and colored on both sides, about 2 minutes. Add the coconut milk and cinnamon stick, reduce the heat to medium, and simmer until the coconut milk is hot and the chicken is just opaque throughout, about 2 minutes longer. Immediately remove from the heat and remove and discard the cinnamon stick. Taste and adjust the seasoning.

Spoon the chicken and its sauce over the noodles, which will absorb the excess liquid. Arrange the papaya over them and scatter the cilantro on top. Serve right away.

BASIC RECIPES

BÉCHAMEL SAUCE

2¼ cups *(18 fl oz/560 ml)* milk

4 tablespoons *(2 oz/60 g)* unsalted butter

3 tablespoons unbleached all-purpose flour

Generous pinch of freshly grated nutmeg

Fine sea salt

MAKES ABOUT 2 CUPS (16 FL OZ/500 ML)

In a saucepan over medium heat, warm the milk until small bubbles appear around the edges of the pan, then remove from the heat. While the milk is heating, in a heavy saucepan over low heat, melt the butter. Add the flour, stir vigorously with a wooden spoon to remove any lumps, and cook, stirring continuously, until aromatic but not brown, about 2 minutes. Remove from the heat and let cool for 3–4 minutes.

Return the pan with the flour to low heat and slowly drizzle in the warm milk, whisking constantly. (If lumps start to appear, either you are adding the milk too quickly or the heat is too high.)

When all of the milk has been added, raise the heat to medium and bring to a boil, whisking constantly and making sure to reach the bottom and sides of the pan. Reduce the heat to medium-low, add the nutmeg and ¼ teaspoon sea salt, and simmer gently, whisking often, until the sauce thickens enough to coat the back of a wooden spoon, about 5 minutes.

Remove from the heat and evaluate the consistency of the sauce. If lumps are still visible, pour the sauce through a fine-mesh sieve into a heatproof bowl. Use right away, or cover, pressing plastic wrap directly onto the surface of the sauce to prevent a skin from forming, let cool, and refrigerate for up to 5 days. To reheat, warm the sauce in a pan over low heat, and whisk in warm milk to thin as needed.

SIMPLE TOMATO SAUCE

2½ lb *(1.25 kg)* fresh plum tomatoes, peeled and seeded, or 1 can *(28 oz/ 875 g)* plum tomatoes, drained

⅓ cup *(3 fl oz/80 ml)* extra-virgin olive oil

6 cloves garlic, bruised *(see page 233)*

Fine sea salt and freshly ground white or black pepper

MAKES ABOUT 4 CUPS (32 FL OZ/1 L)

Coarsely chop the tomatoes, place in a colander in the sink, and let drain for 5 minutes. In a saucepan over medium heat, warm the olive oil. Add the garlic and sauté, pressing with the back of a wooden spoon to release its juices, until it takes on a rich golden color but has not yet turned brown, 1–2 minutes. Remove and discard the garlic and immediately add the tomatoes, ½ teaspoon sea salt, and season to taste with pepper.

Using a fork or potato masher, press down on the tomatoes to break them up until they are in fairly fine pieces. Raise the heat to high and bring the tomatoes to a simmer. Reduce the heat to medium-low and continue to simmer, stirring occasionally, until the tomatoes form a thick sauce, about 20 minutes. Remove from the heat and use right away, or let cool, cover, and refrigerate for up to 3 days.

CREAMY TOMATO SAUCE

Simple Tomato Sauce *(left)*

6 tablespoons *(3 fl oz/90 ml)* heavy cream or 3 tablespoons crème fraîche

MAKES ABOUT 4 CUPS (32 FL OZ/1 L)

Make the tomato sauce as directed. When the sauce is ready, stir in the cream, mix well, cover, and set aside off the heat.

SOY-GINGER SAUCE

½ cup *(4 fl oz/125 ml)* soy sauce

¼ cup *(2 fl oz/60 ml)* mirin

¼ cup *(2 fl oz/60 ml)* rice vinegar

2 green onions, including 2 inches *(5 cm)* of the tender green tops, finely chopped

4 teaspoons peeled and minced fresh ginger

MAKES ABOUT 1 CUP (8 FL OZ/250 ML)

In a small bowl, whisk together the soy sauce, mirin, vinegar, green onions, and ginger. Use as a finishing sauce or dipping sauce, as called for in the recipe.

BASIC TECHNIQUES

CLARIFYING BUTTER

In a frying pan over low heat, melt the quantity of butter called for in the recipe. When it stops sizzling and the solids begin to separate and rise to the surface, skim off and discard the solids. The clarified butter should be golden in color. Watch it carefully to prevent it from getting too dark, which can happen in an instant, and turn off the heat if it begins to darken too much before you have removed all the solids. Pass the clarified butter through a fine-mesh sieve lined with cheesecloth or a coffee filter to extract any solids that remain.

COOKING DRIED BEANS

Pick over the beans and discard any misshapen beans or stones, then rinse the beans under cold running water and drain. Place in a large bowl with cold water to cover by about 3 inches (7.5 cm) and let soak for at least 4 hours or up to overnight. Alternatively, transfer the rinsed beans to a large pot and add water to cover by 3 inches. Bring to a boil, remove from the heat, and let stand for 1–2 hours.

Drain the beans, place in a saucepan with water to cover by about 4 inches (10 cm), and bring to a boil over high heat, skimming off the foam that rises to the surface. Reduce the heat to low, cover partially, and simmer until the beans are tender, 1½–2 hours. The timing will depend on the variety and age of the beans. Use right away, or refrigerate in an airtight container for up to 1 week.

MAKING BREAD CRUMBS

To make fresh bread crumbs, start with day-old country bread. Discard the crusts, tear into pieces, and place in a food processor. Pulse to process into coarse or fine crumbs, 20–40 seconds.

To make dried bread crumbs, start with fresh bread crumbs. Dry the crumbs on a baking sheet in a preheated 325°F (165°C) oven for about 15 minutes. Let cool, process again until fine and then bake, stirring once of twice, until pale golden, about 15 minutes longer.

To toast bread crumbs, start with fresh bread crumbs. In a small frying pan over medium heat, warm 1 tablespoon oil for every ¼ cup (½ oz/15 g) bread crumbs until shimmering. Add the bread crumbs and sauté until golden, about 4 minutes.

BRUISING GARLIC

Using the flat side of a chef's knife, lightly press against the clove until the peel splits. Remove the peel and discard. Using the chef's knife, press down on the clove again until you hear it pop. Pressing the garlic this way allows it to release its flavorful oils during cooking, but keeps it intact for easy removal.

PEELING TOMATOES

Using a paring knife, cut a small, shallow X in the blossom end of each tomato. Bring a pot of water to a boil. Plunge the tomatoes into the boiling water for 15–30 seconds, depending on ripeness, or until the skins begin to loosen. Use the slotted spoon to transfer the tomatoes to a bowl of ice water to stop the cooking. As soon as the tomatoes are cool, remove them from the water. Using the paring knife, and starting at the X, pull off the skin. It should come away easily.

WORKING WITH FENNEL

Using a chef's knife, cut off the stalks and feathery fronds from the bulb. Set aside some of the fronds. Run a vegetable peeler over the outer layer of the bulb to remove any bruised or tough portions. If the outer layer is badly bruised or scarred, remove it entirely. Cut the bulb in half lengthwise. Make a V cut to remove the core from each half, then slice or chop as directed in the recipe.

SNIPPING CHIVES

Discard any wilted or yellow chives. Rinse the chives and pat dry. Gather about 10 chives at a time in your hand. Using kitchen scissors, finely snip the chives into small pieces.

GLOSSARY

BAMBOO SHOOTS An Asian pantry staple, these shoots are harvested from a specific bamboo species. They lend refreshing crunch to stir-fries, soups, and other dishes. Sold packed in water in jars or cans.

BASIL A leafy green herb with mild, sweet tones of anise and cloves. Sweet basil is the type most commonly used in Western cooking. Thai basil has purple-tinged leaves and a more pronounced licorice flavor.

BEAN SPROUTS, MUNG Delicate white Asian sprouts that are excellent in soups, salads, and stir-fries. They perish quickly; refrigerate for up to 3 days in an airtight container.

BOK CHOY A mild and crunchy Chinese cabbage with long, white stalks and dark green, crinkly leaves. Baby bok choy is about half the size and very tender. Both are excellent steamed, braised, sautéed, or stir-fried.

BONITO FLAKES Pale, delicate flakes shaved from a dried and smoked bonito, also known as skipjack tuna. Subtle and aromatic, bonito is an ingredient in Japanese fish stock, dipping sauces, and a common garnish.

BROCCOLI RABE Also known as rapini, this popular southern Italian green has slender stalks, small florets, jagged leaves, and a mildly bitter flavor. A member of the large mustard family and a close relative of the turnip, it is traditionally paired with orecchiette.

CABBAGE, NAPA Also called Chinese or celery cabbage, napa cabbage has an elongated head, pale green leaves, and a pearly white core. Its sturdy texture holds up well in stir-fries and soups.

CHEESES Hard, aged cheeses are best for grating. Semifirm varieties are good all-purpose cheeses for shredding and melting, and fresh cheeses shine when crumbled and tossed lightly with other ingredients.

Asiago A cow's milk cheese made in the Veneto region of Italy. Aged Asiago is a hard grating cheese with a slightly sharp taste; young Asiago is softer, has a gentle tang, and melts beautifully.

burrata A much-sought fresh Italian cheese made by encasing heavy cream and bits of mozzarella inside a "shell" of mozzarella. The name means "buttered," a nod to the exceptionally soft, creamy character of the cheese. A short shelf life makes burrata difficult to find outside of Italy.

caciotta Umbria and Tuscany stake a claim on this lightly ripened farmhouse cheese, made from a combination of cow's and sheep's milk. It has a thin rind with a semisoft, pale yellow interior.

Comté A semihard French cow's milk cheese, also known as Comté de Gruyère. It has a sweet, nutty flavor and firm texture that makes it ideal for shredding and melting.

fontina A semifirm cow's milk cheese from northwestern Italy. A good melting cheese, fontina has a light brown rind, a creamy texture, and a slightly nutty flavor.

goat cheese, fresh This young, soft cheese has a tangy flavor and a smooth, creamy texture. It is sold primarily in logs, thick disks, or pyramids and is sometimes seasoned with herbs, pepper, or nuts rolled in ashes.

Gorgonzola, young A northern Italian blue made from cow's milk. Young Gorgonzola, often labeled *dolce* or *dolcelatte,* is mild, sweet, and creamy. As the cheese ages, its naturally earthy flavor intensifies.

grana padano An Italian aged cow's milk cheese, similar to Parmigiano-Reggiano, but not aged as long. The term *grana*, or "grain," refers to its grainy texture. Freshly grated grana padano has a mild, nutty sweetness that perfectly complements delicate pasta sauces.

Parmigiano-Reggiano The trademarked name of true Parmesan cheese, made in the Emilia-Romagna region of northern Italy. Rich and complex in flavor and possessing a pleasant granular texture, this savory cheese is excellent shaved, shredded, or grated.

pecorino The ubiquitous sheep's milk cheese of central and southern Italy. Pecorino romano, made around Rome, is well aged and sharp. Pecorino toscano, from Tuscany, is mild and creamy when young and stronger and drier when aged. Pecorino sardo, also known as *fiore di Sardegna,* is a grainy, rich Sardinian cheese with hints of caramel.

ricotta A snow-white fresh cheese traditionally made from the whey left over from making mozzarella; commonly used in lasagne and in stuffed pasta fillings. Ricotta salata is salted, pressed, and aged, yielding a crumbly texture and salty flavor.

CHILES, THAI The petite size betrays the intense heat of these slender green or red chiles, which are among the hottest of all chiles. Substitute jalapeño or serrano for less intensity.

CRÈME FRAÎCHE A cultured cream product originally from France, crème fraîche is similar to sour cream but sweeter and milder.

FISH SAUCE Called *nam pla* in Thai and *nuoc mam* in Vietnamese, this flavorful sauce, made from salted and fermented fish, is used to flavor dishes and as a table condiment throughout Southeast Asia.

FLOUR, 00 See page 12.

GREENS Greens are often divided into cooking greens versus more delicate salad greens, although there is overlap. Soak or rinse sandy or gritty varieties in several changes of cold water.

arugula A favorite of Italian cooks, this pleasantly peppery green has deeply notched, bright green leaves that are eaten both cooked and raw. Larger leaves have a more intense flavor.

escarole A member of the chicory family, escarole pairs well with nuts, cheese, and salted meats, or citrus. Enjoy the tender, yellow inner leaves raw, but cook the dark green outer leaves.

Swiss chard A sturdy cooking green, with long, wide stems and large, spreading, dark green leaves. The stems may be ivory, yellow, red, or rainbow striped. Because the stems require longer cooking, remove them from the leaves and cook separately.

Treviso radicchio A crisp, pleasantly bitter, elongated variety of Italian chicory with serrated, ruby red leaves and broad white stems. Its assertive flavor and sturdy leaves are a good match with cheeses, cured meats, anchovies, olives, and capers.

Tuscan kale A leafy, dark green relative of cabbage, with tightly crinkled leaves on long stems. Also known as *cavalo nero* (black cabbage) and dinosaur kale, it is a popular addition to soups. Remove tough stems and rinse thoroughly before using.

KOMBU An edible kelp that is one of the primary ingredients in dashi, Japanese fish stock. The most common form is dried sheets, found in Japanese markets.

MEATS, CURED Italian cured meats appear often in traditional pasta dishes. For authentic flavor, seek them out in delis and specialty food stores.

guanciale Made from the cheek and jowl of a pig, this mildly flavored unsmoked Italian bacon is a popular addition to pasta sauces. Easier-to-find pancetta can be substituted.

mortadella A large, cooked Italian sausage typically eaten as a cold cut and sometimes used in pasta fillings. Made from pork and dotted with pork fat, it is mildly seasoned and often includes pistachios.

pancetta An unsmoked Italian bacon made from pork belly. The most common type is mildly seasoned with a mix of sweet and savory spices and rolled into a cylinder.

prosciutto This thinly sliced Italian ham is cured in salt and air-dried until subtly sweet-salty and velvety in texture. The regions of Parma and Friuli claim the country's finest.

MIRIN A sweet Japanese cooking wine made from fermented rice and sugar, mirin adds a sweet-and-sour flavor to dipping sauces.

MUSHROOMS To prepare mushrooms, wipe them clean with a damp cloth or brush. Varieties with closed caps may be rinsed briefly under running water.

chanterelle A highly prized golden yellow, tender, trumpet-shaped mushroom with a flavor that carries hints of apricot.

cremini Closely related to the common white mushroom, this brown mushroom has a firmer texture and fuller flavor. When allowed to mature, cremini mushrooms are relabeled portobellos.

enoki Tiny, white Asian mushrooms with long, thin stems and caps shaped like pinheads. Available fresh in the winter, or packed in water.

oyster A cream-colored or pale gray mushroom with a subtle shellfish taste. The caps fan out attractively from the stems. Look for smaller mushrooms for the best flavor.

porcini Also known as cèpes, these plump, meaty mushrooms have a rich, woodsy flavor. A brief season makes them difficult—and expensive—to source fresh, but porcini are widely available dried. Soak in hot water to reconstitute.

shiitake A meaty, rich, pale to dark brown Japanese mushroom with a mildly smoky flavor. Always discard the tough stems before using.

OILS When selecting an oil, consider both flavor and smoke point. Oils with high smoke points are ideal for sautéing and frying, while highly flavorful oils like olive and sesame are best saved for drizzling on finished dishes.

Asian sesame oil Full-flavored, amber-colored oil made by crushing toasted sesame seeds. It is used primarily to flavor foods, rather than for cooking, because of its low smoke point.

grapeseed A by-product of winemaking, this mildly flavored oil is made from crushed grape seeds. It has a fairly high smoke point.

olive The first cold pressing of olives yields extra-virgin olive oil, the variety that is the lowest in acid and the purest, with a full flavor that reflects where the olives were grown. Save your best oils for finishing dishes. Use less expensive oils for sautéing and frying.

peanut Oil made from peanuts can be heated to a high temperature before it begins to smoke. It is a good choice for stir-frying and deep-frying.

safflower A flavorless oil pressed from safflower seeds, with a high smoke point.

OLIVES The bitter fruit of a hardy tree, olives must be cured to become edible. Brine-cured olives stay plump, smooth, and relatively firm. Salt- or oil-cured olives become dry, wrinkled, and pleasantly bitter. Color depends on when the fruit was harvested.

Gaeta A brownish black, soft, and smooth salt-cured olive from Italy, with a nutty flavor.

Kalamata Purplish black, almond-shaped, and meaty, this popular Greek olive is cured in brine and then packed in oil and vinegar.

Niçoise Small, brownish black olives from Provence. Brine cured and then packed in oil with lemon and herbs, they have a mellow, nutty flavor.

Picholine Green, smooth, and salty medium-sized olives from France.

Sicilian Large, green, tart, and meaty olives sometimes flavored with red pepper or fennel.

PEA SHOOTS The delicate leaves and tendrils of the snow pea plant, pea shoots are sweet and tender and can be eaten raw or in stir-fries.

PERNOD A sweet French liqueur with an aniselike flavor, Pernod is often used in cooking as a complement to seafood.

SAFFRON This famously expensive spice is the harvested stigma of a crocus flower. The threads infuse subtle flavor, full aroma, and impart a vibrant yellow color.

SALT In these recipes, kosher salt is used for salting the cooking water for pasta and vegetables, and fine sea salt for seasoning sauces and other dishes. The large, flat flakes of kosher salt are made by compressing granular salt. Sea salt, which comes in both coarse and fine grains, is gathered from salt pans on the edge of the sea and has a pronounced, clean flavor.

SHERRY, DRY A specialty of southwestern Spain, sherry is a fortified wine made from the Palomino grape. It comes in eight different types, distinguished by color, flavor, sweetness, and alcohol content. Avoid anything labeled "cooking sherry," which will be low quality.

TAMARI A type of soy sauce made without wheat, resulting in a thicker, more intense sauce with a deep, complex flavor.

TAMARIND PASTE A thick paste made from the fruit of the tropical tamarind tree. It is widely used in the cooking of Southeast Asia and South Asia to add a sweet-tart flavor to dishes. Look for it in jars in Asian markets.

THAI CURRY PASTE Typically made from such ingredients as lemongrass, galangal, chiles, garlic, cilantro, and onions, Thai curry pastes come in a range of colors from red to green to yellow.

TOMATOES, SAN MARZANO A variety of plum tomato grown in southern Italy, the San Marzano is widely acknowledged as the gold standard of sauce tomatoes (both fresh and canned) due to its meaty texture and deep flavor.

TOMATOES, SUN-DRIED Drying tomatoes in the sun intensifies their flavor and yields a dense and chewy texture. Packed in oil, they are flavorful, pliable, and ready to add to cooked dishes. If dry-packed, they must sometimes be rehydrated in hot water before using.

VERMOUTH, DRY A fortified and flavored wine available in red or white and sweet or dry. Dry vermouth is often used for deglazing pans and adds a nice flavor to pasta sauces with seafood.

INDEX

weldonowen

415 Jackson Street, Suite 200, San Francisco, CA 94111
Telephone: 415 291 0100 Fax: 415 291 8841
www.weldonowen.com

Weldon Owen is a division of
BONNIER

WILLIAMS-SONOMA, INC.

Founder and Vice-Chairman Chuck Williams

WELDON OWEN, INC.

CEO and President Terry Newell
VP, Sales and Marketing Amy Kaneko
Director of Finance Mark Perrigo

VP and Publisher Hannah Rahill
Executive Editor Jennifer Newens
Associate Editor Julia Humes
Editorial Assistant Becky Duffett

Associate Creative Director Emma Boys
Designer Lauren Charles
Junior Designer Anna Grace

Production Director Chris Hemesath
Production Manager Michelle Duggan
Color Manager Teri Bell

Photographer Ray Kachatorian
Food Stylist Robyn Valarik
Prop Stylist Christine Wolheim

THE PASTA BOOK

Conceived and produced by Weldon Owen, Inc.
In collaboration with Williams-Sonoma, Inc.
3250 Van Ness Avenue, San Francisco, CA 94109

A WELDON OWEN PRODUCTION

Copyright © 2010 Weldon Owen, Inc. and Williams-Sonoma, Inc.
All rights reserved, including the right of reproduction
in whole or in part in any form.

Color separations by Embassy Graphics in Canada
Printed and bound by Toppan Leefung Printing Limited in China

First printed in 2010
10 9 8 7 6

Library of Congress Cataloging-in-Publication
data is available.

ISBN-13: 978-1-61628-016-1
ISBN-10: 1-61628-016-6

ACKNOWLEDGMENTS

Weldon Owen wishes to thank Linda Bouchard, Carrie Bradley, Shawn Corrigan, Elizabeth Parson, Sharon Silva,
Lauren Stocker, Jane Tunks, Jason Wheeler, and Victoria Woolard for their generous support in producing this book.

Julia della Croce wishes to thank the people of Italy from whom she has acquired the culinary knowledge that forms the
basis of this book. A portion of this content was also adapted from original recipes by Carole Durst, Anna Maria Erenbourg-Weld,
Rita Ghisu, Nathan Hoyt, Paolo Lanapopi, Nick Malgieri, Anna Amendolara Nurse, Susan Purdy, Laurel Robertson, Rick Rodgers,
and Rosa Ross. For recipe testing, many thanks to Nathan Hoyt and Laurel Robertson.

PHOTOGRAPHY CREDITS

All photographs by Ray Kachatorian except:
Jeff Kauck, pages 10, 16–23, 60, 136, 176–177, 202, and 208–209